Social Inquiry After Wittgenstein and Kuhn

SOCIAL INQUIRY AFTER WITTGENSTEIN & KUHN

Leaving Everything as It Is

John G. Gunnell

Columbia University Press *New York*

COLUMBIA UNIVERSITY PRESS

Publishers Since 1893

New York   Chichester, West Sussex

cup.columbia.edu

LIBRARY OF CONGRESS CATALOGING-IN-PUBLICATION DATA

Gunnell, John G.

Social inquiry after Wittgenstein and Kuhn: leaving everything as it is / John G. Gunnell.

p. cm.

Includes bibliographical references and index.

ISBN 978-0-231-16940-0 (cloth : alk. paper)—ISBN 978-0-231-53834-3 (e-book)

1. Social Sciences—Philosophy.   2. Wittgenstein, Ludwig, 1889–1951.   3. Kuhn, Thomas S.
   I. Title.

H61.15.G86 2014

300.1—dc23   2014008130

Columbia University Press books are printed on permanent and durable acid-free paper.

This book is printed on paper with recycled content.

Printed in the Unitsed States of America

C 10 9 8 7 6 5 4 3 2 1

Cover design: Chang Jae Lee

To Aldisa, for her patience and constructive skepticism

If the place I want to reach could only be climbed up to by a ladder,
I would give up trying to get there.

—LUDWIG WITTGENSTEIN

To make light of philosophy is to be a true philosopher.

—BLAISE PASCAL

I just want to know what the truth is.

—THOMAS KUHN

Believe those who are seeking the truth. Doubt those who find it.

—ANDRÉ GIDE

Contents

Preface

THE BASIC PURPOSE OF THIS VOLUME is to present the work of
Ludwig Wittgenstein and Thomas Kuhn as a vision of social inquiry.
The book is addressed primarily to scholars and students in the social
and human sciences and to philosophers of social science, but I hope
that along the way I have made a contribution to the interpretation of
the work of Wittgenstein and Kuhn. My sympathetic reading of their
work has at times made me wonder whether I was clarifying their arguments or whether these arguments had, as Wittgenstein hoped, simply
stimulated thoughts of my own. I have benefited from the vast secondary literature on their work, in both philosophy and social theory, but
that literature has, I believe, in some instances at least, been pushed
dangerously close to crossing the threshold of over-interpretation and
has become the source of a considerable amount of academic folklore.
Approaching Wittgenstein and Kuhn by threading one's way through
this maze of literature can, however, easily lead to intellectual vertigo as
well as inhibit directly engaging their texts, and I have only made sparse
direct reference to that literature.

Evidence of a connection between the work of Wittgenstein and
Kuhn is sketchy. In both chapter 1 and chapter 6, I examine that connection, both conceptually and historically, but my contention is that there
is a basic parallel between, on the one hand, Wittgenstein's approach to
conceptual investigations and, on the other hand, the philosophy and history of science as practiced by Kuhn. They both focused on how concepts
are internally related to, and constitutive of, social practices; addressed
what is involved in the tasks of understanding and interpreting these
practices; and examined both the epistemic and practical relationship

between philosophical inquiry and its subject matter, which are issues
that any form of social inquiry must confront.

Pascal once noted that "the last thing one settles in writing a book
is what one should put in first," and this was the case in formulating this
volume. Wittgenstein noted that in composing the *Investigations*, he had
found that the issues he confronted seemed to intersect in a manner that
made it very difficult to produce a linear presentation that belonged to
a uniform genre. I experienced a similar problem, but despite the diversity among the chapters, they are integrated both thematically and with
respect to the development of Wittgenstein's ideas. I have devoted careful
attention to what Wittgenstein actually said, because one of the most dis-
turbing things about much of the commentary on his work, in both philosophy and social science, has ultimately been a neglect of what Robert
Fogelin (2009) referred to as "taking Wittgenstein at his word." I wanted
to let him speak for himself rather than invent a Wittgenstein for my
own purposes or dwell on, and speculate about, either the influence of the
contexts in which he wrote or putative intentions behind his words. Wittgenstein stressed how language speaks for itself, and I am assuming that
his work also speaks for itself. Consequently, I have given careful attention
to his texts and the shape and flow of his remarks. I have quoted exten-
sively from his work in the course of interpreting it, and some readers
may think excessively, but although it is possible to rephrase, paraphrase,
and summarize many of his remarks, his own words capture the subtleties
involved. It is not, as many seem to believe, that his work is so difficult
to understand, but it is difficult to interpret, that is, to find the language
in which to describe and convey it. Although I have remained sensitive
to biographical information about Wittgenstein, such as in Ray Monk's
(1990) superb volume, various personal memoirs of both Wittgenstein
and his students, and studies of his intellectual and social environment, I
am basically concerned with the content of his work.

There have been many attempts to assess the implications of Wittgenstein's philosophy for thinking about the nature of social science and
social theory, and Kuhn's work has been a constant source of discussion in
these fields. The following chapters, however, are not devoted to an analysis of the reception of their work. I have previously addressed this matter
at length, and it is sufficient to note that despite instances of astute readings and applications, this reception has most typically involved either
seeking support for a variety of prior commitments or negatively charac-

terizing them as progenitors of modern relativism and as a danger to the
search for truth in both science and ethics. Such preconceptions distance
us from understanding their work and recognizing its importance for
illuminating the concept of social inquiry, and, particularly, the manner
in which such inquiry is an interpretive endeavor.

For well over a century, and certainly from at least Max Weber to the
present, there have been variations on a continuing debate about whether
social science is a naturalistic or humanistic form of inquiry. Although
the philosophical myth of a scientific method, on which so much of the
naturalistic argument was based, has been thoroughly undermined, the
alternative has remained only porously articulated. Even though my rendition of Wittgenstein's conception of social inquiry is fundamentally
in conflict with the claim that social science should, or can be, devoted
to causal explanations analogous to those in the natural sciences, my
purpose here is not to reengage that old battle. I do, however, address
the basic criteria of demarcation. My concern is not to legislate with
respect to the details of any specific field of inquiry, but rather to provide
substance to investigations, and images of investigation, based on the
assumption that social inquiry involves the recovery of the meaning of
language and human action. For many years, I have argued that political
theory and political inquiry in general are not, in terms of either theory
or method, sui generis. It is the fundamental principles of inquiry that
are the subject of the following chapters, and most of the positive and
negative implications for specific areas of research will be apparent, even
if not always specified and described. There are aspects of the following
chapters, particularly the discussion of mental concepts, which may be
viewed as excruciatingly detailed, but this is compensation, or revenge,
for the theoretical shallowness of contemporary treatments of such matters in the social and human sciences.

Although Wittgenstein spoke of his work as "a struggle with language," he conceived of language as inseparable from the activities in
which it is entwined, or, as he put it, "words are deeds" (*CV*, 13, 53). His
struggle, however, as well as that of Kuhn, was not simply with understanding language and attending forms of human action but with what *(interpreted*
is involved in interpreting them. While such a struggle is a distinctly *preconstituted*
second-<u>order</u> conceptual investigation and analysis, understanding and *phenomena)*
interpreting Wittgenstein and Kuhn is a <u>third-order</u> endeavor. Conse- *(analyses,*
quently, it may be useful for me to highlight a few selected junctures in *such as phi.*
of soc.
sciences)

my persistent, but somewhat punctuated, involvement with their work. In many respects, I should include Peter Winch, whose first book I discuss at some length in chapter 2, but Winch's third-order statement of Wittgenstein's relevance for thinking about the idea of a social science is valuable more as a guide to approaching Wittgenstein than as a comparable work or an exercise in social inquiry.

My interest in their work began in the mid-1960s, shortly after I completed my Ph.D in the department of political science at the University of California at Berkeley. My major subfield was political theory and my cognate field was philosophy. In those years, the political science department was becoming polarized by a dispute between those who followed more historical and institutional forms of political study and those who embraced the emerging "behavioral" persuasion and its attempt to model political inquiry on what it believed to be the methods of the natural sciences. The philosophy department was also conflicted. A residual logical positivism was being confronted by a new wave of younger postpositivist scholars that included Kuhn, Stanley Cavell, and Paul Feyerabend. I was, at the time, far from fully aware of what was going on in the general field of philosophy, but in the spring of 1962, the same year that Kuhn's *Structure of Scientific Revolutions* was published, Karl Popper was a visitor in the philosophy department. I took his seminar, which was assisted by Feyerabend, whose main task was to oversee student papers (to which he paid minimal attention) and, as a consequence of Popper's distaste for tobacco smoke, to make sure that no one lighted up. Popper's lectures were primarily devoted to an extended critique of the logic of induction, and I had little sense of the general character and context of his arguments—and of the evolving personal and intellectual tensions between Popper and Feyerabend and between Popper and Kuhn—or the more long-standing conflict between Popper, as well as many of his followers, and Wittgenstein.

For many years, I pursued the implications of the work of Wittgenstein and Kuhn for critically examining, and offering an alternative to, the philosophy of logical positivism and empiricism, which had informed the dominant image of science in political and social science (see, e.g., Gunnell 1968, 1975, 1986). In 1998, however, I published an extended argument about what I considered to be a Wittgensteinian approach to various issues in political theory. This work, which also

relied heavily on Winch and Kuhn, was an exploration of what I referred
to as the "orders of discourse" as manifest in the relationships between
philosophy, social science, and politics. I focused particularly on the distinction between what I labeled as the "first-order" practices of fields
such as natural science, which theoretically defined the physical world;
"second-order practices" such as social science and the philosophy of
natural science, which interpreted conceptually preconstituted phenomena; and "third-order" analyses such as the philosophy of social science.
This work also centered on formulating what I referred to as a "theory
of conventional objects," which was predicated on Wittgenstein's basic
claims about linguistic meaning and about words as deeds, J. L. Austin's
(1962) similar but more schematic analysis of speech acts, and Kuhn's
later work on concepts. I attempted to demonstrate the manner in which
this theory provided a basis for the practice of social inquiry as well
as a critique of opposing philosophical and social-scientific positions. I
expanded my earlier arguments about textual and historical interpretation, and I argued that the relativism often ascribed to individuals such
as Winch and Kuhn was based less on worries about epistemic chaos
in practices such as science and politics than on repressed fears about
the authority of philosophy to speak about the grounds of judgment
in these practices. A central argument of the book, however, was that
there was no philosophical answer, either immanent or transcendental,
to the problem of the practical relationship between social inquiry and
the practices that constituted its subject matter.

I increasingly began to deploy what I considered to be a Wittgensteinian and Kuhnian approach to my own work in conceptual history
(e.g., Gunnell 2004a), but I also began a more detailed examination of
Wittgenstein's reception among political and social theorists (Gunnell
2004b). I concluded that most of this literature, whether critical or sup-
portive, and ranging from extravagant, and often ideologically inspired,
attacks to equally implausible images of him as a theorist of radical
democracy and neopluralism, represented less an authentic interpretation of his work than attempts to enlist his name, whether positively or
negatively, in support of a variety of antecedent, but sometimes conflicting, arguments. I remained, however, involved more with analyzing what
I took to be the implications and applications of his work than with the
details of the work itself. It was recognition of the similarity between

Weber's concept of the ideal-type and Wittgenstein's discussion of his philosophical method that prompted a closer textual examination of the *Investigations* (Gunnell 2007a). This was followed by a critical analysis of the growing popularity of attempts to apply the findings of cognitive neuroscience to the study of social and political phenomena (Gunnell 2007b) as well as a more careful examination of Wittgenstein's remarks on the relationship between language and thought and his emphasis on the discursive character of psychological concepts such as emotion (Gunnell 2012). In 2011, I consolidated a group of essays that included an elaboration of the idea of social inquiry as a metapractice; a yet more expansive discussion of the reception of Wittgenstein among social and political theorists; further criticisms of philosophical realism and cognitive neuroscience as a basis of social inquiry; an analysis of Wittgenstein's and Winch's claims about how to do justice to social phenomena in the course of interpreting them; and a historical discussion of the practical relationship between academic intellectuals and politics in the United States. That volume was, however, intended as a prolegomenon to the more dedicated treatment of Wittgenstein's work as a general vision of inquiry in the social and human sciences, which is represented in the following chapters. What has most fundamentally changed for me in the course of writing this book is that while I once turned to his work for philosophical authority in the process of intervening in various academic debates, I now comprehensively simply see and describe both social phenomena and social inquiry differently. This difference is similar to the difference between reading a scientific theory and incorporating that theory into one's vision of the world. What Wittgenstein said in the *Tractatus*, about the book as a ladder that one could discard after climbing it, applies to his other work as well.

The purpose of this biographical excursus is not only to describe the path that led me to the current project, but to allay what might be a reader's quite natural concerns about what I have *not* discussed. In what follows, my concern is not with focusing on every instance where Wittgenstein had something to say that might apply to some particular aspect of work in the social and human sciences. My purpose is to identify the crucial general issues that are common to all forms of social inquiry and to stay on track with respect to how these issues are addressed in his work.

Once I was detached from graduate teaching and faculty interchange on a regular basis, as I have been for the past four years, pursuing
this project has largely been a matter of holding an internal dialogue.
There are, however, three people who have been very important in my
efforts to work through this material. I am very deeply indebted to Linda
Zerilli, at the University of Chicago, who has been a unique and constant
source of encouragement in my efforts to interpret Wittgenstein and
specify his relevance for social theory. I was once a reasonably proficient
reader of German, but over the years, I lost much of that capacity, and I
have relied heavily on translations of Wittgenstein's texts and especially
on editions in the *Collected Works of Ludwig Wittgenstein* published by
Blackwell as well as the Wiley-Blackwell 2009 edition of the *Investigations*. Translations, however, are not always in accord with one another,
and even when they were in agreement, there were a few key instances in
which I concluded that they were infelicitous. In working through some
of the more difficult passages, I have received valuable aid from my former colleague Peter Breiner, who has also consistently helped to sustain
my belief in the importance of this project. I have also gained from my
exchange of thoughts and manuscripts, on various aspects of Wittgenstein's work, as well as that of Winch and Kuhn, with Rupert Read at the
University of East Anglia.

I was fortunate to find in Wendy Lochner an editor whose interests and knowledge encompassed the range of material discussed in this
book. She, Christine Dunbar, Anne McCoy, and Kathryn Jorge have
been helpful and responsive at every turn. I also appreciate the sugges-
tions of the two reviewers chosen by Columbia University Press, and
I benefited from Robert Demke's meticulous copyediting and Andrew
Joron's skillful indexing.

No matter how many times I have reread, and partially rewritten,
this manuscript, I have found places where I could have said more or said
it differently—and where I could have said less. There comes a point,
however, at which it is necessary to realize, as Wittgenstein said, that no
matter how much you try to hit the nail on the head, you will sometimes
miss. It may well be that after reading the following chapters some practitioners of the social and human sciences may continue to believe that
Wittgenstein and Kuhn were dangerous minds, but I hope that they will
at least have a more accurate understanding of what they actually said

and its relevance for thinking about the conduct of social inquiry.

Abbreviations

TITLES BY WITTGENSTEIN

References to *OC*, *PI*, *PPF*, *PPO*, *TL*, and *Z* are to numbered remarks, and references to other titles are to page numbers.

BB *The Blue and Brown Books* (1958)
BT *The Big Typescript* (2005)
CL *Cambridge Letters* (1997)
CV *Culture and Value* (1998)
LC *Lectures and Conversations on Aesthetics, Psychology, and Religious Belief* (1966)
LFM *Wittgenstein's Lectures on the Foundations of Mathematics, Cambridge, 1939* (1976)
LPP *Last Writings on the Philosophy of Psychology*, vols. 1 and 2 (1992)
NB *Notebooks, 1914–1916* (1961)
OC *On Certainty* (1969)
PG *Philosophical Grammar* (1974)
PI *Philosophical Investigations* (2009) [In this edition, material formerly presented as part 2 is designated as *Philosophy of Psychology—A Fragment*, which is cited as PPF.]
PO *Philosophical Occasions* (1993)
PP *Remarks on the Philosophy of Psychology*, vols. 1 and 2 (1980a, 1980b)
PPF *Philosophy of Psychology—A Fragment* (2009)
PPO *Public and Private Occasions* (2003)
RC *Remarks on Colour* (1977)
RFM *Remarks on the Foundations of Mathematics* (1978)
TL *Tractatus Logico-Philosophicus* (2012)
Z *Zettel* (1981)

Social Inquiry After Wittgenstein and Kuhn

Introduction

The limits of my language are the limits of my world. (*TL*, 5.6)
In so far as people think they can see the "limit of human understanding," they believe of course that they can see beyond it. (*CV*, 22)

—WITTGENSTEIN

WHEN PETER WINCH PUBLISHED his *Idea of a Social Science and
Its Relation to Philosophy* (1958), his argument, at least implicitly, was not
simply that Wittgenstein's *Philosophical Investigations* is a significant
guide for thinking about the nature of social science, but that there is
a basic logical, epistemological, and theoretical symmetry between philosophy and social inquiry. In chapter 2, I reconstruct Winch's argument
in detail, but there are grounds for a stronger thesis. A close examination
of Wittgenstein's work after 1930 suggests that part of the alteration in
his vision of philosophy was to conceive of philosophy itself as a form of
social inquiry. This is not to say that the social and human sciences were
his direct object of concern, but rather that his work applies generically
to the study of social phenomena. Although the concerns and subject
matter of particular human sciences differ, their theoretical foundations

and the conditions of inquiry are the same, and Wittgenstein illuminates those foundations and conditions. My argument is that Wittgenstein's philosophy constitutes the basis of a theory and method of social inquiry and that Kuhn's account of transformations in natural science is an example of the kind of investigation that Wittgenstein's philosophy entailed and anticipated.

In the following chapters, there are two central themes that revolve around issues that are endemic to both philosophy and the social and human sciences. These are the relationship between thought and language and the relationship between interpretation and the object of interpretation. Wittgenstein's treatment of these issues constituted a significant dimension of the change in distribution of emphasis that characterized his later work and its relevance for thinking about the nature of social inquiry. Although this book is not a study of the evolution of Wittgenstein's philosophy, a confrontation with some aspects of that evolution cannot be avoided, and I take account of some of the principal continuities and discontinuities. When he claimed in the *Tractatus* that the limits of language are the limits of one's world, he had hopes of demonstrating the capacities of language to reach a clearer grasp of the world, but he eventually came to believe that it was less the "world" than conceptions of the world that were the object of philosophy. There was no way to exceed the limits of the substantive first-order languages in which the world is manifest. Consequently, however, investigating those regions of language, and the practices in which they are embedded, is also, in an important but secondary respect, an investigation of the world.

I argue that the social and human sciences are, by their very nature, interpretive endeavors, but while they are replete with the use of terms such as "language," "meaning," "understanding," "thought," "ideas," "belief," "intention," and "emotion," the concepts to which these words refer have remained ambiguous and, at best, theoretically porous and contested. Wittgenstein's work illuminates these concepts and the relationships between them, but his image of philosophy as a second-order interpretive form of investigation also required coming to grips not only with the epistemic relationship between such inquiry and its subject matter but with the practical relationship as well. Much has been made of Wittgenstein's claim to have rejected "theory" and "explanation" and to have defined philosophy as a mode of description that "leaves everything as it is," but in those instances he was addressing the differences between philosophy and natural science and between his conception of philoso-

phy and traditional metaphysics. Exactly what his image of the relationship between philosophy and its subject matter involved was left somewhat ambiguous, but it constitutes the principal axis of my discussion.
His remark about philosophy leaving everything as it was has remained
ambiguous in part because it did not appear to sit easily alongside his
general therapeutic perspective and his critical analyses of not only philosophy but specific practices such as mathematics and psychology. My
argument is that what Wittgenstein meant was that the subject matter
of philosophy is conceptually distinct and autonomous in a manner that
the subject matter of natural science is not. While natural science conceptually configures the "world," the task of philosophy, and any form
of social inquiry, whatever its particular approach and purpose, is, in the
first instance, to reconstruct a conceptually prefigured form of life. While
the cognitive problems involved in describing and conveying the meaning of such a *Weltbild* is one thing, critically engaging and judging it is
another. In the *Investigations*, Wittgenstein had a limited amount to say
about the latter, but in some of his other work, and especially in *On Certainty*, he not only directly dealt with the nature of judgment and with
how judgments change within a practice but with the issue of conflicts
in judgment between practices. And Kuhn's work constitutes a concrete
engagement with these issues.

Although Wittgenstein and Kuhn have received considerable
attention from social theorists, an understanding of their work has been
deflected by the distortions of some critical commentators as well as by
misinterpretations and reservations among those who have given their
work a more favorable reception. What has made their work so controversial is not some specific doctrinal point, but the fact that they did
not appear to provide an answer to how philosophy could authoritatively
speak about and to its subject matter. The prevalent philosophical ani-
mus toward Wittgenstein and Kuhn has, strangely and almost uniquely,
spilled over into other fields, and even popular culture, and particularly
into the work of individuals who cast their practical concerns in terms of
philosophical issues such as relativism. I will emphasize, and reempha-
size, that the issue of relativism is not actually a problem in social practices, ranging from science to everyday forms of life. It is a philosophical
abstraction and invention, and the very definition of the problem is a
consequence of philosophy's anxiety about its capacity to address matters
such as reality, truth, justice, and the like in a manner that transcends
the criteria that are indigenous to the practices that constitute its object

of inquiry. Philosophy has, however, tended to project this anxiety onto those practices, which in turn have often appropriated the terms in which that anxiety is expressed as part of their self-image. While some practices, such as natural science and religion, seem somewhat immune from this philosophical virus, the social and human sciences have been much more susceptible. I will explain in more detail why this is the case, but the answer resides principally in the fact that, like philosophy, these practices are devoted to the study of other practices and share, and consequently must confront, the question of their own identity and relationship to their subject matter.

It is sometimes suggested that it is contemporary fields such as critical social theory that seek some form of cognitive authority, but this search was at the core of the origins and evolution of the social and human sciences as a whole as well as of philosophy itself. The abiding concern with the practical relationship between social inquiry and its subject matter is ideologically inclusive and involves positions that have both depreciated and valorized the image of natural science as the measure of knowledge. Part of what has elicited the hostility toward Wittgenstein and Kuhn is that they challenged the kind of philosophy from which the social sciences have typically attempted to draw epistemic and practical sustenance. Although Wittgenstein and Kuhn called into question a variety of specific traditional doctrines, such as variations of idealism and realism, a more fundamental problem has been that what they were doing is simply often not easily recognized as philosophy. This has led to strained and futile attempts to fit them into various traditional categories. Because Wittgenstein's work does not reflect the dominant genres, it is not unusual today to find this work only minimally featured in college and university philosophy departments, if not, in some instances, banished altogether. His work is not simply philosophically iconoclastic, maybe in the sense that the work of Martin Heidegger or Michel Foucault might be characterized, but rather it is an outlier of a more fundamental sort.

While the dominant persuasions in philosophy have often cast their identity in terms of their image of the work of iconic figures from the past, they often not only pay little attention to the actual context of that work but project their own academic context backward. Although there may be more than a categorical resemblance between contemporary academic philosophy and some nineteenth-century figures such as Kant and

Hegel, the inclusion of individuals such as Descartes and those further back in the typical philosophical family tree is considerably more dubious. There are, however, fundamental differences between, on the one hand, much of contemporary academic philosophy and, on the other hand, the individuals they count as forebears and the great diversity of practices in which these alleged ancestors were actually participants. Trying to force someone such as Plato into the pantheon, or even characterize him as its founder, is to create a retrospectively defined ancestry that distorts the work of many of the celebrated classical figures and the circumstances in which they wrote. One of the core differences is that much of what we count as the past of philosophy was, unlike the academic and institutionalized forms it takes today, much more rhetorically and practically related to the subject matter that it intellectually engaged. While much of the history of philosophy can be read, as Richard Rorty (1979) claimed, as vainly attempting to mirror nature, there was a practical and persuasive dimension to much of the past literature, which only resonates in the contemporary academic world as a kind of dislocated conversation.

It is interesting that Wittgenstein, as well as Kuhn, had limited regard for, or interest in, most of these putative forebears, but, in the case of Wittgenstein, this was not so much because, for example, he questioned whether Plato was actually "so clever" or because he suggested that Socrates may have been confused (*CV*, 22, 35). He rejected the image of philosophy that contemporary practitioners had derived, and often still retain, from a reading of the authors they claim as their predecessors. The residue of this image still persists in varieties of contemporary representational philosophy, which are devoted to specifying universal grounds of knowledge and judgment, vouchsafing a concept of transcendental reality, and specifying how thought and language make contact with the world, often for the purpose of either underwriting or instructing practices such as science and moral reasoning. It is, however, important not to confuse what I will often refer to as representational philosophy with my claim that the task of social inquiry is representational. The "world" that representational philosophy claims to access is a world that is projected within such philosophy, while the world that is the object of social inquiry is conceptually autonomous. Representational philosophy mistakenly presumes to the status of a first-order discourse. *second order*

It was not simply that Wittgenstein challenged these metaphysical projects, which he so often associated with dogmatism, but that he

was not even playing in the same arena. His later work, despite reten-
tion of the term "philosophy," constituted a quite different endeavor, and
the same can be said for Kuhn. Wittgenstein clearly did situate himself
within the vocation of what he referred to as philosophy, and Kuhn pursued history for what he explicitly said was a philosophical purpose. But
they wished to precipitate a revolution within philosophy. The key to
grasping this difference is not some label such as ordinary language philosophy, analytic philosophy, or the linguistic turn. Wittgenstein himself,
who often puzzled about how to define his enterprise, did not arrive at
any specific designation. So the question is what the work of Wittgenstein and Kuhn looks like when viewed from the inside, as if one had
wandered into such a corpus without a label attached to it and without
preconceived criteria of discrimination. My argument is that their work
is about the nature of the conventions represented in language and various human practices, the epistemological problems involved in accessing
and understanding the meaning of such phenomena, the methodological issue of how to interpret and convey that meaning, and the practical
dimension of the relationship between philosophy and its subject matter.
The picture I have painted is a picture of social inquiry, and Wittgenstein
and Kuhn as social theorists is the central theme of the following chapters. Wittgenstein made it very clear that his first concern was not with
the impact that his work would have on various language communities.
As he put it, "my ideal is a certain coolness. A temple providing a setting
for the passions without meddling with them" (*CV*, 4). This phrasing also
captures Kuhn's sentiment, but this did not mean that they were uncon-
cerned with or did not address the practical issue.

Chapter 1 illustrates how the shadow of Wittgenstein hovers over
issues of social inquiry. This shadow, however, is not an accurate reflection
of the actual form of his argument, and it obscures the terrain on which
it has been cast. Errol Morris's quite public attack on Thomas Kuhn as an
example of how Wittgenstein's work has endangered the concept of truth
is derived from distortions visited on their work by some philosophers. The
concerns that prompted Morris's criticism are worthy of consideration, but
he did not pick an appropriate target. While Morris claimed that Kuhn
threatened the objectivity of science and the search for truth, others have
embraced a line of argument that claims that the practical implication of
Kuhn's work was to foster philosophical complacency and political conformity. These arguments fundamentally misconstrue the work of both Wittgenstein and Kuhn, and they are grossly historically inaccurate.

Chapter 2 presents an overview of how Wittgenstein's work speaks to the practices of the social and human sciences and of what Wittgenstein meant when he stated that philosophy leaves everything as it is. I begin, however, by examining in textual detail Winch's classic rendition of *The Idea of a Social Science*. Winch's text has been clouded by its interpretive history, and although it may be considered somewhat dated and in need of clarification and elaboration, it captures well the general significance of Wittgenstein's work for thinking about the theory and practice of social inquiry. Social phenomena are in certain important respects linguistic phenomena but are nevertheless intrinsically related to forms of social life, and Wittgenstein's work constitutes a theoretical account of the nature of conventional phenomena. When I refer to Wittgenstein's "theoretical account," I am, as I will make clear, fully recognizing his claim that he was not presenting a theory, but I take issue with the manner in which this claim has frequently been interpreted. In this chapter, I introduce a distinction between *first-order/constructive/presentational* and *second-order/reconstructive/representational* forms of inquiry, which, I argue, is the crucial difference between the natural and the human sciences, but which, as I will stress in chapter 7, also has significance for addressing the status of values. This chapter also sets the stage for a further consideration of the concepts of understanding and interpretation.

At the birth of the modern human and social sciences, the fundamental epistemological problem was what philosophers speak of as "knowing other minds." Wittgenstein, however, was committed to the dissolution of the ontological distinction between the "inner" and the "outer." Chapter 3 examines the manner in which his work is a challenge to the dominate views of meaning and interpretation in both philosophy and the human sciences. The chapter begins with a critical discussion of two general accounts, which I refer to as "mentalism" and "interpretism." Notwithstanding the dominance of variations on forms of mentalism, which claim that meaning resides in the world of the mind, it has been consistently countered by claims to the effect that the font of meaning is actually the act of interpretation and that, so to speak, interpretation goes all the way down. The chapter proceeds with a discussion of the evolution of Wittgenstein's account of the relationship between thought and language and the manner in which this account challenges both the orthodox mentalist conception of meaning and the loyal opposition of interpretive determinism, as well as the dichotomous choice that these positions are sometimes taken to entail. I argue that an important dimension of the transformation in Wittgenstein's work, from 1929 to 1948, was the formulation of a new conception of the relationship between language and thought. I then argue that this was the central thesis of *The Blue and Brown Books* and at the core of his rejection of the referential account of meaning. What also began to surface in this earlier transitional work was a theme that would find full expression in the *Investigations*. This was the problem of confusing the means of representation with what was represented, which was the fundamental mistake of metaphysics as well as an inherent danger in any form of social inquiry. In an important respect, the remaining chapters all continue to elaborate his argument about the relationship between language and thought, which I claim is really the central theme of his later work. It was not simply, as so many have recognized, that he claimed that thoughts were accessible because they were expressed in a public language, but that thought as such was located in that language and that language and thought had the same content.

Chapter 4 is devoted to a detailed reading of the *Philosophical Investigations* from the perspective of social theory. In this book, he continued to develop his arguments about meaning; language and mental concepts; the difference and relationship between interpretation and understanding; a basic distinction between words and concepts; the epistemic relationship between inquiry and its subject matter, including the persistent problem of reifying the vehicle of interpretation, which he attempted to solve by the application of what he referred to as perspicuous representations; and a range of other issues that are central to any mode of social inquiry. Although among social theorists there has been a great deal of discussion of Wittgenstein's *Investigations* and although many have a general acquaintance with what is typically recognized as his principal arguments, there is often only a vague sense of the character of the text. And much of the secondary literature in philosophy, which often deals with specialized issues, does not render a clear image of the book as a whole that can be easily grasped by readers in the social and human sciences. In short, familiarity with the text is often more assumed than demonstrated, but it is very difficult to talk about Wittgenstein's arguments without an examination of exactly how they develop in the text. I avoid forcing a particular interpretation, as so many commentators have done when attempting to find support for some favored idea. I have also been uncomfortable with the approaches in much of the secondary philosophical literature, which has attempted to parse the book topically in terms of various standard issues in philosophy, divide it into segments reflecting what is taken to be certain basic internally defined sections, or extrapolate from particular remarks. As useful as much of this literature may be, it often presents a reader with a quite fragmented and accentuated account of what was actually "going on" in this large collation of remarks.

I approach the work more organically and holistically, and I pursue a form of analysis that, I believe, in important ways reflects Wittgenstein's own approach. Rather than positing some structure, either imposed or immanent, I follow how the remarks flow, maybe like a river whose course may not conform to how we might think it should naturally proceed but which rises from a specific location and then carves a path that often bends back upon itself, while still, on the whole, traversing a terrain that we can chart, navigate, and follow to a destination. My purpose in approaching the work in this manner is not to explore every source and tributary or to stop at each bend, but rather to stay within the main current while still sometimes catching eddies that go against the principal movement. When dealing in detail with the text of the *Investigations* and other works of Wittgenstein, such as *The Blue and Brown Books* and *On Certainty*, I have assumed that there are no predetermined sections, and I have exercised interpretive license in segmenting the remarks, much as one might decide to apportion parts of a continuous journey.

My concern, however, is not simply to map the text, but to demonstrate how the work, when viewed at the ground level, is really about issues that are central to the enterprises of the social and human sciences. It is hardly novel to suggest that his work is about linguistic meaning and about what it is both to mean something and to understand and interpret meaning. His analysis applies, however, not simply to language narrowly construed, but, quite explicitly, to conventional phenomena as a whole and to what Weber referred to as the meaningful actions that constitute social facts and to what is involved in interpretation, that is, in second-order claims to knowledge and judgments about such facts. Although one reason for providing (what Wittgenstein might have referred to as) a synoptic view of the *Investigations* is to avoid some of the problems represented in other overviews, I also wanted to avoid conjuring up a nebulous image when referring to the work in later chapters.

Chapter 5 continues to explore Wittgenstein's post-*Investigations* elaboration of the relationship between thought and language as well as his later discussions of interpretation. The remarks posthumously col-

lected and traditionally presented as part 2 of the *Investigations* and later
numbered by Hacker and Schulte and titled a *Philosophical Fragment*, as
well as his later work on psychology, are a distinct development of the
thematic core of both the earlier transitional work and the *Investigations*.
I conclude with the implications of his work for defending the autonomy
of both social phenomena and the practice of social inquiry. I assume
that there are few who would dissent from the claim that the social and
human sciences are, broadly speaking, concerned with the meaning of
social phenomena, despite the various ways in which they may go about
the task of discovering and interpreting such meaning. But despite a
long tradition of claims to the effect that social inquiry is an interpretive
enterprise, these claims have typically been epistemological in character
and not theoretically underwritten. Many of the issues discussed in this
chapter, such as the nature of conventionality and the typology of concepts, deserve greater elaboration, but the purpose here is to situate them
in Wittgenstein's work.

Chapter 6 is devoted to clarifying further Kuhn's still controversial account of science, but I focus on how this account relates to issues
in social inquiry and how it can be read as exemplifying Wittgenstein's
approach to philosophy. I also provide further background for considering Kuhn's actual connection to the work of Wittgenstein. It is not
only the critics of Wittgenstein and Kuhn who see connections between
their works. For example, Wes Sharrock and Rupert Read (2002) have
argued persuasively, and sympathetically, that Kuhn can be viewed in
many respects as a "Wittgensteinian," and Read (2012) has emphasized
the importance of situating Wittgenstein among the sciences. Although
there are significant conceptual and terminological similarities between
the work of Wittgenstein and Kuhn, it is difficult to document a definite
connection. The parallels between Kuhn's argument, and even his language, and Wittgenstein's *On Certainty* are, for example, almost uncanny,
but there is no evidence that Kuhn was, or could have been, actually
familiar with that book when he wrote *Structure*. Although the relationship may be one more of convergence than of influence, the Berkeley
ambience, in which the argument of *Structure* was finalized, cannot be
ignored. And there was more to that context than Kuhn's association
with Stanley Cavell. It was not only Kuhn and Cavell who were together
in the philosophy department at Berkeley in the late 1950s and early
1960s, but also Paul Feyerabend, who, despite a long period as a (some-

what ambivalent) follower of Popper, was in the process of recapturing what was involved in his earlier association with Wittgenstein's work. My purpose is not to say all there is to say about Feyerabend and Kuhn (see, e.g, Hoyhingen-Huene 1993; Bird 2000; Nickles 2003; Markum 2005; Preston 1997; Oberheim 2006), but only to demonstrate that their vision of philosophy was consonant with that of Wittgenstein and that it speaks to basic issues in social inquiry.

When Wittgenstein said that philosophy leaves everything as it is, he was speaking in part directly to the practical issue of its relationship to its subject matter, which involves the critical, normative, and therapeutic aspect of social inquiry, and of how to both speak about matters of justice in social life and do justice to social phenomena in the course of interpreting and explaining them. Chapter 7 turns to an analysis of Wittgenstein's *On Certainty* not only as a philosophical elaboration of the basic kind of premises underlying Kuhn's work but as an entry into the problem of judgment as it is manifest in the social and human sciences and their perennial search for grounds of empirical and ethical evaluation and prescription. As in the case of my discussion of the *Investigations*, my principal goal is to paint a clear picture of the argument that runs through his remarks. This analysis will undoubtedly be read by some as deflationary, because it does not provide the kind of answers, or their substitutes, that have characteristically been pursued and offered. My argument, however, is that there are no such general answers. What Wittgenstein and Kuhn tell us, both implicitly and explicitly, is that making judgments is easy but making them matter always comes down to persuasion both within and between social practices.

Any discussion of Wittgenstein's approach to normativity and normative inquiry cannot ignore the *Tractatus* and its references to ethics. There has, however, in recent years been a major scholarly controversy about how to read the *Tractatus* and how to assess what has been typically referred to as the *Kehre*, or "reversal," in his work after 1929. Some of what are often labeled as the more "standard" readings, which have stressed a discontinuity between the *Tractatus* and the *Investigations*, have become the focus of an extensive critique mounted by variations on what is now often designated, by both critics and defenders, as the "resolute" or "austere" reading as well as the "new Wittgenstein." This latter literature not only emphasizes various continuities between his earlier and later work, but claims that he was not, either explicitly or implicitly, putting forth a philosophical theory but indirectly refuting the possibility of any such project. Much of the argument turns on what he meant by "nonsense" and on placing his own claims in that category. Although this work has significantly contributed to a heightened scrutiny of the *Tractatus* and its relationship to his later work, it is increasingly difficult to determine exactly where the battle lines between the different camps of Tractarian interpretation can be drawn, and those often respectively associated with "standard" and "resolute" readings are far from full agreement among themselves. Although it is important to be sensitive to the problems raised by this now complex body of secondary literature, sorting through all this as a preliminary to approaching the *Tractatus* is beyond the scope of my analysis. I firmly agree with some points of the newer readings, such as stressing the continuity in his work with respect to his therapeutic focus on achieving clarity, his aversion to traditional metaphysics, his rejection of the search for an ideal language, and his emphasis on philosophy as an activity rather than the formulation of doctrines. It seems, however, that in this literature the discontinuities between the *Tractatus* and the *Investigations*, which Wittgenstein himself often stressed, are sometimes suppressed. My response to this controversy is to acknowledge it but sidestep it and avoid the pinball effect of bumping up against and glancing off every interpretive nuance in the secondary literature.

One of my basic claims is that Wittgenstein never fundamentally changed his conception of values, but he did increasingly incorporate them into what we might refer to as the space of reasons. From the beginning, values belonged to what he referred to in the *Tractatus* as what can be "shown" or presented. Although philosophy can represent values, that is, identify and describe the values manifest in human interaction (what he referred to as "absolute value"), these values do not, any more than purely philosophical claims, scientific theories, and the like, represent anything. They are part of the framework within which claims about such matters as right and justice are stated. I argue that his distinction between sense and nonsense was not to deprive ethical claims of meaning but to establish the autonomy of ethics and values. The remainder of the chapter is devoted to exploring how Wittgenstein's discussion of ethics and values provides a basis for critically evaluating what is typically referred in the social and human sciences as normative theory and inquiry.

1

THOMAS KUHN & THE SHADOW
OF WITTGENSTEIN

> Nothing seems to me more unlikely than that a scientist or math-
> ematician, who reads me, should be seriously influenced thereby in
> the way he works. (*CV*, 70)
> This method consists essentially in leaving the question of *truth*
> and asking about *sense* instead. (*CV*, 3)
>
> —WITTGENSTEIN

AT PRINCETON UNIVERSITY on November 15, 2010, the filmmaker
Errol Morris presented a lecture titled "The Ashtray." Morris had been
the recipient of a MacArthur genius grant and had made impressive investigative documentaries, which included the *Gates of Heaven* (1978),
which dealt with the business of pet cemeteries; *The Thin Blue Line* (1988),
which succeeded in exonerating a man who had been sentenced to die;
and *The Fog of War* (2003), which focused on Robert McNamara and the
deceptions involved in the Vietnam War. Morris continued to pursue a
variety of such projects, and his recent book, *A Wilderness of Error* (2012),
was a reexamination of the case of Jeffrey MacDonald, the army doctor who, in 1979, was convicted of murdering his pregnant wife and two

young daughters but who has waged a constant but, so far, futile battle in defense of his innocence.

As a student during the 1970s (at Wisconsin, Harvard, and finally Princeton) Morris had protested the Vietnam War before moving to Berkeley, California, where he eventually began a career in film. In the lecture, he spoke about the manner in which he had always been motivated to search for truth, that is, for "what's really there," but how, in the contemporary era, this type of commitment was in danger of being subverted by intellectual persuasions that threatened to leave us suspended from reality and "lost in language" with a depreciation of the assumptions that there is a "world out there," that "we can apprehend it," and that it is "our job to do so." He argued that for a man told to "take a seat" in the electric chair for a crime he did not commit, the proclamations of the "church of postmodernism," which preach that "truth and falsity are just socially constructed," are of little consolation and simply imply that the accused should "suck it up." Although Morris spoke mostly about his film work, the title and brief parts of his lecture previewed a five-part series that he was preparing for the "Opinionator" in the *New York Times*. The theme of this blog, which began on March 6, 2011, was "does language obscure or uncover the world?," and his discussion pivoted on an incident that occurred in April 1972, during his short period as a graduate student in the History and Philosophy of Science Program at Princeton. His rendition of this incident was designed to point to an issue that is at the heart of contemporary academic discussion in the human sciences but which has also seeped into popular culture. This is the issue of the relativity of truth.

Morris had been studying with the philosopher and historian of science Thomas Kuhn, who had left the University of California at Berkeley in 1964 and moved to the Institute for Advanced Study at Princeton, where he had recently published (in 1970) the revised edition of his highly influential but controversial *The Structure of Scientific Revolutions*. (The original edition was published in 1962.) Kuhn's claim about the "incommensurability" of "paradigms" in the history of natural science "really bothered" Morris, who believed that the claim not only posed a danger to the practice of science but, because of what Morris alleged to be the self-contained character of Kuhn's concept of paradigms, entailed the impossibility of authentically studying the history of science. Morris did not, however, make clear exactly how an argument by an academic philosopher was a threat to science or any other practice concerned with a search for truth. According to Morris, however, Kuhn had forbidden him and other students to attend lectures by the visiting philosopher Saul Kripke. Although Morris apparently did not understand it at the time, Kripke's argument (later published as *Naming and Necessity*, 1980) about the existence and persistence of natural kinds, despite word changes, conflicted sharply with Kuhn's account of revolutionary shifts in science and of how certain words may persist while the concepts to which they refer undergo a change. Morris claimed that things came to a head when Kuhn very critically assessed a paper of Morris's and even called into question his basic scholarly capacity. Morris related that when he attempted to defend his paper, as well as to challenge Kuhn's basic argument about the history of science, Kuhn, a very heavy chain-smoker, became upset and threw an ashtray full of cigarette butts at him and subsequently, in Morris's words, in effect "threw me out of Princeton." It is doubtful that Kuhn was solely responsible for Morris's exit from the program, and it may strain credulity to believe that Kuhn actually attempted to hit Morris with the ashtray. But it is probably safe to assume that the ashtray was launched. Although Kuhn's written work was not polemical and was typically measured and somewhat conciliatory with respect to opposing views, there is much to suggest that personally he was contentious and adamant in defending his argument. He himself noted that in his entire career he had never had a graduate student in philosophy: "I tend to scare them away. I criticize" (1997).

Morris described Kuhn as exemplifying a trend in philosophy, and intellectual life in general, that denigrated the very idea of truth and in which Wittgenstein was deeply implicated. Morris believed that Kuhn could be classified as a "postmodernist," because his "ideas led to the relativity or even the denial of truth—a dangerous idea." There is little to suggest that main currents in postmodernist philosophy were influenced by Wittgenstein, but Morris believed that Kuhn's arguments were derived from Wittgenstein. Morris's commitment was to a philosophical "correspondence theory of truth" that could specify the basis of "the *relationship* between language and the world." His general point of view reflected one pole of a dispute in academic philosophy that had been taking shape while he was a graduate student and that characterized debates in the literature of the philosophy of science. Although it was apparent that Morris had not remained current with the course of the conversation during the following generation, his claims related to what is still a central issue in contemporary philosophy. Partisans of various forms of what is often referred to as representational philosophy use Wittgenstein and individuals such as Kuhn as poster boys for the position that they oppose. Their image of this position, however, is largely a caricature, and in Morris's tertiary rendition, it is even more difficult to ascribe it to any specific individual.

Morris was projecting a philosophical dispute onto practices such as science and other forms of empirical investigation. Certainly scientists, and almost everyone in a practical situation, assume something that might be characterized as a concern about the extent to which hypotheses correspond to facts and whether their theories provide an accurate account of the "world," but many philosophers who defend a correspondence theory of truth are making a claim about truth and reality that not only exceeds any practice such as science but seeks to provide a foundation for such practices. The concerns of the truth-seeker in a particular practice such as science are abstracted and played out on a transcendental stage. Morris was quite correct in sensing that both Wittgenstein and Kuhn were challenging the metaphysical quest for an answer to the question of how language and thought make contact with the world and thereby achieve truth. Kuhn and Wittgenstein were, for example, favored figures in Richard Rorty's (1979) widely discussed challenge to this kind of philosophy, but Morris, both as a graduate student and in later years, misunderstood both Kuhn's argument and its place in the philosophy of science during the last half of the twentieth century. Although Morris's description of Kuhn's argument about paradigms and incommensurability was in some respects simply incorrect, the real crux of the issue that animated the philosophical debate that was reflected in Morris's blog was the question of the relationship between philosophy and its subject matter, in this case the relationship between the philosophy of science and the practice of science. The irony is that an actual practitioner of the search for truth, such as Morris, could believe that philosophy had both the burden and the capacity of sustaining or, as in the case of his perception of Kuhn and Wittgenstein, destroying the criteria for applying the term "truth" in various practices. Philosophy's perennial dream of having an impact on its subject matter had in a strange way become the nightmare of the truth-seeker.

The strong philosophical reaction against the work of Wittgenstein and Kuhn was precipitated by the manner in which their work challenged what Peter Winch (1958) had dubbed the "master-scientist" image of philosophy, that is, the idea of philosophy as establishing a standard of truth and reality that transcends the practices in which concrete truth-claims are advanced and as providing both a justification for such claims and a basis for assessing them. The charge of relativism leveled against arguments such as those of Kuhn and Wittgenstein is not actually motivated by (what appears to be) a concern with the danger of epistemic anarchy in practices such as science and politics, but by the fear of philosophy losing its hopes for cognitive authority and the status of an underwriter and critic of those practices that profess knowledge and truth. For individuals such as Wittgenstein, Kuhn, and Winch, the first task of philosophy was to understand and interpret its subject matter—whether it should affect that subject matter was an open question, to which they did not offer any apodictic answer.

Kuhn obviously had become very frustrated not only with Morris's failure to understand his argument but with his attributing to that argument the Whig or "presentist" view of the history of science that Kuhn had so forcefully attempted to combat, that is, writing the history of science as a story leading up to and justifying the latest reigning scientific theories as coming ever closer to correctly representing the world. Morris's focus was on Kuhn's concept of incommensurability, which Morris took to mean, in effect, that the successive paradigms and theories that Kuhn described were linguistic prison-fortresses that one could neither intellectually escape from nor enter. Kuhn's actual argument, however, was that the history of science revealed a series of paradigm formations and transformations and that the task of the historian was first to understand these formulations on their own terms and then provide an interpretation, which was necessarily couched in the language and conceptual repertoire of the historian/philosopher, a repertoire that, in Kuhn's case, included concepts such as paradigm, anomaly, incommensurable, revolution, normal science, and the like.

Morris began his blog with a quotation from Jorge Luis Borges that stated, "I don't want to die in a language I can't understand"; but a basic premise of Kuhn's argument was that past paradigms were indeed, in principle, understandable even though their concepts might not be the

same as those of the interpreter or fully translatable, which is a fundamental problem in all interpretive endeavors. But another issue hinged on the
difference and relationship between words and concepts, that is, whether
a term such as "truth," despite its universally favorable connotation, is the
name of a thing and has some transcontextual substantive meaning and
criteria of application or whether it is simply a term we apply to claims
in which we have what is considered to be justified belief. Allied to this
issue is the question of whether or not philosophers, as opposed to scientists, political actors, artists, and the like, possess the ability and authority
to assess and justify the use of these terms. The revolt against representational philosophy was not a revolt against the validity of truth-claims
in various practical realms of discourse, but a revolt against a particular
philosophical account of truth-claims and against a particular image of
the vocation of philosophy. Kuhn was not calling into question the objectivity of science, but only a particular philosophical account of objectivity.

Morris suggested that the ashtray incident was precipitated in part
by Kuhn's lingering doubts about his own work and that this hypothesis
had been "reinforced by a recent memoir," *Little Did I Know* (2010), by
the philosopher Stanley Cavell, who had been at Harvard with Kuhn in
the 1950s and subsequently a junior faculty member with him in the philosophy department at Berkeley. Morris claimed that Kuhn, in the process of writing *Structure*, "had Wittgenstein *and* Hitler on his mind," and
Morris posed the question of whether he had been, "like any good Jewish
boy of the period (myself included), struggling with the meaning of the
Third Reich" and wondering "if there are no absolute value judgments to
be made about one historical period (read: paradigm) or another, what
about the Nazis?" Morris claimed that his question derived from an incident Cavell related in his book about a conversation with Kuhn after
Kuhn accompanied him home for a drink after a faculty meeting:

> Talking past midnight Tom was becoming agitated in a way I
> had not seen. He suddenly lurched forward in his chair with a
> somewhat tortured look that I had begun to be familiar with.
> "I know Wittgenstein uses the idea of 'paradigm.' But I do not
> see its implications in his work. How do I answer the objec-
> tion that this destroys the truth of science? I deplore the idea.
> Yet if instruction and agreement are the essence of the matter,
> then Hitler could instruct me that a theory is true and get me

to agree." My reply I cast as follows, using the words I remember using then. "No he could not; he could not educate you in, convince you of, show you, its truth. Hitler could declare a theory to be true, as an edict. He could effectively threaten to kill you if you refuse to, or fail to, believe it. But all that means is that he is going to kill you; or perhaps kill you if you do not convince him, show him, that you accept and will follow the edict. I don't say this is clear. But it is something I cannot doubt is worth doing whatever work it will take to make clear." Tom's response was startling. He arose almost violently from his chair, began pacing in front of the fireplace, saying something like, "Yah. Yah." What causes conviction? What, perhaps rather, may undo an unnoticed conviction?

Part of what is interesting about this passage from Cavell's book is that it does not actually bolster Morris's claim that Kuhn was calling science and truth into question. It simply seems to demonstrate Kuhn's concern about how practical judgments in science or morals are formed and transformed and whether there is any philosophical answer to the problem of adjudicating conflicts between them. Cavell, who would go on to become an eminent Wittgenstein scholar, actually seemed to imply that there was no such answer.

Morris also described how he had recently personally interrogated Cavell "about this passage. About Kuhn and Wittgenstein and about how Wittgenstein had opened the door to relativism." This phrasing, however, rather begged the question, but it was the framework in terms of which Morris interpreted and transcribed Cavell's response:

STANLEY CAVELL: Kuhn really was terribly alarmed that Wittgenstein was denying the rationality of truth. That somehow, everything was going to come down to agreement. It would be circling around that. . . . Which I don't think is a non-issue. I think it's quite real.

ERROL MORRIS: And what were your feelings about it?

CAVELL: . . . that it was a genuine issue, that Wittgenstein was opening up. Part of it was a matter of getting down, in the mud, and figuring out what "agreement" meant.

MORRIS: This would be in "Philosophical Investigations"?

CAVELL: Yes. "Philosophical Investigations." That's what we talked
about. The early Wittgenstein, as far as we were concerned,
was frozen history. Nobody was really interested in trying to
make that work, it was "Philosophical Investigations" that
was really *hot*. The issue about what human agreement could
establish, and how deep that agreement was. Wittgenstein's
quote, "We don't agree in judgment, we agree in form of life."
Whether that meant that knowledge of the universe was
relative to human forms of life. We went around the track
with that a lot, and, why not? The actual quotation is from
paragraph 241 of "Philosophical Investigations": "So you are
saying that human agreement decides what is true and what
is false?"—It is what human beings *say* that is true and false;
and they agree in the *language* they use. That is not agreement in opinions but in form of life." This passage, as well as
many others in "Philosophical Investigations," has produced
extended commentary. But Wittgenstein, notoriously difficult to pin-down, at least in this one instance, seems to be
saying what he's saying. And he opens the door (or the lid of
Pandora's Box) to a relativistic notion of truth. In paragraph
241, it's *agreement* between human beings that decides what
is true or false. It suggests that we could agree that the earth
is flat and that would make it so. So much for the relationship between science and the world. And yet, Kuhn made
peace with this idea. He even made it the cornerstone of his
philosophy of science. A couple of years later in "Structure,"
Kuhn would write, "We may, to be more precise, have to
relinquish the notion, implicit or explicit, that changes of
paradigm bring scientists and those that learn from them,
closer and closer to the truth."

There is no doubt that these then young philosophers were struggling with the implications of Wittgenstein's work, but it is somewhat
doubtful that Morris's report of the conversation is entirely accurate,
because what Cavell supposedly said about truth and falsity being based
on agreement does not exactly coincide with the quotation from Wittgenstein. What is important about the quotation, but apparently misunderstood by Morris, was that in the passage from the *Investigations*,

Wittgenstein was responding to an imaginary interlocutor's conclusion that "human agreement decides what is true or false" and pointing out that agreement was rooted in a form of life that provided the criteria of truth and falsity. Cavell certainly agreed with Wittgenstein's statement, but he made it clear that Kuhn was grappling with the issue of whether there is any external philosophically specifiable basis for assessing the truth of judgments within a paradigm. Although both Wittgenstein and Kuhn believed that there was the possibility of external as well as internal rational critical assessments and defenses of various propositions, it was not the kind conceived by much of traditional philosophy in which concepts denoting what purported to be real in some particular case hovered over an invisible reality that could never, itself, be actually represented. Truth-claims are, perforce, absolute in character. They are only relative when viewed against the backdrop of various forms of representational philosophy as well as in the obvious and benign sense that they are advanced and contested by various people in diverse situations.

Morris made an odd choice in attempting to enlist Cavell as an ally. Not only did Cavell go on to become one of the most influential interpreters and defenders of Wittgenstein, but Morris's selective excerpts and extrapolations from Cavell's autobiography belie how close, both intellectually and personally, Cavell was to Kuhn. Cavell's book also gives some pause to the common assumption that Wittgenstein's work, mediated through Cavell, played a major role in the formulation of Kuhn's basic thesis. Although discussions with Cavell certainly contributed to Kuhn's final version of the manuscript, the basic argument had been formulated before Kuhn arrived in Berkeley. He noted in the preface to *Structure* that the fact that Cavell "should have reached conclusions so congruent to my own has been a constant source of stimulation and encouragement to me. He is, furthermore, the only person with whom I have ever been able to explore my ideas in incomplete sentences. That mode of communication attests an understanding that has enabled him to point me the way through or around several major barriers encountered while preparing my first manuscript." Cavell at that point, however, was actually most deeply involved with the work of the philosopher J. L. Austin.

In his autobiography, Cavell indicated that he had actually gained more from Kuhn than Kuhn did from him, and he said that he realized early on that Kuhn was "doing work that would change things in philosophy" and that his "talents" and dedication to his "project" made "irrelevant" the intellectual "landmines" that were characteristic of American academia. He noted that he and Kuhn were the first faculty members in the philosophy department in "decades" to be "appointed outside the Berkeley ambience," which still bore "the mark of original logical positivism," to which Kuhn's work presented a fundamental challenge. They both critically confronted this intellectual atmosphere and sometimes evoked "outrage" among other faculty members who were still wedded to the correspondence theory of truth that had characterized the dominance of positivism in the philosophy of science. Cavell noted that Kuhn's work on the history of science complemented Cavell's reading of Austin on "how to do things with words" as well as what he referred to as his only "tentative glances at Wittgenstein," while he was still working on finishing his Harvard dissertation. After several years of circulating as a kind of underground tome, a revised form of the dissertation was finally published as *The Claim of Reason* in 1979, and in many respects it paralleled and complemented Rorty's attack on representationalism. Cavell attended Kuhn's classes and did the assigned reading, and he noted that he gained insight from Kuhn's revelation that science actually had a history. Cavell described how, in an early and "formative conversation" with Kuhn, he realized that Kuhn's focus on the manner in which scientific fields are structured by education corresponded to Wittgenstein's account of grammar and language acquisition as well as to what both Austin and Wittgenstein had to say about the grounds of agreement and judgment. But he also noted the degree to which Kuhn continued to agonize about how Wittgenstein "used the idea of paradigm" and that Kuhn had not worked out "the implications in his work" or found an answer to "the objection that this destroys the truth of science." Kuhn had, however, acceded to Cavell's response that someone such as Hitler might possess power but not the intellectual resources to convince someone of the truth of his doctrines, and he had recognized that an important task was to demonstrate how, in fact, fundamental beliefs about what was real and true were both created and displaced.

During the following year, Kuhn and Cavell met frequently and discussed the material that would compose Kuhn's book, and, despite the difference between their personal styles and between the respective details of their German-Jewish family backgrounds, Cavell felt that he had been inspired by these conversations, that he had gained the most from them, and that they had shaped his eventual sense of how language changes and is in certain respects arbitrary but also of how it functions as the "home of the a priori." He believed that *Structure* would make Kuhn "famous"— even if "not *that* famous." As Cavell worked on the last stages of his dissertation, he attempted to incorporate the "shocks" he had received from Kuhn as well as from Austin and Wittgenstein. It is worth noting that, despite Cavell's agreement with Kuhn's work, he has not been the recipient of attacks suggesting that his own work threatens to undermine the concept of truth. One explanation might be that Cavell did not focus on natural science and thus expose that what a significant part of our culture views as the quintessential form of knowledge is open to fundamental transformations that cannot be externally vouchsafed or falsified.

Kuhn did not, any more than Wittgenstein, seek to withdraw the meaning of "truth" from science or from its uses in any other aspect of life; *quite the contrary*, he claimed that the meaning of "truth" derived from its application in these practices rather than from something external to them. Kuhn never relinquished uneasiness about the fact that both within and between human practices the ascription of truth differed and about whether there were, as his critics asserted so vigorously, substantive universal criteria of truth. Unlike, for example, both Rorty and Cavell, Kuhn in his work was not directly devoted to an assault on representational philosophy, but to how what is considered true by scientists undergoes change. What he did, in effect, *was to take the meaning of "truth" away from the province of philosophies such as logical empiricism and bequeath it to science and the other human practices within and between which it is both articulated and contested.* What was implicit in Kuhn's argument, but more contentious, was the suggestion that the basic role of philosophy was more to understand, interpret, and describe claims to truth in science than either to defend or criticize them. This was the source of the philosophical agitation surrounding both Kuhn's work and that of Wittgenstein, which was reflected in Morris's essays.

Carl Hempel, whose covering-law model of scientific explanation became a principal element in the logical-empiricist philosophy of science as well as in the image of science accepted by many peripheral fields such as social science, insisted that to the extent to which this logical and epistemological ideal did not conform to the actual practices of science, it was so much the worse for science. Kuhn, however, claimed, in effect, that the difference was so much the worse for philosophy, and Wittgenstein argued that the dogmatism that characterized much of metaphysics was precisely the consequence of projecting such an ideal onto the actual practices of knowledge. Even at this point of his lecture, Morris did not understand how far the revolt against representational philosophy had proceeded. For example, Hilary Putnam, who Morris referred to authoritatively as a philosophical realist, had not, since at least the 1990s, embraced the views that Morris attributed to him. After many years of flirting and becoming enamored with "many faces of realism," Putnam (1999) had finally committed to what he designated as "pragmatic realism," which he explicitly identified with Wittgenstein's arguments and with claims such as those of Kuhn. And by this time, many philosophers had rejected Kripke's (1982) influential account of Wittgenstein as a rule-skeptic and proponent of the idea that the meaning of rules and the application of terms such as "truth" were grounded in nothing but some kind of community opinion. Wittgenstein's argument was that practices, ranging from common sense to science, and the rules and concepts of truth that are constitutive of such practices, are grounded nowhere but in the practices themselves. How this makes them vulnerable to the worries articulated by Morris is difficult to say. There is an old joke about the Greek boy who asked the oracle, "If Atlas supports the earth, what supports Atlas?" When the oracle replied that Atlas stood on a turtle, the boy asked, "What supports the turtle?" The oracle answered, "It's turtles all the way down." Wittgenstein might have said that it is propositions all the way down.

In the final essay in the blog, Morris described how he had turned for support in his criticisms of Kuhn to the Nobel physicist Steven Weinberg, who, in his extrascientific excursions into the academic "science wars" of recent years, had emphasized the difference between how Kuhn imagined science and how it was actually practiced as well as what he referred to as "Kuhn's radically skeptical conclusions about what is accomplished in the work of science . . . conclusions that have made Kuhn a hero to the philosophers, historians, sociologists, and cultural critics who question the objective character of scientific knowledge, and who prefer to describe scientific theories as social constructions, not so different from democracy or baseball." And, Morris added, "not so different from parapsychology, astrology or witchcraft." The fact is that Kuhn, initially a physicist before turning to philosophy and history, was not at all skeptical of science but only of certain philosophical accounts of science, which were the lenses through which Weinberg perceived and reflected on the practice of science. Simply because natural scientists know a great deal about nature does not mean that they know a great deal about the history and practice of science. Weinberg also criticized what he took to be Kuhn's argument that it was not possible to characterize paradigm shifts as representing cumulative progress in science and that there were no criteria for saying that a particular scientific theory brought us closer to the truth. Weinberg, however, no more than Morris, understood either what Kuhn had actually said or the philosophical context of Kuhn's argument. Kuhn did not challenge what scientists took to be progress, facts, and the like, but only the assumption that there was some determinate, philosophical, trans-scientific basis for making judgments about these matters. As in the case of the application of the word "truth," the criteria of "progress" are internal to science. Kuhn's point was that philosophers are in no particular position to make decisions about what constituted scientific progress.

If Morris had carefully thought it through, rather than seeking a culprit on which to blame what may arguably be a disdain for truth in various elements of contemporary society, which Hannah Arendt had already pointed out a generation earlier in her essay "Truth and Politics," he might have realized that Kuhn was not undermining science, but instead insulating it from some of the very philosophical incursions that Morris believed threatened scientific values, which some tributaries of postmodernism may have come close to manifesting. For philosophers to claim that there is no meaning to "truth" and no basis for truth-claims is as fatuous as the claim that philosophy knows some ultimate meaning of "truth" and how to assess truth-claims. What Morris was actually looking for, in the work of Kripke and others, was a way, other than persuasion, for what is accepted as scientific knowledge to trump its external rivals and its internal forebears, but this was something that Kuhn, despite his personal agreement with what the scientific community deemed as knowledge, argued that philosophy could not supply. What is ironic is that Morris's own career has exemplified the persuasive activity that Kuhn viewed as the catalyst of scientific change. Morris, however, was still not satisfied and concluded, in his words, that in the end "Weinberg fails to drive the stake through the heart of the vampire" who threatened to suck out the life-blood of science and the concept of truth.

Morris then initiated a conversation with Norton Wise, who had been a postdoctoral student at the time that Morris was at Princeton and with whom he had spent many evenings complaining about Kuhn. They reminisced at length about his excessive smoking habit and the adversarial character of his seminars. Morris related that Wise, who later became director of the History and Philosophy of Science Program, described how he had continued his debates with Kuhn and how much of this pivoted on the conflict between the perspectives of the scientist and the historian/philosopher. It is interesting that in a Festschrift for Kuhn from 1993, Wise's contribution did not mention any disagreement with Kuhn. Kuhn had not challenged the scientist's belief in scientific progress and its regulative principle of seeking the truth about the world, but rather only the attempt of academic literature in the history and philosophy of science to tell the story of science as a cumulative building of knowledge that came ever closer to the truth about some abstract concept of the world. Morris also returned to his invocation of Kripke and to what he took to be Kripke's demonstration that "there is an *objective* reality. There is *objective* truth. And there is *objective* history. The beliefs of 6th century B.C.E. mathematicians might be inaccessible to us (or at least, difficult for us to understand), but when Hippasus or one of his contemporaries refer to $\sqrt{2}$, they are referring to the same thing we are." This was actually a poorly chosen example, because it implied the contentious Platonic philosophical assumption, so frontally challenged by Wittgenstein as infiltrating mathematical practices, that mathematical symbols refer to invisible mathematical objects, but the example also once again indicated Morris's failure to distinguish between words and concepts. The word "objectivity" usually carries the same connotation in all contexts, but it involves quite different criteria when applied in different contexts—ranging from officiating sports to quantum mechanics.

In the end, Morris declined to lay the complete blame on Kuhn for what he took, in the wake of such controversies as the continuing contemporary conflict between evolutionary biology and creationism, to be the devaluation of scientific truth and the emergence of a belief in the relativity of truth, but he claimed that Kuhn "shares some responsibility for it." It is true that Kuhn offered no answer to a choice between evolutionism and creationism, any more than his history of science demonstrated that the ascendency of the current understanding of combustion over an explanation based on the theory of phlogiston could be explained by reference to some extrascientific criteria. As Wittgenstein explicitly noted in *On Certainty*, defenders of evolution claim that they have it right, just as antievolutionists hold on to their beliefs, but this dispute is not like that between two rival hypotheses within science that can be judged by commonly accepted theoretical criteria. If philosophy could be called on to authoritatively adjudicate such disputes, we could dispense not only with conflicts within science but between science and theology.

Relativism is not an argument or position that anyone actually embraces, except maybe in sophomore dormitories. It is largely an invention of academic philosophy. "Relativism" is typically a pejorative label for arguments that challenge the belief that philosophy has the inherent capacity to make judgments about the adequacy of claims in various practices ranging from science to morality. It is nearly always ascribed in defense of the authority of philosophy. Scientists, for example, do not worry about, and after some initial resistance usually celebrate, transformations in what is taken to be scientifically true. They do not throw up their hands and complain about the relativity of truth, and they only very occasionally (as Kuhn pointed out) engage in strenuous battles to contest what propositions deserve the label of "truth." Wittgenstein, and Kuhn after him, simply wished to return the property of truth to its rightful owners, that is, to scientists, common sense, and *to people like Morris*. What Kuhn did was to demonstrate that when science changes, much of what scientists, and most of society, mean by the "world" changes. Morris's career has been devoted to demonstrating that such change is possible with respect to what may be the accepted truth regarding something such as a person's guilt. It seems that Morris should have found Kuhn's work less a threat to his enterprise than a confirmation, but instead he joined the chorus of philosophers who have accused Kuhn of promulgating the contemporary "relativist zeitgeist" and the "thesis that knowledge is socially constructed" (e.g., Sokal and Bricmont 1998, 51; Boghossian 2006, 6).

Some, such as Steve Fuller and George Reisch, have gone so far as not only to criticize Kuhn as a threat to truth but to claim that his work undermined the critical socially engaged philosophy of logical empiricism after it emigrated to the United States and that it aided and abetted a conservative American Cold War ideology (Fuller 2000, 2005; Reisch 2005). Fuller alleged that Kuhn had added to the "relativistic" impact of the "radical skepticism of deconstructionism" and "postmodern pluralism," which accelerated the "cancerous growth of specialization" and precipitated a turn away from a search for substantive truth. He charged that Kuhn was "an intellectual coward who benefited from his elite insti-

tutional status in what remains the world's dominant society." Following
Fuller's lead, Reisch argued that the result of Kuhn's work had been to
create an atmosphere of "historical amnesia and political inertia," reward
"intellectual conformity," dull "the critical sensibilities," and precipitate
a situation where an "'acritical' perspective has colonized the academy."
This "paranoid vision" (Richardson 2007, 354) has even prompted the
claim that although Kuhn had not "intentionally plagiarized" the work
of Ludwik Fleck (for which Kuhn later wrote a foreword to the English
translation), the Cold War atmosphere and "political reasons" led to a
"periphrastic" adaption of Fleck's language (Babich 2003, 103–4). These
arguments largely consist of speculations and innuendos (Gunnell 2009).
Although, after the war, Kuhn became largely ideologically disengaged,
there is nothing to suggest that the views that characterized his basically
left-leaning, and even pacifist, early years had ever changed. What is so
disingenuous about these claims is that it was actually logical positivism
that became the dominant image of science among Cold War apologists
and that Kuhn's work significantly undermined that image. But although
Kuhn has been a consistent target of criticism, it is Wittgenstein who is
often presented as the principal author of a spiritual defection from truth,
which has led to a scourge of relativism.

When Pope Benedict XVI delivered his homily to the conclave that
elected him in 2005, he proclaimed that the greatest problem in the contemporary world was the "dictatorship of relativism." He reiterated this
sentiment on World Peace Day in 2012 when he blamed "the culture of
that relativism" for everything from a general social devaluation of moral
truth to the summer riots in Great Britain. One might wonder what
the connection may be between the Pope's pronouncements and similar
claims by secular academicians such as Ernest Gellner, who claimed that
Wittgenstein is the creator of a "spectre [that] haunts human thought:
relativism" and that the answer, for which cultural anthropology must
search, is "human universals" (1984, 83); a philosopher such as Jerry Fodor,
who, in defense of the idea of a human nature based on a universal language of thought, said, "I *hate* relativism. I hate relativism more than
anything else, excepting, maybe, fiberglass power boats" (1985, 5); and the
philosopher Ian Jarvie's claim that we need a "cognitive notion of values" that would serve to counter "the relativistic plague" of contemporary
thought (2008, 279–92). The Pope's concern was with the moral authority
of the church, but it is reasonable to assume that it was his background

as a university professor that in part prompted him to frame the problem as one of relativism.

When academicians speak about the opposition of "rationality and relativism" (e.g., Hollis and Lukes 1982), it is an invidious phrasing, because it implies that the claims that they label as relativism, such as the arguments of Wittgenstein, Kuhn, and Peter Winch, are at best a denial of rationality and at worst a defense of irrationality. What is really at issue in these contrived debates is the criterion of rationality. The line of argument pursued by individuals such as Alasdair MacIntyre, Martin Hollis, Steven Lukes, and many others is that behavior that accords with some (often contemporary) scientific and philosophical logical and substantive criteria of rationality is self-explanatory, while nonconformity must be causally explained (Gunnell 2011, ch. 5). One might understand the Pope's concern about vouchsafing the church's authority, but the source of the sentiments that lead philosophers and many social theorists to seek and defend some form of cognitive privilege might seem stranger. One might ask what dogma and institutional structure they are attempting to protect.

The issue is to some extent the atavistic residue of the past life of philosophy, which like a recessive gene continues to manifest itself. A few centuries ago, the demarcation between what we would retrospectively likely refer to, on the one hand, as practices such as science, politics, religion and, on the other hand, the practice of philosophy was much more difficult to specify. Substantive scientific claims were entwined with a justificatory language designed to defend against rival internal challenges as well as external competing forms of intellectual authority, and philosophy was seldom divorced from speaking about and to various dimensions of political and social life. The language of contemporary science, which is internally paradigmatic and relatively secure from external challenges, has shed this rhetoric of inquiry, but that rhetoric has found a home in philosophy, where it is called "epistemology." The problem of relativism is an invention of the human sciences and rooted in the problem of their practical relationship to their subject matter. Many philosophers and social theorists remain obsessed with maintaining some basis for speaking to, as well as about, the practices from which philosophy has floated free. What it is about Wittgenstein that bothers many people is the fact that his work represents the modern condition of philosophy, where philosophy is no longer part of science and where its relationship to its object of inquiry has been fundamentally problematized. While philosophy's claims to authority are sometimes linked, however vaguely, to actual issues of practical judgment, the search for such authority has often become an end in itself and devoted to jousting with the windmills of relativism in which the ghost of individuals such as Wittgenstein, Winch, and Kuhn are believed to lurk.

Among philosophers and social theorists, and even among rioters in England, there are very few self-proclaimed relativists. Relativism is indeed a specter, but this shade is the evil twin of philosophical foundationalism. It is not really a position at all, but a persona conjured up by metaphysicians, theologians, and rationalists and attributed to those who disagree with the claim that there are philosophically or theologically accessible universal criteria of truth. Those who are engaged in substantive searches for the truth in their respective domains, from social science to investigative journalism, are sometimes frightened by these philosophical bogies and go off in search of metaphysical ghostbusters, but this is also often in part because they, like those practitioners of early science, are less than secure in their claims to truth.

It is very difficult for philosophers to relinquish the idea that there is a way of doing philosophy that overcomes the contingencies involved in the practical relationship between philosophy and its subject matter. Much of the hostility toward Wittgenstein is rooted in his rejection of the image of philosophy as an arbiter of the use of "truth." The relationship between academic philosophy and the various practices it studies is not well understood—even among many scientists and philosophers. Although the facts of science rest on what might sometimes be referred to as "philosophical" assumptions about the nature of things and about how knowledge of those things is gained, this does not mean that the foundations of science are based on the formulations of academic metaphysics and epistemology. And although scientists, such as Einstein, may sometimes, especially in their later years, wax, so to speak, "philosophic" about such matters as whether God plays dice, this has little to do with what goes on in the philosophical academy. But in addition to the confusions that may attend lay understandings of this issue, it is also muddied by both the philosophers' pretensions to science and scientists' pretensions to philosophy.

It is conceivable that members of some isolated society who had developed the capacity to read an anthropologist's account of their culture might begin to reflect comparatively on their lives and have self-doubts—or even members of a religion who had read an academic history of their sect might be prompted to wonder about the truth of their beliefs. It does not appear that Kuhn's work has generated this kind of self-doubt among natural scientists. The kind of anxiety that Kuhn and Wittgenstein seem to induce in some philosophers and in individuals such as Morris, about the very possibility of seeking what is true in some particular case, is distinctly mysterious. It is, however, in part a failure to recognize that "truth" does not refer to a thing at all. When we speak about searching for truth, we tend to become captured by a metaphor that leads us astray. It is not very meaningful to talk about the search for truth apart from the truth about some specific "this" or "that." At most we end up with some abstract formula such as that of Alfred Tarski ("snow is white" is true if and only if snow is white), which, as Wittgenstein pointed out, fails to get us outside of language. Despite the fact that philosophers have devoted a great deal of attention to what they speak of as a general "theory" of truth, there can no more be a theory of truth than, as Wittgenstein noted, "a theory of wishing, which would have to explain every single case of wishing" (*PG*, 19). He denied that "examples give the essence of what one calls 'wishing.' At most they present different essences which are all signified by this word because of certain interrelationships. The error is to suppose that we wanted the examples to illustrate the essence of wishing, and that the counter examples showed that this essence hadn't yet been correctly grasped" (*PG*, 120). And as in the case of wishing, the same could be said of seeing: "For 'naive language,' that's to say our naif, normal, way of expressing ourselves, does not contain any theory of seeing—it shews you, not any theory, but only a *concept* of seeing" (*PP*, 1:1101). So the real question involves the concept of truth, that is, what kind of concept it is.

Simon Blackburn (2005) has conducted an edifying excursion through the history of philosophy from the perspective of a continuing conflict between "absolutism" and "relativism" as a typology of theories of truth and in terms of variations such as realism, constructivism, eliminativism, and quietism. His "guide for the perplexed" may be useful for finding one's way about in the discourse of the contemporary "truth wars," but Blackburn did not provide any definite answer to the problem of truth. As a quasi-realist, he embraced a kind of middle ground, which recognizes a degree of wisdom in both extremes, and he personally opted for a mini-

malist or pragmatic position, which holds that there are indeed truths
in various sectors of judgment but no transcendental truth. Blackburn
seemed to indicate an affinity with Wittgenstein's approach, but although
it might be reasonable to categorize Wittgenstein as a philosophical minimalist, it is important to recognize that in his later work Wittgenstein
rejected the whole idea of a theory of truth. "Truth" is a word that has
uses and that typically functions as a positive signal attached to claims
for which one has what are assumed to be reasons that justify a belief.
We might want to call this analysis a theory, but it would be a theory
only in the sense of a descriptive claim about how certain concepts are
used and how they function in our language. Much has been made of
Wittgenstein's rejection of theory, but, as I will argue in the next chapter,
it is important to be clear about what he was rejecting. In the case of
truth-claims, there are indeed family resemblances among such claims as
well as among certain classes of such claims, but there is no essence that is
common to all and that can be derived as a basis of defending particular
judgments about what is true—or just, or right, or moral.

What has created anxiety about the work of Kuhn and Wittgenstein is not simply that they did not seek to instruct science in the application of the concept of truth but that they did not appear to pursue a
broader social agenda such as that associated with someone such as Karl
Popper. From the point of its prototypical roots, in the work of individuals ranging from Francis Bacon to John Stuart Mill, the philosophy of
science not only has been a normative enterprise but has characteristically reflected ideological motives and motifs. Consequently, it is a short
step from Morris's worries about Kuhn to the conclusion that his work
conceals a conservative ideology that endangers innovation in both science and politics. Popper's perspective appealed to his followers, such as
Gellner and Imre Lakatos, whose political values informed their philosophical approach to science. All of these individuals were bitter foes of
Wittgenstein and what they took to be the relativist implications of his
philosophy, because they were seeking the kind of cognitive authority
that would sustain a form of rational social critique as well as vouchsafe a particular view of social order. Lakatos, for example, had been a
member of the Hungarian Communist Party but was imprisoned for
his revisionist views and, after involvement in the Hungarian revolution,
eventually defected to Vienna and then to England after the Russian
invasion of Hungary in 1956. He gained a degree from Cambridge and

was appointed to the London School of Economics in 1960, where, with
the encouragement of Joseph Agassi and John Watkins, he became part
of Popper's circle. As late as the early 1990s, Agassi, an Israeli, referred
to Paul Feyerabend, who by then was considered a Popperian apostate,
as "just another recruit to the army" of "preachers" of "hate" whose work
raised no bar to ideologies such as Nazism and to what he construed as
similar movements such as the New Left (1991, 36). Gellner had been a
refugee from Czechoslovakia in 1939, and after the advent of the Communist regime, he was devoted to a crusade against Wittgenstein and
relativism. Consequently, it was difficult for many of these individuals
not to read Kuhn's work as embodying yet another form of ideology or,
even worse, as lacking some essential ethical element.

To interpret Kuhn's stress on the manner in which the "firm consensus," and even "dogmatism," underlying "normal" science is a prerequisite
of revolution and essential to the growth of scientific knowledge as participation in Cold War ideology is as strained as assuming, as many others also did, that his emphasis on revolutions reflected the politically dis-
sident atmosphere of the 1960s. What these interpretations share is the
assumption that philosophy is a normative enterprise and that in terms of
neither purpose nor effect does it or should it "leave everything as it is."
This concern about the relationship between philosophy and its subject
matter is the underlying source of the antipathy toward Kuhn's work and
of the worries about relativism that his work has spawned. Both Wittgenstein and Kuhn exacerbated this endemic concern about the role of
philosophy, because while (as I argue in the next chapter) they conceived
of philosophy as a form of social inquiry, they fundamentally problematized the relationship between philosophy and its subject matter.

2

WITTGENSTEIN & SOCIAL THEORY

We might speak of fundamental principles of human enquiry.
(*OC*, 670)
Nothing is more difficult than facing concepts *without prejudice*.
(*PP*, 2:87)

—WITTGENSTEIN

ALTHOUGH THERE IS REASON TO CONCLUDE that in many respects Wittgenstein quite gradually but explicitly rejected much of the conception of, and approach to, philosophy that characterized the *Tractatus Logico-Philosophicus*, there has been considerable controversy about the exact character and degree of change and continuity. I will say more about that shift in chapter 7, but a significant aspect of what he referred to as "turning our whole inquiry around" (*PI*, 108) was what, in effect, was a *conception of philosophy as a form of social inquiry*. This involved avoiding what he repeatedly stressed as the mistake of projecting the language of philosophy, and logic, onto the world and confusing the means of representation with what was represented. Such a projection is an essential characteristic of natural science, but it is a mistake in the case of philosophy, and social inquiry as a whole, to assume such a stance.

It only leads to dogmatism and to a lack of clarity about the object of investigation. In the *Tractatus*, he had already noted that "philosophy is not a body of doctrines but an activity" devoted to "elucidations" (4.112). We might argue about the extent to which the *Tractatus* was a rejection of metaphysics, but while that book struggled with the issue of how thought and language connect with the world, the "world" (*Welt*) is barely mentioned in the *Investigations*. He had early on noted that "the difficulty of my theory of logical portrayal was that of finding a connexion between the signs on paper and a situation outside in the world." He was seeking what he often referred to as a "redemptive" (*ersölende*) concept that would be the "key" to demonstrating how propositions could represent (e.g., *NB*, 39, 54). Some years later, he admitted that "in the *Tractatus* logical analysis and ostensive definition were unclear to me. At that time I thought that there was a connexion between language and reality" (Waismann 1979, 209–10). In the *Tractatus*, he seemed to give up the search for a redemptive concept and relegate the problem to "silence" and to what can be "shown," but he later picked it up again. As late as *The Big Typescript*, he continued to talk about finding such a concept, but, significantly, it is not discussed in the *Investigations*, where it is viewed as a metaphysical pseudo-problem. In the *Investigations*, philosophy was no longer in the business of underwriting natural science or any other first-order discourse, and it was in philosophy, rather than science, that the concept of representation was appropriate. The task of philosophy was to clarify and represent the grammar in which the world was manifest. His concern was no longer with how to represent the world but with how to re-present language-games and the particular conceptual *Weltbild* at the core of a form of life. It was in this respect that Wittgenstein addressed the concept of justice. In his criticism of how James Frazer, in *The Golden Bough*, had distorted the meaning of the exotic social practices he studied, Wittgenstein stated that, as either philosophers or ethnologists, "our only task is to be just" and "not to set up new parties—or creeds" (*BT*, 309). This attitude in no way implied an uncritical approach to the subject matter, but only that, in the first instance, it should be fairly represented.

He noted that calling his new kind of investigation "philosophy" could be misleading, because it was really one of "the heirs of the subject which used to be called philosophy" (*BB*, 28). Philosophy, as he came to view and pursue it, was the investigation of the concepts that informed the conventions of human speech and action, and, as in the case of much of social inquiry, the purpose was often critical and therapeutic, with respect both to the conception of inquiry and, at least potentially, to the subject matter. Although he denied that "philosophy is ethnology," he stated that it is essential to "look at things from an ethnological point of view," which required "taking up a position far outside, in order to see things *more objectively*" (*BB*, 28; *CV*, 45), and many of his examples were drawn from anthropology. In his discussions of mathematics, he stressed the difference between the attitude of the mathematician and that of the philosopher and noted that for philosophy "mathematics is after all an anthropological phenomenon" (*RFM*, 399). He said at one point, "I am trying to conduct you on tours in a certain country" (*LFM*, 44). He viewed philosophy as mapping meaning, and maps assume the autonomy of what is mapped and entail the problem of making an accurate, and useful, representation.

Although one can read the *Investigations* as an inquiry into the vocation of philosophy, it is also an investigation into the conditions that define the very nature of the human sciences, their conceptually autonomous subject matter, and their practical as well as epistemic relationship to that subject matter. While social scientists debate the issue of the proper methods for explaining social phenomena, what Wittgenstein had to say about the nature of such phenomena and what is involved in giving an account of them both includes and transcends any particular method, even though we might have reason to judge some methods better than others. His vision is particularly salient at a point when an interpretive social science continues to remain more an idea than a practice and when, as many theorists are attempting once again to articulate what an interpretive approach might involve, many others are returning to various forms of naturalism, such as cognitive neuroscience and sociobiology, as a ground of explanation and judgment. Peter Winch was quite correct, when more than a half-century ago, he recognized that Wittgenstein spoke to the very idea of a social science, and Winch's argument is still worth examining with care.

WINCH'S IDEA

Winch's *The Idea of a Social Science and Its Relation to Philosophy* (1958) has often become a surrogate for a direct confrontation with Wittgenstein on matters relating to social inquiry. Given the amount of commentary that has been devoted to this book, it may seem redundant to revisit it, but his argument has not, even by many of his defenders, let alone the critics, been carefully reconstructed textually. Often the book has, like that of Kuhn, been represented as a manifestation or symptom of not only a kind of philosophical quietism but a malicious modern form of relativism that has sprung from figures such as Wittgenstein and has become deeply embedded in various aspects of modern thought and culture, including both ethics and science. Winch's work indicates fully the extent to which Wittgenstein speaks both to the philosophy of social science and to foundational issues in the practices of the social sciences themselves, and I take the book as what Wittgenstein referred to as a "signpost." If one has ever hiked in remote areas of the world, they realize that signposts, as well as the gestures of individuals that one may query along the way, are less than certain indicators of how to proceed, but learning how to interpret such *Wegweisen* is a crucial aspect of the journey. Winch's work was that of a young philosopher, and, as he later recognized, the argument was far from perfectly formulated, but as Wittgenstein noted, even though a signpost may not definitively indicate how you should move forward, it is fine if it serves its purpose (*PI*, 87).

What must be made clear at the outset is the fact that Winch did not directly address the practices of social science. He explicitly noted that he was writing as a philosopher about an issue in philosophy rather than engaging in "what is commonly understood by the term methodology" or debates about how social scientists conduct, and should conduct, their activities (136). His book was a contribution to philosophical arguments about the nature of social science. It involved a confrontation between two philosophical *ideas* of a social science and an "attack" on what he claimed had become the dominant "conception of the relationship between the social studies, philosophy and the natural sciences." Apart from brief discussions of iconic figures such as Vilfredo Pareto, Émile Durkheim, and, especially, Max Weber, there was little direct engagement with the literature of social science. Although Winch claimed that "the conceptions according to which we normally think of social events are logically incompatible with the concepts belonging to [natural] scientific explanation" (95), he also had very little to say about natural science. What he characterized as natural science was often a reference less to any actual activity than to the work of individuals such as John Stuart Mill or to a version of the positivist philosophical account of the logic and epistemology of science. What in part made his book relevant for the practices of social science was, as in the case of Kuhn, the fact that the self-image of these fields, as well as their approaches to inquiry, had been significantly influenced by the philosophical position that he criticized.

Winch challenged the "platitude amongst writers of textbooks" that the social sciences were in their "infancy" and had not yet broken away from the "dead hand of philosophy" and embraced "the methods of the natural sciences." He suggested, however, that his conception of philosophy was as "heretical" as his conception of social science. Although he warned against the "extra-scientific *pretensions* of science," such as the claim that it might replace philosophy or that philosophy could be made scientific, he insisted that he was not advancing an "anti-scientific" argument but rather defending the autonomy of philosophy—and, in so doing, the autonomy of social science. His central thesis was that philosophy and social science are logically and epistemologically symmetrical and that consequently "to be clear about the nature of philosophy and to be clear about the nature of the social studies amount to the same thing. For any worthwhile study of society must be philosophical in character and any worthwhile philosophy must be concerned with the nature of human society." It was, however, in his use of the term "philosophy" that much of the misinterpretation of his argument has found its foothold, so it is crucial, as he himself noted, to pay careful attention to his statement of his "philosophical bearings" (1–3).

Winch's equation of philosophy and social science was based on the claim that they both studied other human practices and, consequently, are fundamentally different from natural science. There had been many attempts at demarcation, but Winch's particular argument was somewhat singular. What in part prompted his concern with the role of philosophy was an issue that was prominent at the time he was writing, but it was also an issue in the social sciences as well. Winch claimed that there was a confrontation between two different images of the philosopher: as an "underlabourer" and as a "master-scientist." He argued that although the deficiencies of both of these images were a target of his "heresy," each nevertheless had something to contribute to the idea of a social science. The underlabourer view of philosophy maintained that philosophy was "parasitic" and involved simply the "negative role of removing impediments" in the language of fields such as experimental science rather than contributing to "any positive understanding of the world." This approach to philosophy had actually been derived to some extent from Wittgenstein's work, but part of Winch's concern was to demonstrate that this was not actually the implication of Wittgenstein's argument. Although Winch accepted that philosophy is a secondary practice in the benign sense that it is devoted to understanding other practices, he posed the question of where the underlabourer approach left the more traditional and generalized endeavors of "metaphysics and epistemology" that had once been at the heart of the philosophical enterprise and perceived as directly addressing issues regarding the nature of, and knowledge about, the "world." While some contemporary philosophers suggested that these issues were limited to the concerns of particular subfields such as "the philosophies of science, art, politics, etc.," Winch claimed that these "peripheral" fields would "lose their philosophical character if unrelated to epistemology and metaphysics" more broadly construed (4–7). What Winch was referring to as metaphysics and epistemology was really, as he would go on to make clear, the theoretical dimension of social science—or any science.

Winch suggested that the underlabourer conception of philosophy was largely a reaction against the traditional image of the philosopher as a master-scientist, and he agreed that the excesses that characterized something such as Hegel's "a priori" and "pseudo-scientific speculations" had been "justly ridiculed." But he claimed that the critique of the master-scientist image of philosophy had been mistakenly extended to "a priori philosophizing of a sort which is quite legitimate." He maintained that while "the scientist investigates the nature, causes and effects of particular real things and processes, the philosopher is concerned with the nature of reality as such and in general." What Winch was referring to as the "scientist" and "pure science" were, however, once again, less the actual practices of natural science than the positivist idea of natural science, which had involved a depreciation of theoretical claims, or what Winch referred to as the "*conceptual*" issues, that were prior to "empirical" claims. What he also was referring to was what Kuhn would later dub "normal science," in which theoretical issues were in the background. Although the underlabourer image of philosophy had stressed the importance of language, Winch argued that the distribution of emphasis was incorrect. While clearing up linguistic confusions was important, the essential issue was the intelligibility of reality, and this, in turn, raised questions about "the nature of thought" and "the nature of language" and how they were connected to reality (7–11). Consequently, no field of inquiry could neglect what, maybe metaphorically, were metaphysical and epistemological issues, but what were better designated as the theoretical issues inherent in any practice of inquiry.

It was at this juncture that Wittgenstein first surfaced in Winch's book. Although Wittgenstein's work had been implicated in the philosophy of "ordinary language" analysis, which, in addition to positivism, was a prominent species of the underlabourer position, Winch claimed that Wittgenstein had, even in his early work, pointed to the close relationship between language and the "world." What Winch was alluding to was Wittgenstein's insistence that the "world" was manifest in language and that

> in discussing language philosophically we are in fact discussing *what counts as belonging to the world.* Our idea of what belongs to the realm of reality is given for us in the language that we use. The concepts we have settle for us the form of the experience we have of the world [since] when we speak of the world we are speaking of what we in fact mean by the expression "the world": there is no way of getting outside the concepts in terms of which we think of the world. . . . The world is for us what is presented through these concepts. That is not to say that our concepts may not change; but when they do, that means that our concept of the world has changed too. (15)

This point was strikingly similar to what Kuhn would argue four years later. Winch maintained that this was important for the "philosophy of the social sciences," because "many of the more important theoretical issues which have been raised belong to philosophy rather than to science and are, therefore, to be settled by a priori conceptual analysis rather than by empirical research." This was indeed an awkward, contentious, or confusing statement, but his basic point was that empirical research could not settle conceptual and theoretical issues and that social-scientific inquiry, like any scientific practice, is grounded in basic conceptions of the phenomena it studies and the entailed epistemological criteria of judgment. In the case of social science, this involves such issues as what constitutes social behavior, which is really a "demand for an elucidation of the *concept* of social behaviour" and what is involved in explaining it, and this applies as well to the "historian, the religious prophet and the artist" as well as the "philosopher" and "scientist," who, each in their own fashion, seek "to make the world more intelligible." Winch made it clear that he was not arguing that the knowledge claims of various fields could add up to "one grand theory of reality" or a general "set of criteria of intelligibility." The philosophy of science, for example, is concerned with "the kind of understanding sought and conveyed by the scientist," but he maintained that while "the motive force for the philosophy of science comes from within philosophy rather [than] from within science" and that while its goal is "an increased understanding of what is involved in the concept of intelligibility" embraced by scientists, the purpose of the "*special* study of epistemology" is "to describe the conditions which must be satisfied if there are to be any criteria of understanding at all" (17–21). In the case of the philosophy of social science, in which he was engaged, the task was to elucidate the concept of "understanding" that is relevant to the concept of a "human society." Winch stressed that not only is the social scientist concerned with understanding social reality, but because "social relations" are "permeated with ideas about reality" and are in fact "expressions of ideas about reality," an "understanding of reality" is at the heart of "the concept of a human society." This entailed that a social-scientific understanding of society, despite the claims of structural theorists such as Durkheim, required "an inquiry into the nature of man's knowledge of reality and into the differences which the possibility of such knowledge makes to human life" (22–24).

It was at this point that Winch began his more easily understood discussion of the nature of social phenomena, which he primarily based on Wittgenstein's analysis of language and rules, and of how contact with reality was through the application of language in a "social setting." He turned directly to a discussion of the "nature of meaningful behavior" and to an elaboration of the parallel between philosophy and social science. He defined philosophy broadly as the "study of the nature of man's understanding of reality" and how this study serves to "illuminate the nature of human interrelations in society," and this generic definition sustained his parallel between philosophy and social science. He claimed that Wittgenstein had instigated a "genuine revolution" by his focus on "forms of life" and on the concepts of reality and modes of understanding peculiar to these forms at a particular time and place. While epistemology, as part of the core of philosophy as a discipline, is concerned with the general conditions of understanding such forms and with the "notion of a form of life as such," the "peripheral branches" are concerned with particular contexts of understanding such as science and art. Similarly, the social sciences—in what Winch now specifically and explicitly, and more clearly, referred to as their "theoretical part"—must confront the issue of the "nature of social reality" and the "nature of social phenomena in general." Thus, despite the difference in vocation between the philosopher (qua epistemologist) and the social scientist, he concluded that the latter must eventually be concerned with conceptual and epistemological issues and (again foreshadowing Kuhn) not only, as in the case of natural science, when there is "a revolution in the fundamental theories." Winch, however, in his most provocative phrasing, concluded that this "central part of sociology, that of giving an account of the nature of social phenomena in general, itself belongs to philosophy" and is "really misbegotten epistemology" rather than a strictly "scientific problem" (41–43).

He may have subtly, and rhetorically, been making an argument for the priority of the field of philosophy over the empirical sciences, in an era in which philosophy as an independent field was being depreciated for not being adequately scientific, but what he was referring to as a "scientific problem" was once again narrowly defined. And, for whatever reason, he was again failing to distinguish between philosophy as an academic field and the sense in which social scientists were, in their capacity as theorists, functionally metaphysicians and epistemologists. He had already implied that this is the case even in natural science, but the picture that he painted of natural science as a contrast model still reflected the positivist image. He might have stated the matter differently if he could have had access to Wittgenstein's *On Certainty*. What possibly in part led to this manner of framing his argument was that although he recognized that philosophy and social science are logically and epistemologically symmetrical, he had not quite arrived at viewing philosophy itself as a form of social inquiry and he therefore continued to compartmentalize them. Everything that Winch said really amounted basically to the claim that any science is grounded in theoretical assumptions that inform its factual claims and that the positivist account of both natural science and social science did not recognize the importance of these conceptual and theoretical issues. But Winch was also making the point that what really distinguishes social facts and "meaningful behavior" from natural facts is that the former are both conceptually informed and autonomous and that *social actors* are thus also, figuratively speaking, metaphysicians and epistemologists. As such, they are objects of interpretation, just as the philosopher of science is faced with interpreting the theories and methods characteristic of scientific practices.

Winch's argument in the remainder of the book was a quite straightforward attempt to invoke Wittgenstein's concept of rule-governed behavior and, drawing as well on Weber's account of *Verstehen*, to elaborate a postpositivist, but postidealist, account of social-scientific inquiry that focused on reasons and motives and the manner in which language and social action are a manifestation of publicly accessible concepts. This was offered as an alternative both to the positivist demand of subsuming singular facts under causal laws and to an idealist image of social inquiry as requiring an empathetic grasp of hidden mental phenomena that informed overt behavior. Although Winch's focus on rules has been interpreted by some as an unduly narrow construal of social phenomena, which seemed to entail both formal principles and a reflective self-conscious stance on the part of the social actor, he, like Wittgenstein, used the concept of a rule as broadly equivalent to, or emblematic of, conventional normative phenomena as a whole. Winch, in fact, stressed that most human action is actually habitual and involves tacit knowledge. What he was eliciting from the work of Wittgenstein through the emphasis on rules was the essentially public character of conventional phenomena and the ways in which the "internal relations" between constitutive concepts and forms of social action grounded a society or culture as a holistic entity and provided a repertoire for individual actors. Although he had apparently not quite fully recognized the extent to which Wittgenstein saw only a logical difference between language and thought, Winch's emphasis on the public character of language and rules provided an answer to the persistent problem of knowledge of other minds. This problem is at the heart of the issues of both how intersubjectivity is involved in a society and how social-scientific understanding can be achieved. His point about the relationship between rules and self-reflection was only that social phenomena allowed, in principle, the *possibility* of such reflection, just as social action makes the concepts that inform it open to observation. There was an important respect, closely allied to Wittgenstein's work, in which Winch was seeking to save social science from both behaviorism and intuitionism. The focus on rules also served implicitly to sidestep the persistent debate about whether society and other collective entities or individuals are ontologically prior. What are prior, as Wittgenstein argued, are the conventions that are instantiated in both individual and collective action. Unlike some similar arguments that were emerging at this time, Winch's argument did not imply some abstract form of human agency or subject as the author of action.

The crucial aspect of what Winch specified as the fundamental difference between natural and social science was that in the case of the physical sciences the phenomena that comprise what counts as reality are conceptually constructed and connected by the scientist's theory. This had nothing to do with philosophical idealism but only pointed to the fact that what is meant by "physical reality" is a function of the concepts of natural science or of some comparable conceptual domain. In the case of social science, however, where the subject matter is conceptually and behaviorally prefigured or preconstituted by social actors, the theories and the specific empirical claims of social science come into contact, and sometimes conflict, with the concepts embedded in social practices, as Winch would later emphasize in his essay on "understanding a primitive society" (1964). This is where the danger arises of confusing the means of representation with what is represented. He stressed that in the case of the natural scientist, "we have to deal with only one set of rules, namely those governing the scientist's *investigation* itself," which determines both the practice of science and the theoretical constitution of the subject matter. The only theories confronted are either previous and alternative theories or theories belonging to incommensurable fields such as religion. Winch stressed that to explain social phenomena adequately, social scientists must perforce utilize their own language and concepts, but they must also seek to comprehend and describe phenomena in a manner that clarifies the social actor's vision of the world. Thus, Winch concluded, the relation between the social scientist and a social practice "cannot be just that of observer to observed," but must also in part be like the participation of scientists in their own community or at least like an "apprentice" seeking to learn the rules of the practice (87–88). And they are forced to understand particular forms of social phenomena and come to grips with the cognitive as well as practical tension between those forms and the social scientist's account or explanation.

Some critics have fastened on Winch's somewhat unelaborated assertions about how "a historian or sociologist of religion must himself

have some religious feeling if he is to make sense of the religious movement" or that a "historian of art must have some aesthetic sense if he is to
understand the problems confronting artists of his period." These statements may have been in part an allusion to some remarks of Wittgenstein suggesting that interpreting a conceptual realm requires a certain
degree of commitment to those concepts, but this was not a reversion
to claims about intuitive understanding or to the assumption that the
only way to understand a practice is to engage in it. His point was very
similar to Kuhn's argument about how an adequate interpretation of science must be preceded by understanding the language of the scientist.
Although Winch indicated a certain affinity with the idealist position
of R. G. Collingwood, his emphasis was on affirming the third-person
accessibility of thought. He stressed that the kind of understanding characteristic of social science is, in the end, then, unlike the apprentice's
more unreflective mode of learning, because a "reflective understanding"
by the social scientist must "presuppose . . . the participant's unreflective
understanding." Winch recognized that the epigram at the beginning of
his book, consisting of the injunction of G. E. Lessing that "it is unjust
to give any action a different name from that which it used to bear in its
own times and amongst its own people," is impossible to comply with,
but it pointed to an inherent problem, and even paradox, in both philosophy and social science:

> Although the reflective student of society, or of a particular
> mode of social life, may find it necessary to use concepts which
> are not taken from the forms of activity which he is investi-
> gating, but which are taken from the context of his own in-
> vestigation, still these technical concepts of his will imply a
> previous understanding of those other concepts which belong
> to the activities of investigation.
> (89–90)

This led Winch to claim, yet once more, that the activities of the philosopher and the social scientist, both of whom confront a preconceptual-
ized subject matter, are "closely connected" (91). At this point, however,
Winch turned to the issue of objectivity, which has continued to be the
focus of much of the criticism of his work.

Theorists such as Durkheim and Pareto had stressed that objectivity required the application of a "realist" approach, which depreciated the self-understanding and consciousness of actors within the social forms being investigated in favor of causal explanations. Winch argued that this approach actually leads necessarily to a loss of objectivity because of the projection and imposition of both evaluative and descriptive judgments about the logic and rationality of these forms, which tend to distort or neglect their internal meaning. According to Winch, part of what makes philosophy a model, and analogy, for thinking about the idea of a social science is "the peculiar sense in which philosophy is *uncommitted* enquiry." It not only seeks, at least in principle, to clarify and compare the manner in which different intellectual disciplines, such as science, make the world intelligible but reflects on "its own account of things" and its "own being" and relationship to its subject matter, which tends to "deflate the pretensions of any form of enquiry to enshrine the essence of intelligibility as such, to possess the key to reality. For connected with the realization that intelligibility takes many and varied forms is the realization that reality has no key" (102)—not even that of science. This claim clearly reflected Wittgenstein's comment about how the philosopher is not a citizen of any community and how philosophy is necessarily self-reflective in a manner quite different from natural science. Winch argued that it is not the task of philosophy, or social science, to "award prizes to science, religion, or anything else" (102–3). He directly challenged as "corrupt" any attempt to use a philosophical claim about "scientific objectivity" to support programs of social change:

> While non-philosophical unself-consciousness is for the most part right and proper in the investigation of nature [except at critical and revolutionary junctures]. . . . it is disastrous in the investigation of a human society, whose very nature is to consist in different and competing ways, each offering a different account of the intelligibility of things. To take an uncommitted view of such competing conceptions is peculiarly the task of philosophy. . . . It is not its business to advocate any Weltanschuung. . . . In Wittgenstein's words, "Philosophy leaves everything as it was."
>
> (102–3)

Winch was not advancing a normative claim regarding the practical relationship between social inquiry and its object of inquiry. His concern was with the tendency of social scientists to describe and evaluate societies in terms of the investigator's beliefs and criteria of "sameness" rather than the indigenous criteria of social actors. His point was once again that what distinguishes fields such as philosophy and social science is that they deal with other practices, which forces them to think about their own identity and purposes in a manner that is not relevant in natural science, where the facts are projections of the theories. He noted Collingwood's remark that the work of "scientific" anthropologists often masks "a half-conscious conspiracy to bring into ridicule and contempt civilizations different from their own" (103). What theorists such as Durkheim had advanced as the criterion of objectivity in social science was, Winch warned, actually a threat to objectivity, because it inhibited the investigator from understanding social phenomena on their own terms.

Although Weber's work played a large role in Winch's discussion, Winch did not directly engage issues regarding the practical impact of social science, which were such an important aspect of Weber's discussion of objectivity and the relationship between science and politics. Winch treated Weber as if he were a philosopher of social science, when actually Weber was a social scientist seeking, in part, to justify why the makers of public policy should listen to social science. It was to Weber, however, that Winch turned in clarifying what he meant by "meaningful behaviour," which he suggested was similar to Wittgenstein's analysis of language as "discursive ideas," and it was Weber who Winch characterized as having the most to say "about the peculiar sense which the word 'understand' bears when applied to modes of social life." This was what Weber had called behavior with which "the agent or agents associate a subjective sense" that is "subjectively intended" and related to motives and reasons. Although, given any set of circumstances, it could be doubted that a reason given by an actor was the real reason for a certain instance of behavior or that an actor had in advance formulated and rehearsed such a reason, this account of reasoned action is the "paradigm" case, which gives sense to deviations. But, Winch argued, Weber included more in the concept of meaningful behavior than that for which an actor possessed specific and consciously held and articulated reasons or motives. He again stressed, as Wittgenstein did, that much of social action is habitual and that something such as the concept of "tradition," for example, even goes beyond mere habit. It carries a "sense" of the "symbolic," which allows the idea of an action that extends beyond the description of physical acts and which, by commitment to the rule implied, has some bearing on future patterns of conduct. Although Winch claimed that Weber did not provide "a clear account of the logical character of interpretive understanding" and sometimes spoke of it in ways that seemed as if he were speaking of a psychological technique, he insisted that, in using the term "*Verstehen*," Weber was not talking about something such as "intuition" and that he had maintained that claims about understanding "must be tested by careful observation" (112).

Where Winch believed that Weber could be faulted was his "wrong account of the process of checking the validity" of interpretations by reference to statistical laws. What is needed, Winch claimed, when the interpretation is not, in Weber's terms, immediately plausible is not a statistical test but rather "a better interpretation" that offers greater predictability and that is "far removed from the world of statistics and causal laws" and closer to hermeneutics or relating parts of discourse to the whole in which they are embedded. This criticism, however, indicated again how distant Winch's discussion was from any deep familiarity with the context in which Weber was writing and with the extent to which Weber was strategically attempting to reconcile conflicts between empirical and interpretive modes of social inquiry. Winch noted Wittgenstein's reference to what Winch took to be the suggestion that in our "philosophical difficulties over the use of some of the concepts of our language" we are "like savages confronted with something from an alien culture." He suggested the "corollary" that "sociologists who misinterpret an alien culture are like philosophers getting into difficulty over the use of their own concepts." He claimed that the analogy is "plain," but although he was obviously drawing a parallel between conceptual clarification in philosophy and social-scientific interpretation, he did not elaborate on the similarity (113–15).

Winch credited Weber with emphasizing the fact that "all meaningful behaviour must be social," since it is "governed by rules, and rules presuppose a social setting." He again rejected, however, what he interpreted as Weber's belief that there is no "logical" difference between causal explanations and those that involve "events of consciousness," which, he claimed, violated Weber's own principle of explaining action in terms of internal or subjectively intended meaning. "Social relations,"

Winch maintained, are a function of shared ideas that are in turn embedded in those relations. Although Winch did not reject Weber's uses of external description, which he believed was necessary and could be helpful in various ways and for various purposes, especially in order to draw attention to certain aspects of meaningful behavior, he emphasized that the application of such devices is to clarify and convey meaning and "not to show that it is *dispensable* from our understanding" (117–19). With this corrective in mind, Winch again argued that one of the most persistent criticisms of Weber could be met, that is, the notion that social inquiry involves attending to and grasping some "inner sense," since any such putative sense is the internalization of "socially established" concepts that are, in principle, public in character and open to view (117–20). Winch ended his book by stressing that because the relations between ideas are "internal relations" and because "social relations" exist in terms of ideas or concepts, "social relations must be a species of internal relations too" (123). He claimed that it is in these terms that institutions and forms of social interaction must be approached. But he emphasized once more that when speaking of ideas he was referring to "*discursive* ideas," which have a "straightforward linguistic expression" as well as an expression in the "conventions" governing behavior (128–36).

In the end, Winch's work actually implied a stronger thesis than he explicitly articulated. It is not simply that social science and philosophy are logically comparable and analogous but that philosophy, as conceived by Wittgenstein, is itself a form of social inquiry. As Winch indicated in his later discussion of anthropology, to understand a society is to understand its conception of reality and that entails understanding its language, which was how Wittgenstein conceived of philosophy. "Reality is not what gives language sense. What is real and what is unreal shows itself in the sense that language has. Further, both the distinction between the real and the unreal and the concept of agreement with reality themselves belong to our language" (1964, 309).

LEAVING EVERYTHING AS IT IS

In his book, Winch did not directly confront the problem of the practical relationship between social science and its subject matter, but he took his cue from Wittgenstein when he stated that social science "left everything as it was." What Winch meant by this phrase was, however, far from clear, and this was in part because Wittgenstein's remark that "philosophy leaves everything as it is" was already ambiguous and controversial. The spirit of the remark might seem to go against the grain of the past and present motives and motifs of much of the literature of social theory and social science as well as conflict with what were often Wittgenstein's own therapeutic concerns and his claim that the purpose of teaching philosophy was to change someone's intellectual "taste" (*CV*, 25). Consequently, it is important to interpret the remark in the context of the *Investigations*, as I will do in chapter 4, and elaborate on its significance for thinking about some general issues that are central to the identity of all forms of social inquiry that investigate discursive or conventional objects. These issues include: *the nature of social phenomena*; *the concepts of interpretation and representation that define the epistemic relationship between social inquiry and its subject matter*; *what philosophers often refer to as the problem of knowledge of other minds*; and *what is involved in making descriptive and normative judgments about the subject matter*. Many critics have focused on what they take to be the philosophically conservative and minimalist implications of Wittgenstein's remark, while others have suggested that the remark appears somewhat paradoxical in light of his persistently critical attitude and his claims that he was exposing nonsense, releasing us from a picture that held us captive, destroying houses of cards, and showing the fly the way out of the fly-bottle. There is, however, no paradox involved.

Wittgenstein never denied a practical role for philosophy, and, despite many attributions to the contrary, neither he nor Winch nor Kuhn ever said that one view of the world is as valid as any other. What they did claim was that there is no neutral transcendental philosophical basis for choice and that judgment is always situated in the discourse of some practice and the particularities that attend contexts ranging from science to morals. Once it is recognized that there is no definitive philosophical answer to the issue of the practical relationship between social inquiry and its subject matter, it is necessary to confront directly the actual character of that relationship. Wittgenstein claimed that there is no metaphilosophy, because self-reflection is an inherent element of philosophy. It is inherent because philosophy is a metapractice devoted to investigating other practices. As such, it is necessary to confront the issue of its relationship to the practices that it studies, and, consequently, it cannot avoid thinking about its own identity. While natural science usually leaves questions about the basic nature of its activity, including its relationship to the "world," to philosophers of science, philosophy, as conceived by Wittgenstein, including the philosophy of science itself, as demonstrated by Kuhn, cannot do so and remain authentic. And the same can be said of any form of social inquiry. Institutionalized forms of such inquiry have been marked by perennial crises of identity, and although these have often been directly a consequence of insecurity about their status as a science, that insecurity is rooted in the fact that these fields have characteristically sought to achieve practical purchase by demonstrating cognitive privilege. Sometimes this assertion of privilege is predicated on merely the claim to occupy a more objective position or attitude, but more often it is based on putative access to some universal standard of empirical or normative judgment. The history of the social sciences is replete with examples of these fields attempting to reform themselves in order to better relate, practically as well as epistemically, to their subject matter, and their history could easily be written from that perspective. Wittgenstein noted that the first task of philosophers is to cure many ills of their own and that philosophy is in large part a matter of "working on oneself. On one's own conception. On how one sees things" (*CV*, 24).

When he sometimes talked about philosophical problems disappearing, about philosophy finding peace, and about being able to stop doing philosophy, he was not talking about philosophy stepping away from an investigation of the problems that it might encounter in the course of its investigation of various language regions. He was referring to the kinds of problems that philosophy had typically and historically set for itself, such as determining how it could demonstrate the existence of the external world and what was involved in gaining knowledge about the world. Philosophy had, as Winch indicated, advanced an image of itself as a kind of master-science. This image was often rooted in philosophy's wish either to vouchsafe practices such as science and morals or to claim a title to these practices. Wittgenstein argued that such metaphysical ventures obliterated the difference between what he referred to as "factual and conceptual investigations" (*Z*, 458), that is, that metaphysics purported to be like natural science, when the proper role for philosophy was to understand concepts and undertake conceptual analysis. But this role required a theoretical account of language and concepts.

When Wittgenstein spoke about philosophy leaving everything as it is and when he sometimes insisted on eschewing explanation and rejecting theorizing in general in favor of description, he was almost always distinguishing his endeavor either from explanations in natural science or from metaphysical theories. And he noted that in both of these latter endeavors, explanations took on, as Kuhn would argue in the case of normal science, the character of dogma. Although much has been made of his disclaimers of "theory," discussions of this matter are often quite far removed from his actual uses of the word. In the *Investigations*, he famously renounced "any kind of theory" and "explanation" in favor of "description," but he only used the word "theory" twice more in that work—to refer to set theory in mathematics. What he pejoratively referred to as theory was a very narrow image. He agreed with Goethe's admonition not to "look for anything behind the phenomena; they themselves are the theory" (*PP*, 1:723, 889). As Kuhn would more explicitly claim, there is no ontological difference between theory and fact, and Wittgenstein often referred to interpreting meaning in language as a form of explanation (*Erklärung*). In the *Investigations*, he certainly was propounding what can reasonably be labeled a theory of linguistic meaning as well as an epistemological, and even methodological, account of what was entailed in studying it. Without what might be described as a theory of conventionality and its manifestation in language and action, the kind of "description" of meaning to which he referred would have remained anomalous. When he claimed that such meaning is peculiar to creatures that have "mastered a language" and is embedded in "this complicated form of life [*Lebensform*]" that is distinctly human, that is, a conventional form of life, he was, in effect, advancing an account of the nature of social phenomena, whatever particular historical configurations they might take.

He recognized "the difficulty of renouncing all theory [*Theorie*]: One has to regard what appears so obviously incomplete, as something complete" (*PP*, 1:723). What he in part meant by this statement was that linguistic usages, and social phenomena as a whole, are both idiographic and open-ended. Consequently much of what is often spoken of as theory, which reflects a "craving for generality" and a "contemptuous attitude toward the particular case" (*BB*, 17–18), arises from seeking something essentially common among the things that we "subsume under a general term" rather than simply noting what might be construed as "family like-nesses" or categorical similarity. We become trapped in modes of expression that suggest that general terms necessarily designate the presence of something more than is evident in the things that it encompasses. There cannot, for example, be a theory of politics but only a theory of the kind of phenomena of which a conventional historical practice such as politics is a manifestation. Even less can there be a theory of justice that would be anything more than an argument about how some set of social relations is or should be structured.

In the *Tractatus*, Wittgenstein had referred to theory very generically with respect to a variety of formulations such as his own work, Russell's theory, a theory of judgment, a theory of types, a theory of truth, a theory of symbolism, a theory of color, probability theory, set theory, Frege's theory, theories of rules, concepts, and numbers, Darwin's theory, the theory of relativity, and the like. All of these senses of theory were, however, ones that he eventually claimed were not applicable to the enterprise of philosophy. What they had in common was the manner in which particulars were subsumed under, or disappeared into, definitive generalizations which reduced a phenomenon to an instance or appearance of an archetype that was hidden from view. No matter how much continuity we can read into some aspects of the relationship between his early and later work, there is no getting away from the fact that in some crucial respects there was a significant break. In the *Tractatus*, he may have turned against traditional metaphysics, but there was what we might call a metaphysical claim about the relationships between thought, language, and the world, which amounted to what he later referred to as the "sublimation of logic," and a confusion of what was represented with the means of representation.

What he was, surely, himself doing in the *Investigations* was, however, advancing what we might reasonably speak of as a theory of language and conventions. As he recognized in *On Certainty*, even in the case of natural science, these kinds of claims, despite similarities in grammatical form, are not typical empirical descriptions and generalizations but bedrock conceptions of some dimension of the world. It was the conceptual context in which hypothetical claims, such as those that Kuhn associated with "normal science," are formulated and judged. In Wittgenstein's case, he was speaking about the *kind* of thing conventional phenomena constituted and how they existed and behaved. There is no way to compare such claims with the "world," because they are definitive of what we mean when referring to some dimension of the world, in this case the social world. Like theories in natural science, his philosophical claims about the nature of language are what I will refer to as *presentational* rather than *representational*. When Wittgenstein said that scientific thinking "constructs" (*CV*, 9), he was talking about what we would typically refer to as the formulation of theories in natural science. When he said that his goal was "clarity" and "transparency," this assumed a conceptually preconstructed subject matter, but this also entailed a theoretical account of that subject matter, which was a constructive endeavor. While all theories are *constructions*, specific scientific claims within the framework of a theory, whether natural or social, are *re-constructions* that assume a distinction between the vehicle of representation and what is represented. One way to gain a grasp of what Wittgenstein meant by his rejection of theory and his exemplification of what was involved in philosophical inquiry is to examine his remarks on Goethe's "theory of colors" (*Zur Farbenlehre*, 1810), which he was working on just before his death in 1951.

Newton, in his *Optics* (1704), had claimed that when white light is directed through a prism it is split up into its (at first unapparent) component colors and that, despite appearances, white light contains all the colors. Goethe had experimentally challenged this claim and noted that when he viewed a white wall through a prism, it remained white, and colors only emerged when light came into contact with something dark. Although Goethe saw himself as presenting an alternative to Newton's theory about the nature of light and colors, he was actually studying how colors were experienced and conventionally conceptually discriminated in everyday life rather than speculating about the nature and physical properties of light. Early on he had in fact stated that his concern was not to "explain" colors but to "portray" them and thereby show how colors were perceived, but he still saw himself as presenting a theory in the sense of natural science and as seeking the essence that was manifest in the particular. He undertook a kind of phenomenology of color, but he claimed that the essence of colors was located in the interaction between light and darkness mediated by things such as air, dust, and moisture. It was this dialectic that constituted the *Urphänomen* that he believed was manifest in all colors and from which particular colors derived. While Newton claimed that darkness was the absence of light, Goethe maintained that it was the polar opposite. Despite Goethe's challenge to Newton, there was no real opposition between their projects any more than between natural science and natural history or between physics and aesthetics.

Although Wittgenstein pointedly rejected Goethe's own conception of what he was doing, he saw a considerable similarity between his own approach and that of Goethe, and he agreed that "colours are a stimulus to philosophizing. Perhaps that explains Goethe's passion for the theory of colours. Colours seem to present us with a riddle, a riddle that stimulates [or irritates] us" (*CV*, 76). Wittgenstein said that he believed "that what Goethe was really pursuing was not a physiological but a psychological theory of colours" (*CV*, 26) and that what he was in fact doing was basically describing color concepts. Wittgenstein's own goal was not "to establish a theory of colour (neither a physiological one nor a psychological one), but rather the logic of colour concepts. And this accomplishes what people have often unjustly expected of a theory" (*RC*, 5, 43). He agreed with Goethe that we should not look for a theory behind the phenomena, because, as Kuhn would emphasize, the theory is immanent in the conception of the facts. And in generalizing about social facts, we are typically noting family resemblances rather than manifestations of some underlying identity. "When we're asked 'what do the words 'red,' 'blue,' 'black,' 'white' mean?,' we can, of course, immediately point to things which have these colours,—but our ability to explain the meanings of these words goes no further! What actually is the 'world of consciousness'?—That which is in my consciousness: what I am now seeing, hearing, feeling." Consciousness is not some realm of ineffable qualia that adds up to something such as what some philosophers ponder over as what it is like to be a bat or to be a human being rather than a zombie. Wittgenstein claimed that "the difficulties we encounter when we reflect about the nature of colours (those which Goethe wanted to get sorted out in his *Theory of Colours*) are embedded in the indeterminateness of our concept of sameness of colour." The meaning of color terms is simply a matter of the conventions that govern what people point to as examples of particular colors, and "Goethe's theory of the constitution of the colours of the spectrum has not proved to be an unsatisfactory theory, rather it really isn't a theory at all. Nothing can be predicted with it. It is, rather, a vague schematic outline of the sort we find in James's psychology. Nor is there any *experimentum crucis* which could decide for or against the theory." The nature of color "lies in the concept of colour," and "would it be correct to say our concepts reflect our life? They stand in the middle of it. The rule-governed nature of our languages permeates our life" (RC, 9, 11, 12, 32, 57–58). He claimed "that a physical theory (such as Newton's) cannot solve the problems that motivated Goethe, even if he himself didn't solve them either," because "the difficulties which we encounter when we reflect about the nature of colours (those difficulties which Goethe wanted to deal with through his theory of colour) are contained in the fact that we have not *one* but several related concepts of the sameness of colours" (RC, 45, 49).

Wittgenstein's theoretical account of linguistic meaning did not, any more than a theoretical transition in natural science, leave everything as it was, because it presented us with a very different image of social phenomena. With respect to his therapeutic concerns, it is clear that Wittgenstein did not intend to leave philosophy as it was. The change that he wished to produce was the recognition that the task was one of understanding and interpreting the meaning of concepts and the practices in which they were manifest and that this entailed first clarifying the concepts of "meaning" and "understanding" themselves. At times he agonized a great deal about whether his work could, would, or should have a practical impact on its subject matter. Following his remark about leaving everything as it is, he referred, as an example, to the philosophical analysis of mathematics. From some of his earliest to his latest work, he was involved in criticizing attempts to achieve a philosophical foundation for mathematics and in exposing the Platonic ideas that had infiltrated the field, and he believed that this had been his "chief contribution" (Monk 1990, 466). He acknowledged that "a mathematician is bound to be horrified by my mathematical comments" but that in the end "philosophical clarity will have the same effect on the growth of mathematics as sunlight has on the growth of potato shoots. (In a dark cellar they grow yards long.)," that is, it will inhibit accretions of error (PG, 381). It was not mathematics alone that was open to criticism and the possibility of change. The same could be said of religion, politics, and other aspects of social life. Much of Wittgenstein's last work was devoted to psychology, and in the *Investigations*, he had already spoken about the "barrenness of psychology" and about how the field's "experimental methods" were infused with "*conceptual confusion*." These remarks could very well have been, and today still can be, applied to much of social science as a whole. There is, however, still an obvious ambiguity in claiming that philosophy leaves everything as it is, while, at the same time, making the kinds of critical judgments that characterized much of his work.

When Wittgenstein spoke of philosophy leaving everything as it is, he meant that the claims of philosophy and changes in the conceptual and theoretical repertoire of philosophy do not, by virtue of their performance, either transform or ground the subject matter of philosophy. The implication of his remark was, in effect, to *problematize* the practical relationship between philosophy and its subject matter. He was resisting the imperialism of logic, such as that manifested in the Vienna Circle and in his own earlier work, and this resistance was symbolized in his demand to leave the "slippery ice" and return to the "rough ground" of practical or ordinary language, where one could gain a footing. But if philosophy, in the sense he indicated, leaves everything as it is, it is necessary to specify more fully the differentiating criterion that distinguishes those fields that, by their performance, do *not* leave everything as it is. His answer to this question was also an answer to the basic difference between natural and social inquiry, and it explains to a large extent what he meant when he so often distinguished his work from that of natural science and from the pretensions of metaphysics.

PRESENTING AND REPRESENTING

Someone might suggest that what I am referring to as Wittgenstein's theory of language and conventionality is a form of metaphysics, but this would only be true in the sense that one might speak of scientific theories, or even our common-sense view of the world, as metaphysical. When Wittgenstein referred critically to metaphysics, he was referring to formulations such as realism, idealism, skepticism, solipsism, and the like rather than to the kind of existence claims that characterize theories in natural science and the kinds of "hinge" propositions he discussed in *On Certainty*. It is a mistake to read philosophical doctrines into scientific theories—as one might do, for example, in talking about someone such as Einstein as a realist. Although it is not necessarily odd to talk about a relationship between natural science and nature, such as in the case of speaking about something such as how natural science can, for better or worse, impinge on natural processes, this should not be confused with what is sometimes referred to as the relationship between theories and facts, in which there is no conceptual disjunction. The same issue arises in the case of speaking about natural science as representing nature. Such a manner of speaking is somewhat metaphorical, because what we mean by "nature" is, at least in much of contemporary Western society, largely defined by the language of natural science and the manner in which it has influenced our common-sense view of the world. What plays this role in other societies, as well as in the past of Western society, is, or might be, something quite different. In the case of the connection between natural science and nature, the concepts of relationship and representation do not really apply, because "relationship" tends to imply a certain degree of logical comparability between the parties. When the basic theoretical concepts of natural science change, as Kuhn so effectively argued, some dimension of its conception of its subject matter, that is, what is meant by the "world" or "nature," changes—and some dimension of how many people conceive of the world changes accordingly. The same can also be said of ancient myth, religion, and other (what I will refer to as) *first-order*, *world-presenting*, or *world-constructive* practices.

This is neither a metaphysical claim nor a claim about the inevitability of perspectivity, but rather simply a matter of recognizing that after some authoritative practice—for example, natural science, has given us an account of motion or, alternatively, after religion has claimed to reveal the word of god—we cannot judge these accounts by comparing them with independent facts of motion or the word of god, but only, as Kuhn argued, with some prior, or competing, theoretically incommensurable account. What are referred to as models in natural science are often illustrations of theories, and so we can say that models as well as empirical generalizations *represent*, but theories *present*. The conceptual constitution of the subject matter of practices such as natural science and religion is internal to those practices, that is, there is, we might say, no gap between theory and fact apart from that opened up *within* these discourses. Philosophy and social inquiry as a whole, however, confront a conceptually autonomous subject matter, but the constructive pretensions of traditional philosophy, such as realism, are difficult to subdue, and the same can be said of much of social inquiry, whether empirical or normative.

Wittgenstein's work has been one of the principal impetuses behind the critique of various forms of representational philosophy and its correspondence theory of truth. This kind of philosophy was, and continues to be, distinguished by its claim to be able to speak about truth and reality above and beyond the criteria operative either in the everyday practices of life or in any particular substantive form of inquiry. There is, however, inevitably some potential confusion, or at least irony, in portraying Wittgenstein as rejecting representationalism, because he viewed the task of philosophy as one of representing. The crux of the matter is that representational philosophy did not actually undertake *representing* anything. While it claimed to represent the world, it really sought to present the world. Wittgenstein was certainly concerned with the issue of how language was applied to the world, and thereby gained meaning through those uses, but, in his view, not all linguistic uses were, strictly speaking, representational and relational.

The term "representation," in nearly all its typical contexts and applications, and particularly in Wittgenstein's work, presupposes the conceptual autonomy of the object that is represented. On a recent trip to Rome, I revisited the Sistine Chapel in the Vatican, and it occurred to me that one might be tempted to say that Michelangelo's depiction of god is a representation of god just as one likely might say that Newton's theory of motion is a representation of the physical world. We often use the term "representation" in this sense, but it can be misleading. There are no external criteria for judging such representativeness. These are, respectively, actually *presentations* of god and of the physical world. To speak of them as representations would require being able to specify the object that was being represented quite apart from the representation. I later found that Wittgenstein had made a similar point. He noted that we would not think of Michelangelo's painting as a picture of the deity, and Michelangelo did not actually assume that God looked like this, that is, he did not conceive of himself as engaged in an act of representation. If the painting was a representation, it was of some person who was a model or of an image that the artist had conjured up. The painting was a way of *presenting* the concept of God as creator. To disagree with such presentations, it is necessary to advance another presentation, not to point out a failure to properly represent as one might accuse someone who had failed to paint an adequate portrait or who had failed to describe properly some scientific observation. This distinction was apparent in Wittgenstein's insistence on the need to formulate a "perspicuous representation."

All this is not to say that social inquiry lacks a presentational dimension, or that natural inquiry lacks a representational dimension. Both Wittgenstein's account of philosophy and his account of the nature of linguistic meaning are presentational claims that underlie his approach to clarifying various concepts. But he viewed the practice of philosophy as distinctly representational. The seeds of this distinction between presenting and representing are, as I will argue in chapter 7, in the *Tractatus*. When social inquiry takes on the task of making normative judgments about its subject matter, it is involved, as Wittgenstein said about values in general, in acts of presentation or "showing." In the case of "normal" natural science, as opposed to the theories that support it at any particular time, the claims are representational, because they already presume how the "world" is basically constructed, just as drawing a map is a representation of what we have concluded constitutes the relevant terrain. A map can always be checked for its accuracy in a manner that a theoretical or presentational claim cannot. What separates social science from natural science, the line of demarcation that has so long been a preoccupation of philosophers and social theorists, is not essentially methodological. The criterion of demarcation is that the facts of natural science are *not* conceptually and theoretically autonomous, while social facts, no matter how they are represented, *are* conceptually autonomous. Representation is at the core of the vocations of philosophy and social inquiry, just as it is for landscape and portrait painters, politicians, lawyers, and so on, no matter how they construe, and how well they may be evaluated as undertaking, the business of representing. An impressionist, or even cubist, painting, for example, is still representational even if not realistic.

In the case of philosophy, as conceived by Wittgenstein, and in fields ranging from history and social science to literary criticism, *re-presentation* takes the form of *interpretation* directed toward discursive objects. Wittgenstein claimed that the basic task of philosophy is to achieve *clarity* about such objects, and he likened his philosophical approach to the conduct of descriptive natural history, making sketches of a landscape, and composing an album, which are all distinctly representative activities. The subject matter of philosophy and social inquiry, what Wittgenstein referred to as the "language-games" associated with *"forms of life,"* is, as he noted, "given," and "what has to be accepted, the given, it might be said—are facts of living" (*PP*, 1:630). This is to say that the meaning of social facts is not, at least in the first instance, a product of interpretation.

The problem with much of what has been advanced as an interpretive social science has in part been a failure to recognize that although there are different methods of interpretation, interpretation is not a particular method. The current propensity in social science to parse empiri-

cal/quantitative and interpretive/qualitative forms of inquiry fails to recognize that *all* social inquiry is necessarily, by its very nature, interpretive
and representative. There may be disagreements about the basic adequacy,
in both conception and execution, of some popular method of modeling
and representing social phenomena, such as in the case of rational-choice
approaches, but it is a mistake to believe that these are not exercises in
interpretation. Although Wittgenstein's work has often been characterized as a form of linguistic idealism, he actually maintained that both
the world and language ("grammar") are autonomous, despite the tight
internal relationship between them. It is simply that the world does not
dictate the language applied to it and that the world is only manifest in
the medium language. Wittgenstein used the word "grammar" to refer
both to the subject matter of philosophy and to the practice of philosophical analysis, and this parallel can be extended to social inquiry and
its subject matter. What is involved in interpretation is language describing language and conceptualizing concepts. Wittgenstein made it very
clear that he was illuminating and clarifying meanings rather than determining the correctness of the meanings. The autonomy of grammar and
meaning signifies the autonomy of the conventions that are constitutive
of social objects in general, which are the subject matter of social science,
and it also entails the autonomy of social inquiry and distinguishes it
from natural science.

If the task of philosophy and social inquiry is to reconstruct or
reconceptualize, that is, understand, interpret, and represent, social phenomena, the inevitable question is that of what exactly is the nature of
interpretation and how, in principle, it can be accomplished. What is crucial is to distinguish Wittgenstein's position from both those who view
interpretation as a form of mind reading and those, ranging from W. V. O.
Quine to postmodernists, who claim not only that meaning is a product
of interpretation but that there is an essential indeterminacy in meaning
that requires "radical interpretation," that is, the imposition of meaning.
For Wittgenstein, meaning is no more essentially indeterminate, either
within a practice or with respect to claims about a practice, than any
claim to knowledge, which can always be subject to doubt. While the
language of natural science *does*, so to speak, go all the way down, the
language of social science comes up abruptly—cognitively and practically—against the language and practices that are its objects of inquiry,
and against the problem of interpreting and representing those objects.

Normativity is already embedded in the practices that are the object of inquiry or, as Winch put it with respect to the case of social science, there are two sets of rules—those of the social scientist and those of the social actor. The main point, which Wittgenstein repeatedly emphasized, was that interpretation is always a supervenient claim. It is a *reconstructive* rather than a *constructive* activity.

Confronting the concept of interpretation entails two problems that will be at the core of much of what is discussed in the following chapters. First and foremost is the issue of the location of meaning, and second is the problem of confounding the means of representing with what is represented.

3

MIND, MEANING, & INTERPRETATION

> And nothing is more wrong-headed than to call meaning something a mental activity! (*PI*, 693)
> *Interpretations* by themselves do not determine meaning. (*PI*, 198)
> —WITTGENSTEIN

MUCH OF THE SCHOLARSHIP in the human sciences remains predicated on the basic premises of what may be termed "folk psychology," that is, the assumption that language and action are expressions of ontologically prior and qualitatively distinct mental states involving intentions, purposes, motives, beliefs, and so on. The prevalence of this assumption should not be surprising, because it not only corresponds to our common-sense attitude but is reinforced by various philosophical persuasions. Humans say and do things that only seem explicable by reference to a mental state or process that, it seems, must reside somewhere, which is often referred to as the mind but the identity and location of which seems to remain somewhat undefined. This intentional stance of intending, wanting, hoping, and so on is easily and conveniently applied to animals, and even looking at a darkening sky might lead one to suggest, at least metaphorically, that it *wants* to rain. Many philosophers and psychologists accept the idea that there is a problem of explaining how people are able to know other minds and share thoughts, and they also assume that this is a fundamental problem of social inquiry. Philosophical and psychological answers to the question of the source of the ability to engage in "mind reading" include the alternative claims that humans possess an inherent theory of the mind or that there is genetic capacity for simulation and projecting one's own experiences. Wittgenstein's answer to this "mystery" was basically that what is involved is a sharing of conventions, including those related to learning the use of mental concepts such as belief.

From the work of the early 1930s to his last work on psychology, he progressively rejected his earlier conception of language as a vehicle for the expression of thinking and moved in the direction of claiming that meaning is a phenomenon of language, that language is the medium of thought, and that language and thought are bound together by a common content. We can be said to have intentions only because we share the intentionality of conventions, not because of some prior mental intentionality. He noted, however, that in the case of psychological concepts, we tend to develop images that hold us captive, such as the notion that remembering something is like retrieving it from storehouse. Although recent philosophical ventures in cognitive science ostensibly reject folk psychology and Cartesianism (e.g., Damasio 1994; Churchland 1995), they conjure up a new version of dualism by replacing intentional mental states with states of the brain and suggesting that much of thinking and judging takes place in a subconscious physiological realm, which is comparable to a new version of Freud's unconscious thoughts. What is unconscious might be better equated with the conventions that we follow by training, habit, and disposition. There were some respects in which Wittgenstein admired Freud, but he rejected the idea that there is some kind of deeper consciousness behind what we take to be conscious behavior.

MINDING MEANING

Metatheoretical images and justifications of interpretive practices are typically derived from, or reflect, various, but not necessarily compatible, philosophical renditions and elaborations of what, in the end, amounts to what is sometimes referred to as propositional attitude psychology. Despite considerable ambiguity and disagreement about what exactly constitutes a mental state, mental state explanation is deeply embedded in philosophy as well as in the practices of empirical social science. Mentalism is not only the dominant perspective of most social scientists; it is prominent among literary critics such as E. D. Hirsch Jr. and among intellectual historians such as Quentin Skinner, despite the latter's ostensible embrace of the work of J. L. Austin and Wittgenstein (Gunnell 1998, ch. 5). They both advance classic arguments to the effect that the task of textual interpretation is a matter of recovering the mental state of an author, whether this is to be accomplished by deciphering the meaning behind the words of a text or by closing the context in which the text was produced. Although mentalism may serve well in many practical circumstances, it can be misleading when it is transformed into a philosophical dogma and then applied as a theory of interpretation. Nietzsche once said that "thinking, as epistemologists conceive it, simply does not occur; it is a quite arbitrary fiction," but this fiction has a long genealogy, the basic lines of which are worth recalling.

Although there is room to question how literally we should interpret Plato's description of thinking as the soul talking with itself about objects in the world, his formulation certainly contributed to a view of thinking as a discourse in a special language that takes place in a realm designated as the mind. In his treatise *On Interpretation*, Aristotle stated that "spoken words are the symbols of mental experience, and written words are the symbols of spoken words. Just as all men have not the same writing, so all men have not the same speech sounds, but the mental experiences, which these directly symbolize, are the same for all, as also are those things of which our experiences are the images." This basic account of the relationship between thought and language persisted and dominated, as Wittgenstein demonstrated in the *Investigations* by his analysis of the claims of St. Augustine. Descartes's mind/body dualism has probably been exaggerated in some respects, because he argued that only humans, unlike machines and animals, are capable of thought and that thought was inseparable from language. But even though he did not conceive of thought as a private realm only accessible to the subject, he perpetuated the assumption that language is the sign of thought. Mentalism, however, was in many respects formalized in the work of John Locke in his classic account of the "new way of ideas."

Locke's *An Essay Concerning Human Understanding* was presented
not only as an approach to the explanation of perception and knowledge
but, explicitly, as a theory of linguistic meaning. After his attack, in book
1, on the theory of innate ideas and following his discussion of the origins and types of ideas and the difference between simple and complex
ideas in book 2, he began, in book 3, to address "Words or Language
in General." At the end of that book, he noted that "there is so close a
connection between Ideas and Words . . . that it is impossible to speak
clearly and distinctly of our Knowledge . . . without considering, first,
the Nature, Use, and Signification of Language." In book 3, he claimed
that "words in their primary or immediate Signification, stand for nothing but the Ideas in the Mind of him that uses them, how imperfectly
soever, or carelessly those Ideas are collected from the Things, which they
are supposed to represent." According to Locke, although words signify
ideas and ideas represent objects, there is no natural connection between
words and ideas. The connection is voluntary and arbitrary. For Locke,
marks and "articulate sounds," such as a parrot might make, were empty
and not sufficient for language. What was required to endow words with
life and impart meaning was to use words as signs of "internal Conceptions." Language was also the "great instrument and common Tye of
Society," because it allowed "the Thoughts of Men's Minds to be conveyed from one to another." People wanted their words to have a "double
conformity"—to external objects as well as to the ideas of others—and
this could be achieved, particularly with respect to simple ideas, by fixing
the signification of a term by reference to some standard in nature, even
though much could go wrong because of the ambiguity of signification
and the imperfections of language. Although words referred to external
reality, it was in a secondary sense that relied on the capacity and willing-
ness of individuals to make the proper connection.

Although much of social science employs what it claims are scientific methods, such as survey research, it is typically assumed that much
of the data represent the causal role of hidden beliefs, motives, attitudes,
and preferences, as well as other mental states that are, however, undefined. And many philosophically, ideologically, and methodologically
disparate practitioners of human sciences remain wedded to the basic
assumption that language and action are to be interpreted as expressions
of prior ideas. Much of the postpositive literature in social theory, which

began to emerge in the late 1950s and 1960s and has sometimes been referred to as the "interpretive turn" (Hiley and Bohman 1991), reflected a growing concern with developing a hermeneutic or interpretive approach to social inquiry. Much of this movement, however, including the work of individuals such as Charles Taylor (e.g., 1971), not only retained the mind-first bias, but, in reaction to behaviorism and empiricism, accentuated the role of intentions and purposes as teleological, subjective, non-causal explanations of texts and actions.

The contemporary philosophical influence of what is often referred to as intention-based semantics can be in large measure attributed to a series of essays by Paul Grice (1957, 1968, 1969, 1975, 1981, 1982). What is somewhat ironic, however, is that Grice's early work did not explicitly state that he was offering a psychological account of intentionality. One can read Grice as simply describing how intentional agents invoke linguistic conventions and thereby convey meaning. In his later work, however, Grice tentatively concluded that language was in fact an expression of mental states and that maybe it had evolved as a way of communicating such states. Grice distinguished between "natural" meaning, such as the manner in which certain physical symptoms signify or mean the presence of disease, and "non-natural" meaning, as manifest in the case of a speaker intending an utterance to produce an effect by the listener recognizing the speaker's intention. He later refined this account by claiming that meaning was a matter of the speaker intending that the audience should believe that the speaker believed a certain thing and that the speaker intended to convey that intention to the audience. He continued to focus on the difference between a speaker's meaning and the conventional or "timeless" meaning of the words that a speaker might use to impart an intention or the speaker's meaning, and he emphasized the concept of "conversational implicature" and what he referred to as the "cooperative principle" that allowed a speaker to impart intentional meaning by drawing upon a repertoire of conventions.

The work of Jerry Fodor (e.g., 1975, 1983, 1990) could be viewed as a systematic attempt to formalize the basic theory that many have assumed is implicit in Grice's essays. Fodor's influential philosophy of psychology has passed through several phases, but he has remained, following Noam Chomsky, one of the strongest supporters of "Cartesian linguistics" and the assumption that the human ability to acquire and utilize language is lodged in an innate mental capacity and the presence of mental representations. In many respects, Fodor's work could be read as a defense of the theoretical coherency of folk psychology and as updating Locke, and it probably comes close to constituting a philosophical counterpart to how many social scientists and social theorists tend to conceptualize the realm of the mental. For Fodor, language and actions are expressions of thought and intentions that gain meaning from functionally corresponding mental states that can be physically realized in multiple ways but that both represent and are caused by external objects. These mental representations are, Fodor claims, cast, through a computational process, in symbols of a syntactically structured "language of thought" that he labels "mentalese."

Steven Pinker, a prominent psychologist and cognitive scientist, has also argued strongly for the existence of universals in human culture and particularly for a "language instinct," which he advances as the core of the "mind," and he is adamant in defending the independence and priority of thought (1994, 1997, 2002, 2007). He rejects what some have termed the Standard Social Science Model, or what he characterizes as the image of the "blank slate," which he claims has contributed to the false assumption that there is no "human nature" and to the propagation of the idea that the mind is a social product. Like Fodor, he claims that "in an important sense, there really are things and actions out there in the world, and our mind is designed to find them and label them with words." He argues not only that language does not determine thought but, like Fodor, that there is "nonverbal thought" or "mentalese" that exists before and without natural languages and that transcends the cultural variations among these forms. His version of "mentalese" is a universal language of thought consisting of ideas in the form of abstract, a priori, Kantian-like categories including space, time, intention, and so on. His argument is based in part on the existence of linguistic devices such as metaphor and indirect communication, which, he claims, imply the existence of mental meanings behind language.

Probably the most articulate and consistent attempt to rescue the traditional idea of the mind from what he construes as various forms of linguistic idealism and relativism is the work of the philosopher John Searle (1992, 1995). He designates his position as "biological naturalism," which, by his definition, entails the claim that although all mental states are ultimately rooted in neurobiological processes in the brain, the mind is the seat of consciousness and qualitative subjective experiences that cannot be reduced to physical phenomena. He argues that conscious mental states and processes constitute an emergent, higher, and autonomous, but not experimentally accessible, level. Consciousness and intentionality, he claims, are real phenomena distinguished by a first-person ontology, which gives rise to a sense of self and a capacity for "intrinsic" intentionality. For Searle, mental causation is a basic fact of the world. What is especially important for Searle is to account for "collective intentionality" or the "we-intentions" that characterize institutional facts but that transcend basic individual intentionality. Although he claims that "language is essentially constitutive of social reality," he stresses that there are thoughts that are independent of and prior to language and from which the intentionality of language derives. Although Searle has devoted a great deal of effort to elaborating Austin's account of linguistic meaning, Austin did not actually claim that the intentional force of illocutionary speech-acts was grounded in psychological states.

The core of mentalism is the assumption that language and our concepts mediate, and in some respects constitute a barrier, between thought and the world. It is worth paying closer attention to the legacy of this position and especially to the concepts of intention and intentionality, which feature so centrally in the claim that language and action are expressions of thought. "Intention" as a philosophical term of art is not exactly the same as how intentionality is conceived by mentalism as a kind of explanation of meaning, but there is a connection. Intentionality is often defined as the capacity of the mind to be about or represent things or states of affairs—either real or imagined—that is, to mean something in the German sense of *meinen*. The term derives from the Latin *intentio* and from the verb *intendere*, which referred to being directed toward something. At least from the time of the work of Franz Brentano, intention has often been viewed as the distinguishing feature and power of the mind, and it has been a common answer to what it is to be in a mental state and possess mental and normative propositional content, that is, content that can be judged as either correct or incorrect. The term was originally used to talk about what we now are likely to speak of as concepts, which indicate both mental entities and the external things that are present to the mind.

CONSTRUCTING MEANING

Despite the dominance of variations on the above perspective, there has been a consistent and popular line of argument to the effect that the meaning of texts, as well as social facts as a whole, is an endowment of the interpreter and that the recovery of authorial intention is impossible, because it is either nonexistent or inaccessible. The literature embodying this kind of position is in many ways as diverse as varieties of mentalism, and my concern is not to probe it very deeply, but only to indicate the general character of this type of claim. Although this view transgresses the orthodoxy of mental state explanation, it still pivots on the problematic of that conception, that is, whether or not it is possible to divine the mind of an author. This basic argument has been prominently associated with the work of H.-G. Gadamer (1975, 1976), who rejects the notion that there is any point in talking about a correct interpretation conforming to an author's intention, because a text is always detached from the contingency of an author. He claims that meaning is a product of the fusion of the "horizon" projected by a text and the horizon constituted by the "effective history" of the interpreter, but the meaning of a text is ultimately a function of its interpretation.

The more widespread challenge to the norm of recovering authorial meaning is, however, versions of what may be labeled poststructuralism, postmodernism, and deconstructionism. These involve a variety of claims to the effect that *tout est déjà interprétation*. For those who embrace some form of this persuasion, intentionality and meaning are dissolved into the act of interpretation. For example, Michel Foucault defends what he refers to as the "essential incompleteness of interpretation" and claims that "interpretation can never be brought to an end . . . because there is nothing to interpret. There is nothing absolutely primary to interpret, because at bottom everything is already interpretation. Each sign is in itself not the thing that presents itself to interpretation, but the interpretation of other signs" (1990, 64).

There is no need to sort out all the differences between various views of interpretism (which might include Jacques Derrida, Stanley Fish, Rorty, and even a semioticist such as Umberto Eco, who seeks to put some limits on interpretation and halt interpretive drift), but what they have in common is the notion that the object of interpretation is in some fundamental respect created by the discourse of interpretation.

As much as these claims about the endlessness of interpretation might seem to challenge the duality of thought and language, they are strangely dependent on this position. All the talk about linguistic porousness, the elusive, undecidable, and indeterminate character of meaning, the slippage between sign and signified, what always escapes particular interpretations, and so on seems to presuppose the existence of the very thing that cannot be reached. And while individuals such as Hirsch and Skinner seek to curtail indeterminacy by recovering the mental states of authors, postmodernists and poststructuralists seek their own form of determinacy through the interpretive imposition of meaning.

These highly selective and truncated sketches of mentalism and interpretism are offered only as a backdrop for examining the extent to which Wittgenstein's work presents a fundamental alternative to the core of both basic positions and their various permutations. Wittgenstein's work is not alone, but it has significantly contributed to a wider challenge to traditional conceptions of mind and meaning.

THE REVOLT AGAINST REPRESENTATIONALISM AND MENTALISM

Rorty's *Philosophy and the Mirror of Nature* (1979) featured discussions of Wittgenstein, Kuhn, Wilfrid Sellars, and Donald Davidson in support of a critique of traditional representational philosophy. Despite some significant differences between these individuals, what they had in common was not only a challenge to traditional metaphysics but a rejection of any fundamental divide between thought and language. It is unclear just how much Sellars, in his famous essay "Empiricism and the Philosophy of Mind" (1963), derived his criticism of the "myth of the given" and philosophical foundationalism as well as his arguments about language and thought from Wittgenstein. Similarly, Davidson's relationship to Wittgenstein is equally less than clear, even though his later work seems to acknowledge an affinity and suggest something like a social theory of the mind. There is, however, in many respects a remarkable congruence between their work and Wittgenstein's treatment of language and thought.

Sellars began his "argument with an attack on sense datum theories," which was only his "first step in a general critique of the entire framework of givenness," or the idea that there is an indisputable foundation of knowledge based on some form of immediate experience (128).

After a long discussion devoted to dispensing with the assumption that there are such primitive "inner episodes" as sensing, Sellars turned to the issue of what is involved in learning a rudimentary language such as that described by Wittgenstein in the *Investigations* when presenting his hypothetical example of the "builders" and their use of "slabs" as well as in his critique of Augustine's account of how a child learns its first language. Sellars argued that although we may tend to assume that those initiated into a natural language already occupy a "logical space," which provides a basic picture of the world, the idea of an "awareness of logical space prior to, or independent of, the acquisition of a language" is a myth. He was not saying that concepts and words are the same, that is, that there is a word for everything that we discriminate as an element of the world, or that thinking is exactly the same as speech, but he was saying that what we typically speak of as human thinking cannot be divorced from language and that there is no epistemic contact with the world that is prior to language (161–62). Like Wittgenstein in *On Certainty*, he claimed that although "there is clearly *some* point to the picture of human knowledge as resting on a level of propositions—observation reports—which do not rest on other propositions in the same way as other propositions rest on them," the metaphor of "foundation" is misleading. It inhibits us from seeing "that if there is a logical dimension in which other empirical propositions rest on observation reports, there is another logical dimension in which the latter rest on the former." He claimed that "in characterizing an episode or a state as that of *knowing*, we are not giving an empirical description of that episode or state; we are placing it in the *logical space of reasons*, of justifying and being able to justify what one says" (169, emphasis added). The foundational "picture is misleading because of its static character. One seems forced to choose between the picture of an elephant which rests on a tortoise (What supports the tortoise?) and the picture of a great Hegelian serpent of knowledge with its tail in its mouth (Where does it begin?). Neither will do. All empirical knowledge, like its sophisticated extension, science, is rational, not because it has a *foundation* but because it is a self-correcting enterprise which can put *any* claim in jeopardy, though not *all* at once" (171).

Sellars argued that we must give up the idea of "even a vague, fragmentary, and undiscriminating . . . awareness of the logical space of particulars, kinds, facts, and resemblances, and recognize that even such 'simple' concepts as those of colors are the fruit of a long process of publicly reinforced responses to public objects (including verbal performances) in public situations." He argued "*that instead of coming to have a concept of something because we have noticed that sort of thing, to have the ability to notice a sort of thing is already to have the concept of that sort of thing, and cannot account for it.*" He rejected the claim that language is simply a vehicle for expressing thoughts, but he did not deny, unlike some behavioralists and philosophers such as Gilbert Ryle, that there are inner episodes or aspects of thinking that are distinct from "verbal episodes." These inner episodes are not something given in immediate experience, but they are not ineffable. They are "effable" in "intersubjective discourse." He noted that his position "could be represented as a modified form of the view that thoughts are *linguistic* episodes," and he claimed that we attribute intentionality (aboutness and referentiality) to thoughts because they possess the same semantic structure as language (175–78). Wittgenstein could not have said it better.

At this point, Sellars introduced his extended parable about what might have been our language-using Rylean or behaviorist ancestors who initially had no notion of the existence of mental episodes. Onto the scene, however, came a man named Jones who observed that his fellows often appeared to act intelligently even when they did not announce what they were doing. This led Jones to develop a theory of internal episodes, based on a model of inner speech. Sellars claimed that the lesson of this story is that "the ability to have thoughts is acquired in the process of acquiring language and speech and that only after public speech is well established, can 'inner speech' occur without its overt culmination" (188). He was not claiming that concepts pertaining to thinking are actually unobservable theoretical entities such as those sometimes posited by natural science, but only that we can make sense of them by looking at them in this light. After Jones had taught others to interpret one another in this way and, in effect, to become mind readers, he added a language of sense-impressions and other mental concepts. Our ancestors soon adopted mental language as a model of self-description, which they also used to perform a "reporting role" in communicating with one another and which explains the asymmetry between first- and third-person descriptions of what one is doing and the notion of so-called privileged access to one's own thoughts:

As I see it, this story helps us understand that concepts pertaining to such inner episodes as thoughts are primarily and essentially *intersubjective*, as intersubjective as the concept of a positron, and that the reporting role of these concepts—the fact that each of us has a privileged access to his thoughts—constitutes a dimension of the use of these concepts which is *built on* and *presupposes* this intersubjective status. My myth has shown that the fact that language is essentially an *intersubjective* achievement, and is learned in intersubjective contexts . . . is compatible with the idea of "privacy" of and privileged access to "inner episodes." It also makes clear that this privacy is not an "absolute privacy." For if it recognizes that although these concepts have a reporting use in which one is not drawing inferences from behavioral evidence, it nevertheless insists that the fact that overt behavior *is* evidence for these episodes *is built into the very logic of these concepts*, just as the fact that the observable behavior of gases is evidence for molecular episodes is built into the very logic of molecule talk. (189)

Sellars said that he used his myth to kill another myth, "the myth of the given."

Sellars's position entails that all awareness is linguistic and that there is no logical space independent of language. Thoughts are inner episodes with conceptual content, and although not all that we call thinking is identical to silent speech and verbal imagery, the concept of thinking cannot be explicated except analogically. Although we tend to speak of animals as if they behaved in the space of reasons, this is metaphorical. There may be an evolutionary continuity from animal to human, but it is a mistake to reverse the relationship and attempt to explain the latter in terms of the former or to talk of things such as a hidden biological brain that thinks and underlies our linguistic thinking. There is experimental evidence that suggests that claims such as those of Sellars have a historical, anthropological, and psychological basis.

In *A Man Without Words*, Susan Schaller (1991) tells the fascinating story of her work with a man in his late twenties who was totally deaf and who possessed neither a natural language nor sign language. He was beyond the age when many assume that a person without language can ever actually acquire it, and her initial attempts to teach him sign language failed. He would simply look at her in a puzzled manner and repeat the sign, because miming had been his basic, but torturous, manner of communication. Unlike, for example, someone playing charades, his gestures were not semantic symbols. After many intense days of contact with Schaller, however, he finally achieved a Helen Keller moment and grasped the game of naming and how there could be a connection between words and things, from which he eventually went on, through learning sign language, to think and act conceptually. When asked to recall and describe his thoughts before he possessed language, he said it was only "darkness." Equally significant was research (Senghas and Coppola 2001) conducted in Nicaragua. In this case, a group of deaf adolescents who were isolated from their hearing peers had created a rudimentary language based on gestures—maybe somewhat comparable to that of Wittgenstein's builders. The children, however, were lacking any gestures for mental concepts such as belief, thought, and so on. When presented with a puzzle that was designed to test recognition of false beliefs, they failed the test. Subsequently, a later generation of deaf children was introduced to sign language at a relatively early age, and this language included sophisticated signs for mental concepts such as "I know that you know" and "you do not know what I know," and they passed a form of a common type of psychological experiment that is sometimes referred to as the Sally/Ann scenario.

This often involves spectators watching a staged drama or puppet show in which a child is playing with a toy that the child hides before temporarily leaving the room. Meanwhile, another child comes into the room, finds the toy, and, before leaving, hides it elsewhere. When the first child returns, spectators are asked where the child will look for the toy. The results seem to indicate that while adults will of course typically say that the child will look for the toy where it had been originally hidden, young children are likely to say that the returning child will look where the toy has actually been placed. While some conclude that humans are in some way naturally mind readers, a Wittgensteinian answer to this problem would be along the lines of his claims about how language acquisition is predicated on initiation into the language-game of naming. In the case of the Sally/Ann experiment, what might explain the mistake of the young children is that they have not really learned the conventions involved in the game of hiding.

Donald Davidson's very influential philosophy is more complicated, but it points in the same direction as Sellars argument (1980, 1984,
2001). What Sellars referred to as conceptual capacities is much like what
Davidson, following Bertrand Russell, referred to as propositional attitudes. These are modeled on language and do not correspond to neu-
rophysiological events. They involve a special kind of intelligibility in
which reasons are justifications for beliefs, desires, and so on and do not,
for example, explain particulars by subsuming them under general laws.
Although Davidson claims that, in principle, the mind and mental states
belong to the general universe of physical causation, he maintains that,
in practice, it is impossible to transcend the mind's "anomalous" status
and reduce the connection between thought and action to physical laws.
This is what led him, in his early work, to claim that reasons, desires, and
intentions, defined in terms of semantic content, can be factored out and
treated as causes of action. He argues, however, much like Wittgenstein,
and as in the case of Hilary Putnam's later work, that language connects
us directly to the world. While representationalists such as Fodor and
Pinker, and many who now subscribe to some form of cognitive science,
claim that natural languages are simply the clothing of an internal language of thought, Davidson argues that language and thought are mutually entailed and have the same content. His conception of "propositional
attitudes" is very similar to what Wittgenstein referred to as thoughts.
Despite important differences between Wittgenstein and Davidson,
they both claimed, in effect, that there is no thought without language
and that only those who possess language can, except in some functional
sense, be said to think. Davidson claims that thought involves a mastery
of mental concepts and the connections between them, which in turn
explains the intersubjectivity of language and the normativity of rules
and conventions. He posits a basic identity between thought and speech,
in that he claims that "beliefs and intentions are like silent utterances"
and that thought presupposes a speech community.

WITTGENSTEIN AND MENTAL CONCEPTS

Wittgenstein's turn after 1929 was not only toward looking at philosophy
as a form of social inquiry; it was also a fundamental transformation in
his conception of the relationship between thought and language. This
transformation was more radical than merely the recognition that mean-

ing is expressed in a public, intersubjectively accessible language. What he basically had to say about these matters is present in *The Blue and Brown Books* and the *Investigations*, but the transition that led to this later work was already apparent in the *Philosophical Grammar* (1933) and in various remarks compiled in the *Zettel* between 1929 and 1948.

He suggested that although intentionality may be "an extension of primitive behaviour. (For our *language-game* is behaviour.)," it is nevertheless a function of language. He noted that "there is nothing astonishing about certain concepts only being applicable to a being that e.g. possesses a language": we might say that "'the dog *means* something by wagging his tail.'—What grounds would one give for saying this?—Does one also say: 'By drooping its leaves, the plant means that it needs water'?" And "we should hardly ask if the crocodile means something when it comes at a man with open jaws. And we should declare that since the crocodile cannot think there is really no question of meaning here" (*Z*, 520–22). Human behavior can be described and explained "only by sketching the actions of a variety of humans, as they are all mixed up together. What determines our judgment, our concepts and reactions, is not what *one* man is doing *now*, an individual action, but the whole hurly-burly of human actions, the background against which we see any action." This requires "seeing life as a weave," but "this pattern . . . is not always complete and is varied in a multiplicity of ways. But we, in our conceptual world, keep on seeing the same, recurring with variations. That is how our concepts take it. For concepts are not for use on a single occasion" (*Z*, 520–22, 567–68).

It is a mistake to assume that understanding an intention is a matter of reading off "a representation from something or other and that intention is an emotion, a mood, sensation, image, or state of consciousness" that one could speak of as having "duration and other such features." To describe an intention is a matter of "describing what went on from a particular point of view, with a particular purpose. I paint a particular portrait of what went on." Wittgenstein asked, if "someone . . . could look into your mind [would they be] able to see that you *meant* to say *that*? Suppose I had written my intention down on a slip of paper, then someone else could have read it there. And can I imagine that he might in some way have found it out *more surely* than that? Certainly not" (*Z*, 23, 34, 36, 45). In speaking of thought, we cannot get outside language. He claimed that the word "thought," like other mental or psychological concepts, has a variety uses, but it does not refer to anything that is theoretically distinct from language. It is, however, very difficult to convince people, including many philosophers, that there is no such separate domain or a special kind of thought-language that precedes, and finds expression in the conventions of, speech. Wittgenstein very early on had noted that "now it is becoming clear why I thought that thinking and language were the same. For thinking is a kind of language" (*NB*, 82). Later, however, he rejected this phrasing, because while speaking and thinking are "categorically" different concepts, categorical differences are not necessarily ontological ones (*PP*, 2:7). He suggested that "the human body is the best picture of the human mind" and that the idea of the inner world of the mind is just "part of the mythology stored in our language" (*PO*, 133). If we wished to know if someone could understand something or play a game such as chess, we would not be looking for an inner process but rather for the manifestation of a certain grasp of rules and the ability to deploy them.

Although he had always argued that, in some basic way, thought and language were connected, he was, through the point of the *Tractatus*, still under the spell of the assumption that thought is a psychic realm of representations of possible states of affairs and that language is both an expression of thought and a logical picture of reality. He claimed that one of the principal tasks of philosophy is to clarify the thoughts that were expressed in language. His later work might in some respects be construed as compatible with these early claims, but there was a distinct rejection of any fundamental bifurcation of thought and language. The key point in Wittgenstein's later treatment of this issue was that there is only a logical difference between thought and language. With respect to the relationship between language and the world, he claimed that they are both autonomous. The world does not determine how it is presented, and our language does not determine the world—even though the world is only manifest in language and many words gain meaning by being applied to objects in the world. He claimed that "like everything metaphysical the harmony between thought and reality is to be found in the grammar of the language" (*PG*, 112).

For Wittgenstein, "meaning," like "thought," did not name a specific thing but functioned as a family-resemblance concept. What is typically translated as "meaning" in his work includes designating a particular object, meaning something by a phrase, and so on. It is important to distinguish his use of *meinen* to indicate "intending," "believing," and so on, his use of *Bedeutung* to refer to semantic meaning, and his use of *Absicht* to refer to an intention to do something. These are, however, connected in that Wittgenstein rejected the notion that any of these uses typically refer to either physiological or epiphenomenal mental states or processes. Pascal once said that "meanings receive their dignity from words instead of giving it to them," and Wittgenstein was making a similar point. What are meaningful are signs, which in their use embody meaning. It is, however, as he stressed, very difficult to "get free of the idea that the sense of a sentence accompanies the sentence: is there alongside of it" and to jettison the assumption that the signs seem empty unless we assume that there are intentions or interpretations that give them content (Z, 139).

It might seem that there is still something distinctly counterintuitive about his argument, because it might appear that he was denying the existence of thought. What he was denying, however, was that human thought is something different from operating with signs and having learned a language, which provides the capacity to use signs either overtly in speech and writing or without such physical expression. It is a mistake, despite the grammatical similarity, to conceive of mental states and processes in terms of the paradigm of, or as a parallel to, physical phenomena. There is no prior language of thought that is expressed in natural languages, and it is impossible to detach what we typically refer to as thought from these natural languages. Mental concepts do not apply, except in a secondary manner, to anything other than human beings who have mastered a language. He maintained that, like meaning and understanding, thinking is "a widely ramified concept. A concept that comprises many manifestations of life. The *phenomena* of thinking are widely scattered." The word "think" may refer to "thinking out loud," "thinking as one talks to oneself in the imagination," "a pause during which something or other floats before the mind," "a thought expressed in a sentence," "the lightning thought which I may later 'clothe in words,'" "wordless thinking as one works," and so on, but all this entails language. And "if we are to speak of an experience of thinking, the experience of speaking is as good as any. But the concept 'thinking' is not a concept of an experience" such as a sensation. In the case of human beings, there is nothing that we refer to as thinking that does not involve operating with conventional signs, and it is a mistake when "the concept 'thinking' is formed on the model of a kind of imaginary auxiliary activity." Despite the claims of someone such as William James, Wittgenstein maintained that there is no evidence that would "convince one that it is possible to think without a language" (Z, 96, 106, 109–10).

Wittgenstein once noted that "one of the most dangerous ideas for a philosopher is, oddly enough, that we think with our heads or in our heads." For Wittgenstein, it was important to dispel the notion that there is some process in the brain correlated with thinking in such a way that it would possible "to read off thought-processes from brain-processes." Although there are observable phenomena associated with something such as seeing, the "psychological verbs" do not signify such phenomena. There are certainly things going on in the brain, as well as other parts of the body, but these cannot be an explanation for the conventions involved in "our thoughts, and hence for our talking and writing," because "physiologically nothing corresponds to them." Such a notion is the result of "primitive interpretations of our concepts," which is often a consequence of worrying that accepting anything other than a physiological explanation would be a reversion to some idea of a "soul *side by side*, with the body, a ghostly soul-nature" (Z, 444, 464–65, 471, 605, 608–11).

He noted that, like the terms thinking and meaning, "the concept of understanding is a fluid one," that is, it is a family-resemblance concept. There would be a considerable difference between, for example, understanding an order and understanding a musical theme or something such as Lewis Carroll's poem "Jabberwocky." But at the core of his argument was his insistence that understanding is categorically and conceptually different from interpreting. If, in some instance, an understanding of speech or action is called into question, an interpretation might be required, but an interpretation is a "rider" and "something that is given in signs." It is an argument and an account of meaning, but it is not the bearer of meaning. In the case of understanding, what happens is that typically

> I do no interpreting. I do not interpret because I feel natural in the present picture. When I interpret, I step from one level of my thought to another. If I see the thought symbol "from outside," I become conscious that it *could* be interpreted thus or thus; if it is a step in the course of my thoughts, then it is a stopping-place that is natural to me, and its further interpretability does not occupy (or trouble) me. As I have a railway

time-table and use it without being concerned with the fact
that a table can be interpreted in various ways.

The explanation of meaning is a matter of locating "the place of a word
in grammar," which is the autonomous home of meaning even though it
is "something made up of heterogeneous elements" and even though "the
way it meshes with life is infinitely various." Like Austin, he stressed the
difference between the "purpose," or "effect," of a word, that is, its "role in
human life," as opposed to its meaning, which is a matter of "conventions"
and the uses that are "constantly fluctuating." He maintained that this is
particularly apparent in the use of a word such as "'good' (in an ethical
sense)," and the only reason that such a word can be treated as referring
to a single concept is that the uses can be construed as related. There is
no object or one thing to which an evaluative word such as "good" refers.
The word tends to have a residual universal meaning, but the criteria of
application differ widely. And it does not refer to any object or property
of an object, even though a particular property could be the criterion of
its application (*PG*, 5–6, 9, 23, 29, 32, 36, 99, 138; *Z*, 229).

Wittgenstein was intent on dispelling what seems to be the almost
irresistible urge either to seek a mental state as the source of meaning
or to assume that the only way the indeterminacy of meaning can be
overcome is to make interpretation the locus of meaning. He noted that
people tend to "regard understanding as the essential thing, and signs as
something inessential.—But in that case, why have the signs at all? If you
think that it is only so as to make ourselves understood by others, then you
are very likely looking on the signs as a drug which is to produce in other
people the same condition as my own." One might read Grice in this
manner, but Wittgenstein argued, for example, that "the expression of a
wish can be the wish" and "the expression doesn't derive its sense from the
presence of some extraordinary spirit." When a person gives an order, it is
usually the case that the words are sufficient, and neither the person giving the order nor the recipient assumes that "this is only the words" and
not the meaning. The person giving the order has nothing but the signs,
because "when I think in language, there aren't meanings going through
my mind in addition to the verbal expressions; the language is itself the
vehicle of thought." He cautioned that we should not "think of understanding as a 'mental process' at all.—For *that* is the way of speaking that
is confusing you. Rather ask yourself: in what kind of case, under what

circumstances do we say 'Now I can go on,' if the formula has occurred to us?" He suggested that "thinking is quite comparable to the drawing of pictures" and that it is "an activity, like calculating," that can be done with or without paper, speech, and so on. The point, which he reiterated constantly, is that "*language must speak for itself*" (emphasis added), and he even suggested that one could say that "*meaning drops out of language*; because what a proposition means is told by yet another proposition" and "the mistake is to say that there is anything that meaning something consists in" (emphasis added). A request for the meaning behind words could signify asking for an explanation of what one was doing with words or how the words were applied and used. One might have reason to wonder in some instance if a certain set of words represented an order or a question, or what one wanted to accomplish by giving the order. This might call for clarifying a sentence by conveying the use in equivalent words, or maybe might require explaining that it really was not an order after all. Sometimes we alternate between gestures and words and use one to explain the other, or employ another "symbolism" or "mode of representation," but we do not get outside of signs and language. Austin spoke about how we do things with words, but Wittgenstein also emphasized how we say things with what we do. The point is to recognize that what Wittgenstein was talking about was not language narrowly conceived but the conventions expressed in symbolization. There is no symbolism that belongs exclusively to what we tend to call the mind, and "hence it would be stupid to call meaning a 'mental activity,' because that would encourage a false picture of the function of the word." There may be all sorts of what might be construed as "psychological processes" that accompany speech, but these do not explain meaning, which is a matter of grammar (*PG*, 2–3, 7, 103, 112–13, 124; *Z*, 16, 20, 227, 446).

THE BLUE AND BROWN BOOKS

Although *The Blue and Brown Books* (1958) were a preliminary to the composition of the *Investigations*, they in some respects more directly, systematically, and prosaically pursued the themes of mind, meaning, understanding, and interpretation that, I will argue, continued to form the core of the *Investigations*. If we follow the discussion as it evolves in this earlier work, it becomes clear that the principal concern was not simply to disestablish the assumption that meaning is correlating words and objects and to emphasize how meaning is a function of how words are used, but to dispel the belief that the meaning of a word is a mental act or process that accompanies a word or action and that takes place in the mind, the head, or the brain.

As in the case of the *Investigations*, Wittgenstein began the *Blue Book* by asking, "What is the meaning of a word?" He noted that "a substantive makes us look for a thing that corresponds to it," or else, it seems, we get caught up in a succession of "verbal definitions." But the difficulty is that many words simply do not have satisfactory "ostensive definitions," and because such definitions can be easily misunderstood, it is often necessary to "*interpret*" what a particular gesture or words such as "this" or "that" may designate. This in turn leads to the assumption "that there are *certain definite* mental processes" that give meaning to words and without which "the signs of our language seem dead." We assume that the connection between language and objects is "psychological" and "that the action of language consists of two parts; an inorganic part, the handling of signs, and an organic part, which we may call understanding these signs, meaning them, interpreting them, thinking," which "take place in a queer medium, the mind." It seems as if a thought can bring about various effects such as an action and that it "can either agree or disagree with reality." We might believe that we can solve the dilemma of this apparently "occult" character of thought by assuming that a word evokes and refers to a "mental image" of an object, but this does not solve the problem, because the image is just another sign. We could "replace every process of imagining by a process of looking at an object or by painting, drawing or modeling; and every process of speaking to oneself by speaking aloud or by writing." Frege formalized this common organic notion of meaning by speaking of it as the "sense" that is "added to dead signs" in order to give them meaning, "but if we had to name anything which is the life of the sign, we should have to say that it was its *use*" (1–4).

Where a particular sign derives its life or meaning is from "the system of signs, from the language to which it belongs. Roughly: understanding a sentence means understanding a language." The problem in clarifying meaning is not like a "scientific one," that is, a matter of determining the nature of some hidden "mechanism of the mind." What we might speak of as "the activities of the mind lie open before us" in the things we say and do rather than existing in some parallel mental universe. Confusion about mental terms is similar to that of how a noun such as "time" often leads us, in the absence of an object, to look for its hidden nature, when the real issue is typically a matter of clarifying the "grammar of that word." Consequently, "it is misleading to talk of thinking as a 'mental activity,'" when actually "thinking is essentially the activity of operating with signs," an activity that is "performed by the hand, when we think by writing; by the mouth and larynx, when we think by speaking; and if we think by imagining signs or pictures." There is "no agent that thinks" and no place in which thinking takes place. To say that the thinking occurs in the mind is only a "metaphor" and a manner of speaking. The word "mind" does not refer to anything, but simply designates a category of functions that we can perform without vocal sounds, without making marks on paper, or without bodily actions. Although this point might be conveyed by saying that thinking takes place in the "head" or "brain," it can be confusing if we believe that there actually is a particular place that corresponds to the general term "thinking." We are tempted to believe that if a sentence has a locality in language, a thought must also be a "*something*" and have a locality.

We might be inclined to say that a thought cannot be the same as a sentence, because the same thought could be expressed in two different languages, but if people are asked to specify what their thoughts are apart from the sentences they speak or write, there is no answer. The word "thought" has a "*use*, which is of a totally different kind from the use of the word 'sentence.'" This is not to deny that there may be underlying neurological and physiological processes taking place when we speak, but, Wittgenstein asked, "in what sense can the physiological processes be said to correspond to thoughts, and in what sense can we be said to get the thoughts from the observation of the brain?" An experimenter might correlate the observations of a subject's brain with the subject's verbal expressions, and we might say that both are manifestations of thought, a physiological one and a linguistic one. But there are actually only two phenomena involved and no third element that is the bearer of both, such as "the thought itself," of which brain activity and words are symptoms and on which one could have two different perspectives. The word "thought" simply does not name things, either material or immaterial, even though we may use it to refer to a category of things, which might include something such as making mathematical calculations without making any marks on paper (5–8).

Although it can be perfectly intelligible to say, in a figurative sense, that thinking takes place in the head or in the mind, this is only to distinguish it from overt behavior. The mistake is to assume that, because of the similarity in linguistic form, such statements actually refer to "*the* locality" or the "*real* seat of the activity of thinking." Rather than attempting to provide any general account of what is involved in operating with signs, it was in this context that Wittgenstein introduced the concept of "language-games" as a way of using signs that was "simpler than those in which we use the signs of our highly complicated everyday language" but similar to "the forms of language with which a child begins to make use of words." He claimed that the study of language-games is the "study of primitive forms of language or primitive languages" from which more complicated ones might be constructed. He was already using "language-games," as he would in the *Investigations*, to refer both to what an observer might specify as actual forms of linguistic practice and to what might be invented for illustrative and interpretive purposes. In both cases, however, the concept was a tool for the purpose of dispersing "the mental mist which seems to enshroud our ordinary use of language." This approach was designed to avoid the "craving for generality" and "contemptuous attitude toward the particular case" that arise from seeking something common among the things that we "subsume under a general term" such as "thinking" rather than simply noting what might be construed as "family likenesses." We become trapped in modes of expression that suggest that general terms necessarily designate the presence of something more than is evident in the particulars that it categorizes. This leads to problems such as confusing a hypothetical mental state such as thinking with a sensation such as a pain, and it often derives from a "preoccupation with the method of science" and "mathematics." He noted that "philosophers constantly see the method of science before their eyes, and are irresistibly tempted to ask and answer questions in the way that science does. This tendency is the real source of metaphysics, and leads the philosopher into complete darkness." He claimed that the task of the philosopher is "purely descriptive" and not to "reduce" or "explain" things in the sense that natural scientists seek to subsume things under general laws. He suggested that much of this confusion was related to the ambiguity attaching to the word "kind," which is sometimes used to denote the properties of natural entities but sometimes refers to "grammatical structures." In the former case, there may be definite standards of "completeness," but in the latter case, when, for example, talking about kinds of "games" or about mental terms such as "thinking," "understanding," and "meaning," there may be a variety of uses without particular limits or a "sharp boundary." He argued that "the idea that in order to get clear about the meaning of a general term one had to find the common element in all its applications has shackled philosophical investigation." In philosophical inquiries, we are dealing with grammatical and conceptual matters, and "here we strike rock bottom, that is we come down to *conventions*" (15–24, emphasis added).

Much has been made of the manner in which Wittgenstein identified language with rules, but his use of the concept of a rule was as an ideal-type. There might be cases in which strict rules of grammar have been taught in school, but these were not the rules with which he was concerned. He actually stressed that "we don't use language according to strict rules—it hasn't been taught us by strict rules, either," but there is a tendency to "constantly compare language with a calculus according to exact rules." The reason that "we are unable clearly to circumscribe the concepts we use" is "not because we don't know their real definition, but because there is no 'real definition' to them." We may puzzle about things such as how to define "time" (St. Augustine) or "knowledge" (Socrates), because there are "apparent contradictions" in grammatical uses of the term, but a definition will not remove the problem. "Philosophy, as we use the word, is a fight against the fascination which forms of expression exact on us." It is important, as Lewis Carroll's Humpty Dumpty insisted, to "not forget that a word hasn't got a meaning given to it, as it were, by a power independent of us, so that there could be a scientific investigation into what the word *really* means. A word has the meaning someone has given to it" while using it. We should not seek "ideal languages" to improve on or replace "ordinary language," but only to eliminate confusions such as those arising from someone claiming that a definition solves the problem of determining the exact use of a common word (25–28).

Much has been made of Wittgenstein's references to ordinary language, but there is little to suggest that what he meant by "ordinary" was some specific kind of language. What is often translated as "ordinary language" actually included several different terms. His most often used word was *gewöhnlichen*, which may be best translated as "everyday," "common," or "customary," but which he sometimes used to distinguish it from a specialized language such as that of physics. What is sometimes translated as "ordinary" also includes *Umgangssprache*, which typically means "colloquial"; *Sprache des Alltags*, which is similar but also means "everyday" or "common"; and *alltäglichen*, which again means "common" or "everyday." What Wittgenstein was referring to was not some basic, universal, common-sense language. His primary point in using these terms was to emphasize the difference between the language of philosophy and the language of its subject matter, whatever linguistic domain might be at issue, and to stress that the concern was neither to construct an ideal language nor to approach understanding language from such a perspective. What his work may suggest, however, is that some form of everyday language is chronologically prior and that more specialized languages, such as those of science, are derivative. Since his later work did not employ an esoteric philosophical language, this might suggest the possibility of greater practical contact between philosophy and its subject matter, but philosophical discourse is still not the discourse of its subject matter, which was a distinction that he consistently stressed.

Before one can investigate what people are thinking, and maybe critically assess what they are thinking, the investigator must be clear about the concept of thinking and mental terms such as "intention." Even if we accept the claim that meaning something is a matter of use or what one is doing with words, rather than a mental act, one might still ask what was the intended use and still speculate about something mental attached to the words. But Wittgenstein maintained that although one might suggest, for example, that what made painting a portrait of a particular person was the "*intention*" of the artist, such an intention is "neither a particular state of mind nor a mental process." He noted that there are many actions and attitudes that we might speak of as intentional and that there is no general answer to how we determine what a person is doing with words. It may become apparent from the context, a person may overtly state what action was being performed, a person may have written down what was planned, and so on. There is, however, no general method for determining meaning, and the intention and meaning are located nowhere other than in language and action. What Wittgenstein was attempting to demolish was the persistent image of meaning, sense, intention, and the like, on the one hand, and of saying, doing and the like, on the other hand, as separate but parallel processes that take place "in two different spheres."

If the answer to meaning is not an operation of the mind, it might seem, as so many have concluded, that, in the end, the meaning of a symbol must be provided by an "*interpretation*," but Wittgenstein stressed the infinite regress involved in this assumption. Because "whenever we interpret a symbol in one way or another, the interpretation is a new symbol added to the old one." An interpretation is simply an account of meaning and not the source. In order to halt the regress of interpretation, we might say that meaning is the "last interpretation," but that strategy does not actually solve the problem. In the end, then, there is no "distinguishing mark between a *sign* and the *meaning*." There may be a case in which we could imagine "a conscious process" running alongside spoken words, such as speaking in one language aloud and supplying the meaning by speaking inwardly in another, but there is no such process of translating from some imaginary realm of nonlinguistic thought to language. But because we can speak about both saying something and meaning something, we tend to hold on to the notion that we are referring to "two parallel processes." We may accompany words with various forms of expression and feeling in the way that the tune of a song accompanies the words, but it is a mistake to pose a question about meaning as if it were a "metaphysical question" or to "express an unclarity about the grammar of words in the *form* of a scientific question." Because, for example, we can speak of sentences in two different languages as having the same "sense," we may believe that the sense is something different from the sentences, "a shadowy being," which is the object of thought, maybe like a picture that we understand without interpreting it. But "the sentence itself can serve as such a shadow." We tend to speak of "meaning or thinking as a peculiar *mental activity*," with "the word 'mental' indicating that we mustn't expect to understand how these things work" unless we can provide a scientific answer, but this just propels us down the wrong path (32–40).

There are various manners of speaking that, if taken literally, lead us astray, such as the notion of being guided by an idea or having an idea in or before one's mind or mind's eye and wishing to find the right words to express it. To say that we want to express an idea implies that "we are trying to express in words what is already expressed, only in a different language," a language of thought. What is really involved is either that we have not actually arrived at what we want to say or that we have not really made a choice between different forms of speaking. Wittgenstein noted that what he had been trying to do was dispel the assumption that "there '*must be*' what is called a mental process of thinking, hoping, wishing, believing, etc., independent of the process of expressing a thought, a hope, a wish, etc.," and that if one were puzzled about such matters, simply "substitute for the thought the expression of the thought." He posed the question of whether it is possible to say one thing and mean another, and he concluded that this could be the case in that words can be variously understood and interpreted, or in that it could be like "asides" in a play where the actor might say one thing and whisper the opposite. But meaning and thinking are only private experiences in the sense that one need not give them public expression, not in the sense that there is a language of thought. Thinking and speaking are not analogous to the words and melody of song, whereby one "could leave out the speaking and do the thinking just as one can sing the tune without the words." One can speak without thinking, that is, without accompanying speech with images, alternative words, and the like, but one cannot engage in what we typically consider as an instance of thinking without language. The point of all this is simply that if we carefully analyze the use of mental terms, it "rids us of the temptation to look for a peculiar act of thinking, independent of the act of expressing our thoughts, and stowed away in some peculiar medium." It leads us to recognize "that the experience of thinking *may* be just the experience of saying" and that it is a mistake to be captured by certain "pictures embedded in our language." A word such as "meaning" has various "odd jobs" in our language, and philosophy gets into difficulty when it attempts to find "regular functions" for such words. The basic problem is one of confusing language regions and seeking pseudo-scientific answers to questions such as what constitutes thinking (41–44).

Wittgenstein argued that philosophy had gone awry by seeking a kind of general and final certainty and completeness and by assuming that "ordinary language is too coarse." It was actually philosophy that often had made things appear "boggy and unsafe," and "as soon as we revert to the standpoint of common sense this *general* uncertainty disappears." He offered the example of how adopting the particle physicists' account of "solidity" was meant to "explain the very phenomenon of solidity," but it only created confusion by choosing one grammatical structure over another. And when philosophers and psychologists seek generality and certainty in the case of mental concepts, they end up positing "two kinds of worlds, worlds built of different materials; a mental world and a physical world." The former is conceived as the name for something that is "gaseous, or rather, aethereal." Because mental terms do not seem to correspond to any object, philosophers look for one basic material that underlies everything and pose oxymoronic questions such as whether there can be unconscious thoughts. The consequence is the metaphysics of realism, idealism, and solipsism. It is in part "our ordinary language, which of all possible notations is the one which pervades all our life, holds our mind rigidly in one position, as it were, and in this position sometimes it feels cramped, having a desire for other positions as well." But metaphysics and natural science are not the solution. They only exacerbate the cramps. The solution is to recognize that words function as "different instruments in our language" and are characterized by their "use" and that "a great variety of games is played with the sentences of our language: Giving and obeying orders; asking questions and answering them; describing an event; telling a fictitious story; telling a joke; describing an immediate experience; making conjectures about events in the physical world; making scientific hypotheses and theories; greeting someone, etc., etc." The basic problem is that we either confuse these types with one another or seek some fundamental common ground among them. We find, for example, that when we use the word "I" as a subject we are not naming the physical aspects of a person, but "this creates the illusion that we use this word to refer to something bodiless, which, however, has its seat in our body." And then, in opposition, one might claim that there is only a body, and thus the fruitless metaphysical contest proceeds. "The word 'mind' has meaning, i.e., it has a use in our language," and it makes sense to speak of "mental activities," but it is mistake to assume that we are speaking of something outside the realm of language (44–73).

The *Brown Book*, part 1, was devoted to demonstrating yet more fully what was involved in operating with signs and how this, rather than some "mental experience" or "state of mind," was the source of meaning. Here Wittgenstein adumbrated both his discussion of Augustine that would be more fully developed in the *Investigations* and his discussion of how to construct and analyze hypothetical "language-games," such as the example of the "builders," which were similar to the games used in training children in their first language. It was also possible to "imagine such a simple language to be the entire system of communication of a tribe in a primitive state of society," and he stressed once more that these language-games were not intended to represent incomplete parts of a language but a complete, although rudimentary, system. He began to insist that even in the case of emotion, there is no distinction between meaning and expression, and "the utterance of an emotion" is not "some artificial device to let others know that we have it" and that can be separated from "the natural expression of emotion" such as weeping. These contrived examples also demonstrated how problems such as those revolving around what is meant by past, present, and future arise from "asymmetry in the grammar of temporal expressions" rather than from any real problem about, for example, "the nature of the future" that could be conceived in a scientific manner. But his principal focus was on dispelling the assumption that the meaning of terms such as "reading" referred to something that was happening "if not in conscious states, then in the unconscious regions" of people's "minds, or in their brains."

In part 2 of the *Brown Book*, he continued at length to focus on the "superstition" that there is a "mental act" of "thinking, wishing, expecting, believing, knowing, trying to solve a mathematical problem, mathematical induction, and so forth" that, so to speak, makes us "capable of crossing a bridge before we've got to it" and that enables us to, for example, follow a rule. It might be more like a "decision," but even this can be misleading and incline us to assume that something must be making us do what we do, some "cause." We may have "reasons," but in many cases "*we need have no reason to follow the rule as we do.* The chain of reasons has an end." He concluded that there was "a kind of general disease of thinking which always looks for (and finds) what would be called a mental state from which all our acts spring as from a reservoir." While our words may be accompanied by a certain tone, gestures, forms of expression, and so on, they are not accompanied by mental acts and experiences of meaning, remembering, reading, understanding, etc. (145).

Wittgenstein focused on how the mythology of mentalism has arisen from the manners of speech that characterize everyday language, but also on how this mythology had been perpetuated and accentuated by both philosophy and the scientific pretensions of psychology. The problems and mistakes that he specified, such as the dualism of language and thought, the assumption of mental causation, the identification of the mind with the brain, the belief that definitions establish meaning, and the failure to distinguish between understanding and interpretation, were passed on to the social and human sciences, where they became deeply embedded.

The Blue and Brown Books point in a significant manner to how to read the *Investigations* as constituting a theory of social phenomena, as an account of what is involved in explaining such phenomena, and as a guide to the epistemological and practical relationship between social inquiry and its subject matter, and they signal the extent to which Wittgenstein's critique of the theory of meaning in the *Investigations* centered on the mistaken image of meaning arising from a mental event. But for a social scientist, or any practitioner of the human sciences, there is much in the *Investigations* that further clarifies both the nature of such forms of inquiry and the problems involved.

4

INVESTIGATING THE *INVESTIGATIONS*

Think of the multifariousness of what we call "language": word-
language, picture-language, gesture-language, sound-language.
(*PG*, 179)

—WITTGENSTEIN

WITTGENSTEIN WAS NOT talking about language and meaning in
any narrow sense but rather in terms of the conventions involved in all
human actions and activities. In the preface, he noted that he had made
"grave mistakes" in his earlier work and had considered republishing the
Tractatus along with the *Investigations* in order to demonstrate the "contrast." A significant element of this contrast was a much broader view of
language in the later work, which in part was the result of his conversations with Frank Ramsey and P. Straffa. The work was the "precipitate
of philosophical investigations [*Philosophischer Untersuchungen*] into the
concepts [*Den Begriff*] of meaning [*Bedeutung*], of understanding [*Verstehen*], of a proposition and sentence [*des Satzes*], of logic, the foundations [*Grundlagen*] of mathematics, states of consciousness [*Bewßtsein-
szustände*], and other things," which were all important to any approach

to social inquiry. Although he had initially wished to "proceed from one subject to another in a natural, smooth sequence," this plan turned out to be against what he experienced as the "natural inclination" of the "remarks" (*Bemerkungen*), because the "nature" of the investigation made it necessary to "criss-cross in every direction over a wide field of thought." This resulted in what might seem like an "album" consisting of "a number of sketches of landscapes," which he hoped, however "unlikely," might possibly "bring light into one brain or another" and "stimulate someone to thoughts of his own" and not "spare other people the trouble of thinking." One might wonder whether these investigations or "surveys" were *by* philosophy or *of* philosophy, but these endeavors were interdependent. He stressed that philosophical investigations are conceptual investigations, and it would indeed be odd to assume that he saw the future of philosophy as simply reflecting on its own conceptual difficulties. He maintained that language was inseparable from the activities in which it was embedded, and it was less words that were being investigated than concepts that were at the theoretical core of all claims about both the nature and particulars of social or conventional phenomena. Such an investigation might be best understood as an exercise in philosophical anthropology and as logically prior to a wide range of particular forms of "anthropological" inquiry, including, as he indicated, mathematics and psychology, to which he devoted a great deal of attention.

Wittgenstein famously began the *Investigations* by noting that his "earlier concept of meaning" in the *Tractatus* was based on "a primitive philosophy of language" that was exemplified in St. Augustine's account of the "learning of language." Although he had noted that this account contained "a calculus of our language," the calculus was not sufficient for explaining "everything that we call language" (*PG*, 19). Augustine related how as a young child he had learned the meaning of words by correlating the "sound" that adults made with the "thing" to which they "meant" to "point." He said that he came to recognize their "intention" by observing the "bodily movements" that were the "natural language of all peoples" and that expressed their "state of mind." By hearing words and locating them in sentences, he claimed that he came to "understand" the "objects that the words signified" and that consequently he had learned to form those same "signs" in order to "express" his own thoughts. Wittgenstein confronted the limits, and mistakes, of this basic, but still common and persistent, account of linguistic meaning, that is, first, that "the words in a language name objects—sentences are combinations of such names" and, second, that language is a vehicle for the expression of the thoughts that endow words with meaning. This last point would be central to the entire work, but the remnants of the whole conception of meaning that he subjected to such intense criticism are still widely entangled in the theory and practice of social inquiry.

Wittgenstein did not deny that linguistic meaning was related to a connection between words and objects. The application of language to things in the world was in large measure the function that language performed, and this connection was the key to the initial "learning of language." But it would definitely be misleading to say that language was a way of representing the world—as if one could specify the contents of the world in some nonlinguistic manner. World and language are internally related. A basic problem with Augustine's account was that it did not allow for all the different "kinds of words" and for the ways in which they are, and might be, used or applied in various practical situations, and it did not distinguish between a person's first acquisition of a language and translating from one language to another. Wittgenstein maintained that since it is impossible to separate linguistic meanings from the activities in which they are manifest, describing the "acts" that someone might perform with certain words and situating them in their appropriate context provides an "explanation" (*Erklärungen*) of their meaning. He immediately presented a hypothetical example of how language use or application (*Verwendung*) is tied to an action and its circumstances, in this case sending someone to a store with the message "five red apples." The "meaning" (*Bedeutung*) of these words in this situation was a function of how they were employed (*gebraucht*) (*PI*, 1).

Since the idea of meaning as a correlation between a word and an object was a correct but nevertheless limited and "primitive idea of the way language functions," he further explicated it through another extended constructed example, which had been adumbrated in *The Blue and Brown Books*. This involved imagining "a language more primitive than ours," dealing with communication between a builder and an assistant. He offered this as a way of demonstrating the danger of universalizing the characteristics of one "circumscribed area" of usage, and he elaborated the point by discussing the uses of a word such as "games," which, despite some similarities, might refer to quite different kinds of things. He emphasized that it is necessary to recognize how the imposition of some "general concept of the meaning of a word surrounds the working of language with a haze which makes clear vision impossible," but "it disperses the fog if we study the phenomena of language in primitive kinds of use in which one can clearly survey the purpose and functioning of the words." By the use of these examples, Wittgenstein was accomplishing a number of things. He was beginning to employ what he would later describe more fully as his philosophical method of constructing language-games as instruments of interpretation. But the examples principally demonstrated how meaning is a function of use and illustrated what is involved in teaching someone a first language, a process that is more accurately labeled "training" (*Abrichten*) than "explanation," because it does not presuppose a prior language. Augustine's account more closely reflected what is involved in learning a foreign language. It presumed that a person acquiring a first language is naturally endowed with a language of thought that, through translation, allows access to a natural language. Although a child first learns to associate words with objects, it is less a matter of "ostensive definition," as might be the case in learning a foreign language, than of "ostensive teaching," which provides the platform for later language learning, deployment, and innovation (2–6).

He wished to demonstrate how children learn their native language and the uses of words by engaging in "*language-games*" that consist "of the language and the activities into which it is woven." He acknowledged that the examples might seem to be incomplete, because they did not include all that we might think of as language, but, no more than in the case of any other human artifact or institution, is there any a priori criterion of completeness that would include all the present and possible future semantic and syntactical elements of a language? "Our language can be regarded as an ancient city: a maze of little streets and squares, of old and new houses, of houses with various extensions from various periods, and all this surrounded by a multitude of new suburbs with straight and regular streets and uniform houses." And, he added, to imagine a language means to imagine a "form of life" (*Lebensform*) and the broader contexts and circumstances in which language is used. This entails that understanding and explaining meaning is always a matter of attending to situational particularities. Wittgenstein viewed words as gaining meaning in the sentences in which they were used, but even the character of sentences is variable and can conceivably consist of only one word, as in his example of the builders and the use of "slab" as an order. He posed the question "How many kinds of sentences are there?" And he answered that "there are *countless* kinds; countless different kinds of use of all things we call 'signs,' 'words,' 'sentences.' And this diversity is not something fixed, given once and for all; but new types of language, new language-games, as we may say, come into existence, and others become obsolete and get forgotten." And within and among the manifold possible categories of language-games, or what we do with words, such as stating, questioning, describing, judging, ordering, and so on, there are also infinite variations and forms of expression. He emphasized once more that "the word 'language-*game*' is used here to emphasize the fact that the *speaking* of language is part of an activity [*Tätigkeit*] or of a form of life" (7–24).

At this point, he did not get deeply involved in complicated issues regarding the differences between humans and animals, such as whether animals can be construed as conscious and possessing the capacity to think, but he noted that the essential difference was simply that animals "do not talk. Or better: they do not use language—if we disregard the most primitive forms of language," while "giving orders, asking questions, telling stories, having a chat, are as much a part of our natural history as walking, eating, drinking, or playing." The natural history of human beings is a history of the conventions that they create and transform and in terms of which they think and act, and the explanation of meaning always involves locating it in within this history. The human encounter with the world is mediated by language, and learning the conventional names of objects is an important part of how one is "trained" in "preparation for the use of a word." Words do not have meaning standing on their own, even though there is often what might called a residual meaning attaching to some words as a result of the manner in which they have been typically employed. He recognized that in this respect certain words may take on a particular conventional character, but the meaning of words is a function of the speech-acts explicitly and implicitly conveyed in sentences. Although an individual is initiated into a repertoire of language usage and although conventions of usage can be highly institutionalized and in some respects constraining, he stressed that such training is also preparation for "inventing" and transforming linguistic meaning and engaging in other forms of social construction. Wittgenstein emphasized, however, the limitations of ostensive definitions in fixing meaning, because pointing "can be variously interpreted in *any* case." He maintained that this problem attends all definitions, which work only if one is already familiar with the language-game in which they are employed, that is, "it only makes sense for someone to ask what something is called if he already knows the use of the name." There are many types of definitions, but those that are typically contained in a dictionary do not so much explain what something is as record how a word is, or has been, used, and this requires determining its place in a language-game rather than simply correlating a word with an object (25–31).

He often used hypothetical anthropological examples, and he suggested how "someone coming into a foreign country will sometimes learn the language of the inhabitants from ostensive explanations." But he noted that it would nevertheless often be necessary "to *guess* how to interpret [*deuten*] these explanations." He stressed that because what one "means" is something that takes place "only in a language," it is impossible to specify what "bodily action" is necessary to establish meaning by pointing to something that we wish to name. But he also again stressed that meaning does not come from some mysterious place often referred to as the mind. There is, however, a tendency, as in the case of Augustine, to fall back on the notion "that a *mental, spiritual* [*gestige*] activity corresponds to these words." Wittgenstein noted that although there seems to be a "strange connection of a word with an object," which often leads one "to imagine meaning to be some remarkable mental [*seelischer*] act, as if it were the baptism of an object," this assumption, in both philosophy and everyday life, "only arises when *language goes on holiday*" and we confuse one language region with another. The meaning of a name, like any other word, is a function of the language-game in which naming takes place, and it is only the "tendency to sublimate the logic of our language" (which was what he had come to see as his mistake in the *Tractatus*) that prevents us from realizing that there is no single act that constitutes naming and no "simple" thing that a name signifies. He pointed out that it is a mistake to "confound the meaning of a name with the *bearer* of the name" or the thing named, that is, to confuse words with objects, even though "the *meaning* of a name is sometimes explained by pointing to its *bearer*." For example, we might designate a certain liquid as "water" or a certain metal as "gold," but, as Kuhn would also emphasize, it would be a mistake to assume that we have exhausted the meaning of these words or established some necessary connection between the words and the objects. At this point, Wittgenstein simply summed up explicitly what he had been getting at all along, that is, that it is a mistake to identify meaning with the thing that corresponds to a word and that "for a *large* class of cases of the employment of the word 'meaning'—though not for *all*—this word can be explained in this way: the meaning of a word is its use in the language" (25–43).

He did not, however, conceive the concept of use in a narrow utilitarian manner. There is more than one use of "use," but from the Greeks through the work of the early Wittgenstein, and even in contemporary philosophy ranging from logical positivism to recent forms of realism, there have persisted variations on "the idea that names really signify simples" that form the "constituent parts of reality." He emphasized that words such as "simple" and "composite" are themselves used in "an enormous number of different, and differently related, ways." This point explicitly introduced one of his most important themes—the function of paradigms in explaining or interpreting language-games, which both complemented his emphasis on language-games as tools of interpretation and related to his insistence on not confusing what is represented with the vehicle of representation. Interpreting social phenomena requires paradigms as a means of representation, but it also creates the danger of reifying the paradigm. He noted, as an example, "there is *one* thing of which one can state neither that it is 1 meter long, nor that it is not 1 meter long, and that is the standard meter in Paris," but this was "only to mark its peculiar role in the game of measuring," which is its function as a means and standard of representation and judgment. The same holds true for many color statements that are predicated on samples operating as a measure and form of representation and serving as "a paradigm [*Paradigma*] in our game; something with which comparisons are made," a "means" or "mode" of representation. While the word "red" might function as a name for a certain element in a color chart, the color chart could also be a guide to or the expression of a rule for using the word "red." This point was followed by a parenthetical remark that related to his broader account of games and rules. One could say that "a game is played according to a particular rule," but this might mean either that the rule was an "aid" in teaching someone how to play a game or that it was a "tool" in playing the game. It could also mean that an observer might attempt to discern the rule that was operating in the course of the game—where it might appear to be "like a natural law governing the play." In the latter case, however, there is a question of how an observer could, apart from judging the reactions of the players, distinguish between correct and incorrect moves. He noted that "a paradigm that is used in conjunction with a name in a language-game," such as the king in chess, "would be an example of something which corresponds to a name and without which it would have no meaning" (44–55).

This discussion of how names gain meaning in language-games raised *"the great question that lies behind all these considerations"* (emphasis added), that is, the question of what is "essential to a language-game" and what various language-games have in common. His answer was, in effect, that "language-game" did not refer to a particular thing but rather to a class or category of things and that "instead of pointing out something common to all that we call language, I'm saying that these phenomena have no one thing in common in virtue of which we use the same word for all—but there are many kinds of *affinity* between them." The concept of a language-game was a means of representation, and the tendency to confuse the means and object of representation and to mistake categorical terms for designations of things was a consistent target of Wittgenstein's therapeutic efforts. He devoted a great deal of attention to the different ways in which the word "same" could be deployed, and it was at this point that he introduced the concept of "family resemblances" as a way of considering why we might refer to various activities such as "games" as the same kind of thing even if there was nothing that was essentially the same among them. He was using the concept of family as a taxonomic category, not as a designation for entities that are genetically related. The elements of what he conceived as a language-game are connected by what an observer might discern as "a complicated network of similarities overlapping and criss-crossing." In this way, one might distinguish, for example, a "family of games" or a family of "numbers." There are, however, no fixed boundaries to such categorical concepts. He noted, for example, that it is possible to give the "concept of number rigid boundaries," but, as in the case of games, "the extension of the concept is *not* closed by a boundary." This is especially the case with a family-resemblance concept, which can be reshaped without changing its basic identity, and the playing of a particular game, such as tennis, "is not bounded everywhere by rules" and allows variation while still remaining tennis. Family-resemblance concepts are very different from many of the theoretical concepts employed, for example, in natural science. The concept of an atom is not a taxonomic concept and does not have the same sort of flexibility and possibility of extension as a categorical concept. But although "the concept of a game is a concept with blurred edges," this should not lead to the conclusion that it is not "a *concept* at all." In these instances, "*seeing what is in common*" is a matter of concern and perspective or of "seeing in *this* way or *that*." He claimed that this is the "position" in which persons find themselves "in ethics or aesthetics" when they seek "definitions that correspond to our concepts." A word such as "good" has definite similarities in its usage, but its criteria of application vary among language-games, and it is a mistake to treat it as if it were a theoretical concept. There is no object to which "good" refers any more than in the case of truth, certainty, justice, and so on. What he was in part stressing was the extent to which it is impossible to avoid the particular circumstances attaching to matters involving ethical judgment. Here, there is no escape from particularity to universality (56–77).

By focusing on words such as "*knowing* and *saying*," Wittgenstein continued to illustrate how meaning is relative to the various uses of words and especially how it is a mistake to seek some common foundation of such usage. While individuals might both "know" and "say" how high a particular mountain is, they might not be able to describe the sound of a certain musical instrument even though they "knew" it when they heard it. There is even "fluctuation of scientific definitions," which demonstrates once again that a definition does not necessarily fix or reveal some essential meaning and that the rules for the application of words differ, that is, the words may refer to different concepts. A distinction between words and concepts was an important part of the background of his remarks. For example, his use of the word "rule" did not usually refer to some rigid calculus but was emblematic of conventions as a whole, and it could be used to designate quite different concepts. He noted that he had come to realize that "logic was a 'normative science'" and that although philosophers "often *compare* the use of words" with situations in which there are "fixed rules," it is yet another example of the danger of reifying paradigms. Language use cannot be accounted for and evaluated against the background of some "*ideal* language." We can, for various purposes, "*construct* ideal languages," but not for the purpose of judging "everyday language" on the assumption that meaning and understanding equate to operating "according to definite rules" any more than "playing a ball-game" always entails such rules. What he was in part stressing was the extent to which normativity and logic are already built into the practice of language, and it is this normativity that philosophical analysis should attempt to illuminate. Although he placed great emphasis on the many ways in which rules are involved in language, he continued to stress that the application of a word is "not everywhere bounded by strict rules" and that even when a rule is specified, what constitutes following it might be in question. "A rule is like a signpost," but a "signpost does after all leave room for doubt"—notwithstanding the fact that it is "in order—if, under normal circumstances, it fulfills its purpose," because "no ideal of exactness has been envisaged" (78–88).

Up to this point, Wittgenstein had been addressing general issues relating to language and meaning, but he had not directly addressed the question of what he himself was doing with words and in what kind of language-game and activity he was involved. He began by explicitly rejecting his former assumption that formal logic is "something sublime," has a "universal significance," is the invisible "foundation of all the sciences," and "explores the essence of all things," of "everything empirical," including the ultimate meaning behind natural languages. He proposed now not to "seek to learn anything *new*" in the sense of discovering something deeper than the meaning of actual language use but only "to *understand* something that is already in plain view." He was not referring to what everyone is aware of or what is in some way self-evident, but rather to the fact that the meaning of language, as encountered by the philosophical observer, is preconstituted and that an indigenous logic is already immanent in linguistic usage. The purpose of philosophy is not to explain the nature and existence of the phenomena to which words refer, but to recover the meaning of the words. Wittgenstein demonstrated this point by referring to how Augustine, when he posed his famous conundrum about the nature of time, made the mistake of treating it like a problem in natural science rather than a problem revolving around the concepts to which the word "time" might refer. Philosophy is not directed "towards *phenomena*," but instead toward "the *kinds of statement* that we make about phenomena," which entails that "our inquiry is therefore a grammatical one" that focuses on analyzing "our forms of expression" and "sheds light on our problems by clearing misunderstandings away . . . concerning the use of words" induced by confusions about such things as the relationships among different "regions of our language" (88–90).

Two points were implied here. First, many of the problems of philosophy are rooted in these confusions, and his intention in this respect was therapeutic. Although the same sort of confusions might be present in various everyday uses of language and therefore important with respect to understanding those uses, the therapeutic task of philosophy was not, at least in the first instance, external, that is, directed toward social actors. It was directed toward the problems involved in explaining social phenomena. His point about the concept of time can be illustrated by a recent public television program that focused on what the narrator referred to as the "illusion of time." The thesis of the program was that our everyday use of the word "time" and our sense of temporality in life are based on an illusion that a scientific investigation can expose. This claim was comparable to the story of Eddington's table and the suggestion that our perception and conception of its solidity are an illusion based on a failure to recognize its underlying atomic composition. Wittgenstein had already (*BB*, 45) pointed out a similar mistake about the use of the word "solid." To refer to time as an illusion is really to make the same error as Augustine, that is, to assume that there is, or in this case is not, an object that determines the meaning of a word and to assume that the word always refers to the same concept and belongs to the same kind of language-game. Wittgenstein was once again directly confronting and rejecting the position he had taken in the *Tractatus*, and he insisted that his goal now was not to achieve either a "final analysis of our linguistic expressions" or a "state of complete exactness," but rather "to understand the nature of language," not in the sense of some "*essence*" that is hidden below the surface but in terms of how it functions at any particular time and place (91–93).

Although from the outset he had emphasized that meaning no more comes from the "mind" than from a correlation with objects, he now began to focus more directly on arguing that it was a mistake to attempt to locate some mental "intermediary" between the "*sign*" and what it signified. Again rejecting his former claims in the *Tractatus*, he argued that such an approach was just another instance of the "sublimation" of logic and the "pursuit of chimeras." He claimed that it was a mistake to posit "thinking" as the source of meaning, whereby "thought, language, now appear to us as the unique correlate, picture, of the world. These concepts: proposition, language, thought, world" seem to "stand in line behind the other," but although these words have various "humble" uses, there is no language-game that makes this philosophical scheme intelligible. And he argued that it is a mistake to view formal logic as the essence of thinking and to assume that it represents the "a priori order of the world" and the foundation of experience. The goal of philosophy should not be *"striving after* an ideal" that we believe "*'must* occur in reality," but to accept the fact that "our language 'is in order as it is.'" He had made this last claim in the *Tractatus*, and in both cases his point was not that language lacked order, but that understanding it required achieving clarity about the conventions of our language.

Ideals may have explanatory applications, but Wittgenstein maintained that such ideals in the case of philosophy or any interpretive endeavor are a means of representation, and the great mistake, as he relentlessly emphasized, was to confuse what was represented with the means of representation, which not only was a problem in philosophy but was endemic to all the human sciences. It is endemic because social inquiry is a matter of representing conventional phenomena by means of other conventions. Wittgenstein was claiming not that practical language never went astray or was unambiguous, but rather that the problems that might emerge are not caused by a failure of such use to correspond to some object, thought, or ideal that is the real source of meaning. The function of ideals in his philosophical approach was to illustrate and convey the uses of language, and it is crucial to avoid the tendency in philosophy in which "one predicates of the thing what lies in the mode of representation [*Darstellungsweise*]." As an example of this problem, he referred to Faraday's statement that "water is one individual thing—it never changes." Wittgenstein's response was that such a scientific definition of water does not necessarily determine the use of the word "water," even though such a use might be characteristic of a particular scientific community:

> The more closely we examine actual language, the greater becomes the conflict between it and our requirement. (For the crystalline purity of logic was, of course, not something I had *discovered*: it was a requirement). The conflict becomes intolerable; the requirement is now in danger of becoming vacuous.—We have got on the slippery ice where there is no friction, and so, in a certain sense, the conditions are ideal; but also, just because of that, we are unable to walk. We want to walk: so we need *friction*. Back to the rough ground!
> (94–107)

The old view of logic could "only be removed by turning our whole inquiry around" on the "pivot of our real need," which was to look at the particularities of "the spatial and temporal phenomenon of language" and the immanent and variable logic of how it functions in the games that people play. This turn in the conception of the vocation of philosophy was in effect to transform philosophical investigations into a form of social inquiry. Wittgenstein insisted that his concerns were not "scientific ones" in that the aim was not "hypothetical" or to "advance any kind of theory." What he was referring to as a contrast model were both the hypothetical claims of natural science and the super-scientific claims of logic and metaphysics. He stated that "all *explanation* must disappear, and description alone must take its place," but for Wittgenstein, description and clarification, as in the case of language use, as he so often explicitly stated, constituted explanation. His point was that philosophical problems are not "empirical" in the sense that natural science might be considered empirical. They are "solved through insight into the workings of our language" and by struggling "against the bewitchment of our understanding by the resources of our language." There were, as the title of the book might be taken to imply, two dimensions of what Wittgenstein took to be philosophical problems. One dimension consisted of the problems that were internal to the practice of philosophy, and the other dimension involved problems encountered in the course of philosophical inquiries. What he rejected were the kinds of problems that traditional philosophy had set for itself, such as specifying the logical and metaphysical foundations of language. Despite the continuing dispute about whether Wittgenstein's work was primarily therapeutic or descriptive, there is no reason to choose between these alternatives. There is no doubt that it was meant to be *philosophically* therapeutic, but he did not attempt to specify the social role of philosophy. He made it clear that the conceptual muddles in which philosophy often found itself were not generically different from those in others pursuits such as mathematics and psychology as well as in everyday life. And part of philosophy's task was to describe and explain these practices. He insisted, however, that before philosophy could approach any other particular region of language, it was necessary to cure its own "illusions," which were "as deeply rooted in us as the forms of our language" and where often "a *picture* held us captive." We become caught up in an expression, such as a "simile," that has become "absorbed" into our language, and we assume that what is not really the same actually "*has to be!*" Philosophy's path of escape was "to bring words back from their metaphysical to their everyday use," and this involved, for example, continuing to make it clear that meaning is neither something dictated by the objects in the world nor some mysterious mental "aura" surrounding a word, but a matter of the application of language (108–16).

He was sensitive to the extent to which his investigations might seem to "destroy everything interesting," and he noted in another place that "it occurred to me today as I was thinking about my work in philosophy & said to myself: 'I destroy, I destroy, I destroy—' (*CV*, 19). What he was destroying were the metaphysical issues that philosophy had characteristically embraced, but he claimed that in the end, "we are only destroying houses of cards and we are clearing up the ground of language on which they stood" and exposing the "nonsense" that arises from "running up against the limits of language," where we attempt to peek over and see what is on the other side. The point was to examine the "language of every day," by which he meant practical or applied language in general, and not chase after some ghostly meaning that accompanied the use of words and provided them with sense (117–20).

These self-reflective questions about the nature of philosophy are of a type that would not typically be addressed in a practice such as natural science, in which there is no question of either cognitive or practical conflict with the subject matter and in which issues are settled by unilateral definition and decision. He noted that the "difficulty of philosophy is not the difficulty of the sciences, but the difficulty of a change of attitude. Resistance of the will must be overcome" (*PO*, 161). Such issues are unavoidable in the case of philosophy, which deals with human activity (*Verhaltens*) and its particular circumstances. He insisted, however, that there is no "second-order philosophy." What he was in part getting at was that, as he constantly stressed, philosophical surveys are grammatical in character, and consequently "philosophy" is inherently concerned with words and concepts. But his more important, but less explicit, point was that philosophy is, by its very nature, a metapractice, because its subject matter is a preconstituted grammatical and conceptual world, and the task is one of understanding and interpreting that world. When Wittgenstein spoke of "grammar," he was sometimes referring to philosophical analysis and sometimes to the subject matter of philosophy. This bound investigation and its subject matter together, but there was even a yet more subtle aspect to this remark, to which he had already alluded. Philosophy must be a self-reflective enterprise, because it deals with a subject matter that is conceptually autonomous, and consequently its own identity is an issue. But it is one thing to specify the nature and aim of philosophy and another thing to confront the issue of its method or how to go about pursuing that aim.

Wittgenstein stated that "a main source of our failure to understand [*Unverständnisses*] is that we don't have *an overview* [*Übersehen*] of the use of our words.—Our grammar is deficient in surveyability [*Übersichtlichkeit*]. A surveyable representation [*Darstellung*] produces precisely that kind of understanding which consists in 'seeing connections.' Hence the importance of finding and inventing *intermediate* links." There are various ways to translate *Darstellung*, but "representation," "depiction," "account," "description," "interpretation," "picture," and "rendering" all seem appropriate and compatible with his use of the word. He was speaking about finding a way not only to solve a puzzle but to describe and communicate the results to some audience. This approach, he insisted, was of "fundamental significance," because it "characterizes the way we represent things." He asked if this was a "Weltanschauung," and he seemed, at this point, to conclude that it was, because it functioned as a perspective on something that is conceptually preconstituted. It was designed to solve problems arising from a failure to "know my way about" some linguistic terrain. Wittgenstein made a consistent distinction between, on the one hand, the way that we look at and represent or interpret something and, on the other hand, what we take something to be, that is, how we theoretically conceive it. And, again, what is represented and the means of representation are two different things. This, however, raised the issue of why one wished to find one's way around and what the implications of such an exploration might be. The answer that Wittgenstein offered was one that has troubled many commentators (121–23).

He went on to say that "*Die Philosophie darf der tatsächlichen Gebrauch der Sprache in keiner Weise antasten, sie kann ihn am Ende also nur beschrieben.*" This was originally translated by Anscombe as "Philosophy may in no way interfere with the actual use of language, so it can in the end only describe it." Hacker and Schulte subsequently chose "must" rather than "may," but "must" and "actual" are still ambiguous. The basic sense of the remark might be better conveyed by a somewhat freer translation: "Philosophy *is in no position* to interfere with the *prac-*

tical application of language; it *therefore* in the end can only describe it." Wittgenstein then said, "For it cannot justify [*begründen*] it either. It leaves everything as it is." Although this statement might appear to conflict with his often therapeutic attitude, his basic point was that, unlike the claims of natural science, the claims of philosophy do not, simply by their performance, transform the identity of the subject matter. He made this clear by noting, for example, that philosophy "leaves mathematics as it is," which reflected his arguments against the search for the transcendental and logical foundations of mathematics. He certainly hoped to supply some light to the practice of mathematics, but there was no assurance that the light would penetrate the practice. And most mathematicians have been reluctant to confront his criticisms. This remark was not intended to limit the scope of philosophy, but simply to point out that there is no philosophical answer to how philosophy can influence its subject matter. What Wittgenstein's statement did in effect was to grant autonomy to both philosophy and its object of inquiry, but a consequence was to open up a range of choices with respect to the relationship between them. In his case, the intention of philosophy was certainly not to leave philosophy as it was, but whether or not philosophy had practical consequences was an issue that was necessarily open to discussion, dependent on circumstances, and impossible to settle by any philosophical decision or discovery. Philosophy's basic problem was not, for example, to solve contradictions in an activity such as mathematics, but, for example, to illuminate "the civic status of a contradiction, or its status in civic life." He once again stressed that "philosophy just puts everything before us" rather than seeking an underlying explanation or advancing "*theses*"—its task is more like that of the study of history, that is, one of "marshaling recollections." He noted that "the real foundations" of our object of inquiry are often "hidden"—not because of a lack of deep causal explanation, but because they are embedded in and constitutive of the practices themselves (124–29).

The question of how to achieve the kind of survey or overview that Wittgenstein proposed could be neither avoided nor definitively answered, but he returned to the epistemological and methodological issues of how philosophy might go about the business of representing its subject matter without superimposing some external scheme. He urged a particular technique that is in part endemic to the nature of philosophy and other human sciences, but it also in part reflected a particular choice that he pursued. It is endemic in that philosophical accounts of meaning, that is, interpretations, are, as Max Weber had recognized, necessarily couched in the language of inquiry. The choice is with respect to the language and vehicle of interpretation. It was at this point that Wittgenstein again made it very clear that when he spoke of language-games, it was not just about the object of inquiry, but about what he took to be an essential element in the method of inquiry, such as his parable of the builders. He had already emphasized how important it is to distinguish between these two kinds of language-games, and he maintained that "our clear and simple language-games" are not a preliminary to the "regimentation" of language but, instead, are "*objects of comparison*" designed to illuminate the "features of our language." These were ideal-types that served as a "model" (*Vorbild*) in aiding understanding and advancing an interpretation rather than a "preconception to which reality *must* correspond." The latter approach had led to what he referred to as the kind of "dogmatism" that had characterized so much of philosophy. The proper task of philosophy, he argued, is to find "an order in our knowledge of the use of language," that is, an immanent order. This could not be an order in language as a whole or an order that did not change. The basic purpose was neither to "reform" language nor to achieve a final account of rules, but to "*emphasize* distinctions" and confront "confusions" that arise when language is "idling." The goal was the kind of "*complete* clarity" that would allow "philosophical problems" to "*completely* disappear." But, once again, the problems to which he referred at this point were not primarily those that philosophy might encounter in its exploration of various forms of language use, but those that had defined traditional philosophy. He stated that "the real discovery is the one that enables me to break off philosophizing when I want to.—The one that gives philosophy peace, so that it is no longer tormented by questions which bring *itself* into question," that is, the questions that had defined traditional metaphysics. He argued that "a method is now demonstrated by examples," but "there is not a single method, though there are indeed methods, different therapies." What vehicle might illuminate language use in some particular situation was always something to be formulated and negotiated. There was, however, still much to be said about what constituted the meaning that was the object of philosophical inquiry as well as what was involved in understanding and interpreting meanings, and here the concepts of understanding and interpreting, as well as the important distinction between them, became crucial (129–33).

He noted that when we "understand" (*Verstehen*) a word in a particular instance, we seem to "grasp the meaning at a stroke," which might evoke a particular picture (maybe like the lightbulb in a cartoon balloon), but there is no conflict between this image and the idea of meaning as use, because we do not grasp all the possible uses or applications of the term or even of the picture. Although there are "abnormal" cases of usage, there may, in "normal cases," be little or no doubt about meaning, because our concepts often reflect both our "characteristic expression" of things, such as sensation and emotion, and "extremely general facts of nature"— otherwise "our normal language-games would thereby lose their point." But there is no going outside language in order to more directly encounter the world. The task of philosophy is not to picture the world, but instead to picture the language in which the world is pictured. Meaning, however, both in the practice of a language-game and in the practice of interpreting a language-game, is always open to question and can be changed by altering a person's "*way of looking at things.*" But in addition to not confusing the meaning of a word with an object, what Wittgenstein principally wished to combat and *what most consistently occupied his attention in the remainder of the book* was the illusion that understanding, knowing, and similar terms refer to mental states in the sense of "an apparatus of the mind" or "brain"—even though knowing or understanding might reasonably be spoken of as either a "state of mind" or a "disposition" to act in a particular way. He emphasized that what is basically involved in "understanding" is "to have 'mastered' a technique," such as how to proceed in constructing a series of numbers. There is not some mysterious "mental process" hidden behind the "circumstances" that "we count as manifestations of understanding" (134–55).

In order to explain more fully the character of certain concepts that are often associated with meaning, but confused with an obscure mental process, Wittgenstein presented a very lengthy analysis of the use of the word "reading," by which he referred to actions of "rendering out loud what is written or printed; but also of writing from dictation, copying something printed, playing from sheet music, and so on." Given all the senses in which the word "reading" is used, we might be tempted to believe that there is something essential to them all, that reading "is a quite particular process" or "experience," which can be explained in terms of "what goes on in the brain and the nervous system." But in fact we "use the word 'read' for a family of cases. And in different circumstances we apply different criteria for a person's reading." The issue of reading also relates to the general question of what is involved in "being guided" or "influenced" and whether there is anything common among the experiences that might be associated with such terms. In the case of something such as knowing how to go on in the course of some practice, what is involved differs among various language-games, despite what may be the family-resemblances. What is important is to focus on "*how the words are used*," and "it would be quite misleading . . . to call the words a 'description of a mental state.'" The words are a "signal" to be judged by whether they are appropriately applied in a particular game. It is simply that "the role of these words in our language is other than we are tempted to think," and specifying "this role is what is necessary in order to understand and solve philosophical paradoxes. And this is why definitions usually aren't enough to resolve them; and even less so the statement that a word is 'indefinable.'" A word is always definable. The problem is to specify the kind of definition and its use (155–82).

Throughout the *Investigations*, there is a close connection between Wittgenstein's critique of the referential theory of meaning and his discussion of mental concepts. It is not that he was denying the existence of something we might call "thought"; rather, he was pointing out that it is a word that has various uses in our language and that it is a mistake to attempt to fix the meaning by assuming that it refers to something like an event in some room to which an individual has private access or to some physiological or neurological phenomenon. He was confronting the problems that often arise from a certain manner of speaking about such things as what is involved in meaning something, which often leads to the assumption that in the case of, for example, giving an order "your mind, as it were, flew ahead and took all the steps" and that the steps "were in some *unique* way predetermined, anticipated—in the way that only meaning something could anticipate reality." He said that philosophers tended to "misinterpret" the way people use mental concepts, and, he suggested, in this respect they "are like savages, primitive people, who hear the way in which civilized people talk, put a false interpretation on it, and then draw the oddest conclusions from this." They tend to confuse different language-games and consequently to assume that "understanding" and "misunderstanding the use of the word" refer to "an odd *process*" that is not open to view. Although there is actually nothing "astonishing" or "strange" involved in understanding the use of a word, there is a tendency to "think that the future development must in some way already be present in the act of grasping the use and yet isn't present," just as one might think that in intending to play a game such as chess that all the rules of the game are somehow present in the intention. Wittgenstein was making two basic points here. The first was that intentions and meaning something are not mental acts, but rather are embedded in the conventions of a game and in the rules involved in teaching and playing it. But he was also opening up the issue of the nature and functioning of rules, which was so essential to his account of language-games and which also led to an elaboration of the distinction between understanding and interpreting (182–97).

How, he asked, can a rule teach one what to do, when any action "can, on some interpretation, be made compatible with the rule"? His answer was that "every interpretation hangs in the air together with what it interprets, and cannot give it any support. Interpretations by themselves do not determine meaning." A person typically goes by a rule, or follows a "signpost," because the person has been trained to do so and because this training initiates the person into "an established usage [*Gebrauch*], a custom [*Gepflogenheit*]." He claimed that following a rule is not something that only one person at a particular time could do, but this was simply to make the logical point that "to follow a rule, to make a report, to give an order, to play a game of chess, are *customs* (usages and institutions). To understand a language means to have mastered a technique." He acknowledged that while it might seem a "paradox" that an action could not be definitively identified by a rule—because under some interpretation "every course of action can be brought into accord" or "conflict" with the rule—understanding a rule and interpreting a rule are two different things: "there is a way of grasping a rule which is *not* an interpretation [*Deutung*]" and "is exhibited in what we call 'following the rule' or 'going against it,'" and consequently "one should speak of interpretation only when one expression of a rule is substituted for another." He claimed "that's why 'following a rule' is a practice [*Praxis*]. And to *think* one is following a rule is not to follow a rule. And that's why it's not possible to follow a rule 'privately.'" This difference between understanding a rule and interpreting a rule demonstrated the extent to which "language is labyrinth of paths. You approach from *one* side and know your way about; you approach the same place from another side and no longer know your way about." Acting within a language-game and giving an account of a language-game are two different, but sometimes related, activities. Achieving an understanding of a game might be a prerequisite for providing an adequate interpretation, and an interpretation might aid or influence an understanding of a game (198–203).

He again made it clear that it would be impossible to speak about people possessing intentions apart from and prior to the rules and conventions in which they participated and were "trained" to follow or had learned to invoke. If an "explorer" came into a country that was inhabited by people possessing an unknown language, the "shared human behaviour [*Handlungen*] is the system of reference by which we interpret an unknown language." What he was referring to was the "regularity" characteristic of typical conventions in the human form of life, such as giving, obeying, and rebelling against orders, along with the language that might correspond to these activities. And if someone who spoke a foreign language did not understand what the "*concepts*" of regular or same mean with respect to rules, it would be necessary to "teach" the person "to use the words by means of examples and exercises." This indicated an important distinction between words and concepts, but he was also illustrating how providing an example of how to go on in a particular case, by an expression such as "and so on," did not suggest that the rule involved "*points beyond*" the example to a "deeper explanation," in the manner that "mathematicians sometimes think" when speaking of "infinity," or when one interprets "what is not limited as a length that reaches beyond every length" (204–9).

He continued to emphasize that it is important to resist the temptation to assume that what is understood by a person who offers an explanation of an action is, any more than in the case of exchanges among individuals involved in some practice, a matter of grasping some mental event that stands behind the action and the reasons provided. When the reasons "give out . . . I shall act without reasons" or in some circumstances follow an order "without concern about the reasons or motivations behind it." Someone might, of course, have doubts about how to proceed in continuing with what might appear to be the beginning of a series of numerals, but in most circumstances, and as a matter of principle, one would not start with various possible interpretations of a rule and choose among them on the assumption that there is some fundamental indeter-minacy. The answer is not to assume some mysterious "intuition" about how to go on. This, however, raised an issue that occupied much of Witt-genstein's attention, that is, how to apply the concept of "*the same*" and what constituted "identity" with respect to a rule. "Same" might mean numerically identical, generically comparable, having similar attributes, theoretically the same, functionally the same, and so on. The question of how one is able to follow a rule is not about causal explanation. It is about "justification" (*Rechtfertigung*), but having "exhausted the justifica-tions [*Begründungen*], I have reached bedrock, and my spade is turned. Then I am inclined to say: 'This is simply what I do.'" Further explanation would be simply ornamental. Although there might be a temptation to think of the "beginning of a series as a visible section of rails invisibly laid to infinity" corresponding with the "unlimited application of a rule," this should only be "understood symbolically" as indicating "*how it strikes me.*" Because in most instances, "when I follow the rule, I do not choose. I follow the rule *blindly.*" It is a matter not of intimation, compulsion, or in some way being guided by the rule, but of being taught and accus-tomed to act in a certain manner. "The rule can only seem to produce all its consequences in advance if I draw them as *matter of course.*" Witt-genstein then posed the very question that so many commentators, such as Errol Morris, have directed toward his argument, that is, is it "that human agreement decides what is true and what is false"? His answer was that "what is true or false is what human beings *say*; and it is in their *language* that human beings agree. This is agreement not in opinions, but rather in form of life" and in the attending "definitions" and "judgments" (210–42). We do not hold a town meeting to decide on the criteria for the application of "true" and "false."

Wittgenstein again returned directly to the concept of mental states, which was really the issue that had precipitated much of his dis-cussion of rules. He presented what is usually referred to and discussed as his argument about the impossibility of a private language, that is, a language in which the words refer "to what only the speaker can know— to his immediate private sensations." A great deal of literature has been devoted to analyzing this argument, but the underlying point was actu-ally the simple fact that the very idea of a private language is oxymoronic, because language is a public conventional phenomenon. It is, neverthe-less, difficult to shake off the idea that there is something like a language of thought that is expressed in natural languages. This was assumed in Augustine's claims as well as in Wittgenstein's own early work. Wittgenstein did not deny asymmetry between first- and third-person claims about pain; he only maintained that first-person statements are reports rather than corrigible claims, and that although it might at times be an intelligible manner of speaking for people to say that they "know" they are in pain, it makes little literal sense. People might express a sensation such as pain in various ways, and the verbal expression of pain is an alternative to or refinement of something such as crying. Sensations are, by definition or grammar, private, but their expression is public and can be genuine or feigned. What people might say about such things as pain is the "raw material" of philosophical inquiry, but he again made clear the distinction between philosophy and its subject matter by noting that "what a mathematician is inclined to say about the objectivity and reality of mathematical facts is not a philosophy of mathematics, but something for philosophical *treatment*"—"the philosopher treats a question . . . like an illness" (243–57).

He went on at great length to illustrate his point about pain by saying that if a person chose to keep a "diary" of sensations such as pain, it would have to be in a public language in which the person participated or in a coded form of that language. Similarly, whatever a person's experience of color might be, the expression and criteria of color statements are public and something that is learned by example. He recognized that his argument might sound like behaviorism and as if he were identifying pain with "*pain-behavior*," but his purpose was to reject the dualism of mind and body and stress "that only of a living human being and what resembles (behaves like) a living human being can one say: it has sensations; it sees; is blind; hears; is deaf; is conscious or unconscious." It is not the body, a part of the body, or the mind (*Seele*) that experiences pain, but a "human being," and to be a human being is to be engaged in language-games such as those involving sensation and pain. In cases of reporting pain, there is usually no issue of "justification," and "to use a word without justification does not mean to use it wrongly." He noted that "what we call 'descriptions' are instruments for particular uses," and one does not describe one's sensations in the way that one might describe a "room" to which one has privileged access. These are two different language-games (258–92).

Here, Wittgenstein presented a hypothetical example of a group of individuals who each claimed to have a beetle in a box, to which no one

else had access, and claimed that they knew what a beetle was by looking in their particular box. He pointed out that they might, in fact, have
different things, or nothing, in their box, but the word "beetle" would still
have a use in the language-game even though in this case it was not necessarily the name of a "thing" or even a "something." His point was that
these were reports, and that it is a mistake to view the "grammar of the
expression of sensation on the model of 'object and name'"; "the object
drops out of consideration as irrelevant." Wittgenstein expressed this by
saying that a sensation such as pain is "not a Something but not a Nothing either," yet a "Nothing would render the same service as a Something." What might seem to be a paradox disappears once we "break
with the idea that language always functions in one way, always serves
the same purpose: to convey thoughts" (293–304).

He denied that "the picture of an inner process gives us the correct
idea of the use" of a word such as "remembering," but he stressed that
rejecting such a "*grammatical* fiction" does not entail either denying the
existence of something that might be referred to as mental activity or
accepting behaviorism. The problem begins when "*we talk of processes and
states, and leave their nature undecided,*" *which is the* "*decisive moment in the
conjuring trick*" that makes it seem that by denying the fiction one has
denied the very idea of mental processes, when the "aim in philosophy"
is only "to show the fly the way out of the fly-bottle." It is an "illusion" to
believe that there is some "*private* exhibition" of pain, real or feigned, that
is different from the public expression, that in order to find out what the
word "think" refers to "we watch ourselves thinking," or that there is a
parallel between crying as an expression of a pain and uttering "a sentence,
an expression of a thought." Similarly, thought and speech, or writing, are
not typically "*detached,*" even though in certain instances we may conceive
of thinking as an activity. We are, for example, misled if we assume "that
understanding is a specific, indefinable experience" or that thinking "in
words" involves "'meanings' in my mind in addition to the verbal expressions; rather language itself is the vehicle of thought" and "what constitutes thought here is not some process which has to accompany the words
if they are not to be spoken without thought." He suggested, much as Sellars did later, imagining "people who could think only aloud. (As there are
people who can only read aloud)." What might be considered thoughtful
speech would be analogous to singing with expression. "We sometimes
call accompanying a sentence by a mental process 'thinking;' nonetheless,

that accompaniment is not what we call a 'thought.'"The common notion that there are "meanings" in our mind for which we seek verbal expressions, as if we were involved in a process of translation or description, is very misleading, as in the case of "a French politician" who "once wrote that it was a peculiarity of the French language that in it words occur in the order in which one thinks them" (305–36).

He reiterated that an "intention [*Absicht*] is embedded in a setting, in human customs and institutions. If the technique of the game of chess did not exist, I could not intend to play the game of chess. To the extent that I do intend the construction of an English sentence in advance, that is made possible by the fact that I can speak English." He stressed that "in order to want to say something, one must also have mastered a language; and yet it is clear that one can want to speak without speaking. Just as one can want to dance without dancing." Thus "thinking is not an incorporeal process which lends life and sense to speaking, and which would be possible to detach from speaking." What would constitute such an incorporeal process is impossible to specify, and while it might serve as a metaphor for distinguishing the grammar of "think" from that of a word such as "eat," it is in the end "an inappropriate expression." It is a "sure means of remaining stuck in confusion" and smacks of the kind of philosophical Platonism, common among mathematicians as well as philosophers, that holds that "numerals are actual, and numbers are nonactual objects." To grasp "how a word functions," it is necessary to jettison the "prejudice" of essential meaning and "to *look* at its application" and to recognize, for example, that "speech with and without thought is to be compared to playing a piece of music with and without thought." He insisted that there was something fundamentally amiss with William James's attempt, much like that of Augustine, "to show that thought is possible without speech," which James tried to do by recounting the recollections of a deaf-mute who claimed to recall "wordless" thoughts that he had experienced before he had learned to write. The fact is that "the words with which I express my memory are my memory reaction," and "our criterion for someone's saying something to himself is what he tells us, as well as the rest of his behavior; and we say that someone talks to himself only if, in the ordinary sense of the words, he *can talk*. And we do not say it of a parrot; or a gramophone" (337–46).

We may believe that we know in our own particular way what it is to have a thought, but there is no actual experience of thought. It is a myth to believe that a deaf person knowing "only a sign-language" talks "inwardly in a vocal language"—or that a deaf person, or a child, prior to leaning sign language, can really be said to have thoughts. Wittgenstein said that "the point is not that our sense impressions can lie to us, but that we understand their language. And this language, like any other, rests on convention [*Übereinkunft*]," which is characteristic of the kind of "behaviour of a living being" to which we attribute a "mind." The idea of "the domain of the mind" as something that bestows meaning and sense is only "a dream of our language." We might say that dogs and machines do not think, but despite common assumptions to the contrary, that is not an "empirical statement" open to experimental evidence, because, except metaphorically with respect to things like "dolls" or "ghosts," "we say only of a human being and what is like one that it thinks." This is because humans partake of and deploy conventions and symbols. The issue of what may be *like* a human being is, however, contentious. One criteria of discrimination might be whether we could say of something that it can "talk silently" to itself, but this kind of question might lead us astray by tempting us to try to locate "what goes on" when this happens, because "this is where the illusion lies." We assume, like Grice, that "communicating" is a process whereby the point of it is that "someone else grasps the sense of my words—which is something mental"—and, "as it were, takes it into his own mind." But this leaves us with the assumption that "mental processes just are strange." Wittgenstein asked, "Is calculating in the head less real than calculating on paper?" He suggested that someone might be apt to say that it is and that it consists of "some mental process *corresponding* to" the calculation on paper. His answer was, again, that there is an identity of mental and linguistic content, and, consequently, for example, "a mental image is the image which is described when someone describes what he imagines." Thought and its expression cannot be conceptually disentangled. The answer to what "thinking" is or what "imagination" is does not involve pointing to a mental "process," but rather is a matter of clarifying how these words are "used," that is, "*essence* [*Wesen*] is expressed in grammar," and "grammar tells what kind of object anything is. (Theology as grammar)." We cannot transcend language by seeking meaning in the mind any more than in some deeper logic or reality behind language. "The only correlate in language to an objective necessity is an arbitrary rule." By "arbitrary," Wittgenstein did not mean whimsical, but only that there is nothing accessible beyond the language in which reality claims are couched (347–73).

The answer to puzzles such as what would constitute various people having the same thought or the same images of a color is to refer neither to physiological facts nor to "an inner ostensive explanation." A person "could not apply any rules to a *private* transition from what is seen to words." Such "rules would really hang in the air; for the institution of their application is lacking." The best answer to how a person can have the same thought as another person is to say that "I have learnt English" and thereby learned the use of a word such as "red" or the "*concept* of pain." Sameness is grammatical, that is, conceptual, and the task of inquiry is not to "analyze a phenomenon (for example, thinking)" but to analyze the concept of thinking, that is, the "application of a word." We have an image of a color not because we have been shown such an image or because we have conjured up such a "phenomenon" by thinking, but because we have learned the "concept" and the application of a paradigm (374–84).

Returning to the issue of calculating in one's head, he noted that if we came across some "tribe" in which people only calculated in their head, it might lose its significance as a "limiting case" and require replacing the "paradigm [*Vorbild*]" of making marks on paper. When we ask ourselves questions about what constitutes calculating or seeing the color "red," it is often that "the *deep* aspect readily eludes us" as "the analysis oscillates between natural science and grammar." We do not accomplish such things by consulting a "*mental image*" that is some kind of "superlikeness." Such "image-mongery" only leads to "a lack of clarity about the role of *imaginability*" and about "the extent to which it insures that a sentence makes sense." Making sense is really a matter of "representability in a particular medium of representation." Wittgenstein insisted, as he had in his earlier work, that it is a mistake to assume that there is an "I" that looks within and imagines or sees objects, as if one were in a private "visual room," because such a "room" has no owner, no occupier, and no inside or outside. What one discovers in the visual room is actually only "a new way of speaking" and a "new conception" that one takes as "seeing a new object. You interpret a grammatical movement that you have made as a quasi-physical phenomenon that you are observing," but it is more like inventing "a new way of painting" or "a new kind of song." When someone says that they "have" a "visual image," it is not a reference to some inner world, but rather a manner of speaking that announces an experience; but this disjunction between "expressions of ordinary language (which, after all, do their duty)" and the "picture" they may evoke is "what disputes between idealists, solipsists, and realists look like. The one party attacks the normal form of expression as if they were attacking an assertion; the others defend it, as if they were stating facts recognized by every reasonable human being." It is confusions about such matters that lead to "the feeling of an unbridgeable gulf between consciousness and brain process" that philosophers posit when speaking, for example, about "turning my attention on to my own consciousness" as if "gazing" at an object—such as in the case of William James's account of "introspection" and the "self," which still persists in some philosophical extrapolations from research in neuroscience. Wittgenstein noted that what he was offering were "really remarks on the natural history of human beings; not curiosities, however, but facts that no one has doubted, which have escaped notice because they are always before our eyes" (385–415).

"Consciousness," he claimed, is not, in its typical use, a name for some intangible thing that "automata" lack, but simply a term for indicating a variety of human attributes and capacities. He suggested that when we speak of consciousness, we should not imagine a "picture" that leads us to ask questions, for example, about the constitution of the "mind [*Seele*]." What happens is that "a picture is conjured up which seems to fix the sense unambiguously," but it inhibits grasping the "actual use of these expressions." While it is reasonable to ask what someone is thinking, we go astray in taking literally a question about what is going on in a person's "head" or about "what a strange thing" a "thought" seems to be and how it might be conceived as having "captured reality." Wittgenstein insisted that "the agreement, the harmony, between thought and reality" is grammatical, that is, it is in the application of language. Yet there tends to remain the worry that there is some kind of gap—such as "between an order and its execution" or between a wish, belief, or expectation and its fulfillment—that is "unexpressed" and must be filled by some mental event such as a thought, an intention, or "the process of understanding." It may be that "every sign *by itself* seems dead"; "*What* gives it life?—In use it *lives*" and has "breath." The same basic issue is involved in the case of asking how a sentence can represent, and he noted that "surely you see it when you use one"—"nothing is concealed" or "hidden." Wittgenstein was not legislating the application of mental terms, but simply demonstrating how "it is easy to get into that dead end in philosophizing where one believes that the difficulty of the problem consists in our having to describe phenomena that evade our grasp . . . where we find ordinary language [*gewöhnliche Sprache*] too crude" (416–36).

It is a mistake, for example, to assume that an expectation is something in addition to the language and behavior of expecting, because "it is in language that an expectation and its fulfillment make contact." But he recognized that it is difficult to "shake oneself free of the idea that using a sentence consists in imagining something for every word" and entails an accompanying mental process or image. No more than in the case of an arrow used for the purpose of pointing is meaning some "mental thing," some "hocus pocus that can be performed only by the mind." It is a function of someone's "application" or use of the arrow. To mean [*meinen*] something is to do something—"like going towards someone." He claimed that "what I want to teach is: to pass from unobvious nonsense to obvious nonsense," and much of this nonsense derived from misinterpreting the use of mental concepts. Although "human beings do in fact think," it is not really very helpful to ask "why" they think and to look for "causes"; rather, it is helpful to seek the "reasons" (*Gründe*), such as those, for example, for holding a particular belief. In the end, however, we often operate simply on the basis of "certainty" (*Sicherheit*). Although this is often a matter of past experience, "justification by experience comes to an end. If it did not, it would not be justification" (437–90).

Wittgenstein stressed an analogy between language and tools. Without language humans could not communicate, conceive and execute plans, and influence one another, and "to invent a language could mean to invent a device for a particular purpose." It could also be likened to the "invention of a game" in which interaction is a matter not of "physical causation" but of grammatical conventions. It is important to note once again that for Wittgenstein "grammar" referred both to the grammatical practices of language and to an account of those practices. In that second sense, "grammar does not tell us how language must be constructed in order to fulfill its purpose, in order to have such-and-such an effect on human beings. It only describes, and in no way explains, the use of signs." With respect to the first sense, he insisted that "the rules of grammar may be called 'arbitrary' [*willkürlich*], if that is to mean that the *purpose* of grammar is nothing but that of language," that is, it has no intrinsic purpose or function. Particular instances of language use can

have a purpose and effect, but this is different from their semantic meaning or what one is doing linguistically as opposed to what one is using
language to accomplish. But Wittgenstein stressed that the "boundary"
between what is part of language, that is, meaning, (*Sinn*) and what is
not is variable. He continued to emphasize, however, that the purpose
of language is not to express thoughts and that the sense or what one
means does not come from something such as a picture (*Bild*) "behind
the words" or the "signs [*Zeichen*]," even though the words are open to
"interpretation [*Deutung*]." Similarly, understanding (*Verstehen*) a sentence is not a particular mental state. Mental states and processes are, in
themselves, as dead as signs, but it is also not interpretation that determines meaning. Understanding might involve "various kinds of things,"
but he suggested that it is "akin to understanding a theme in music."
The meaning of such a theme is, however, more than its structural use
in the music. It involves expression and the evocation of a feeling or
experience. Although he denied that mental terms refer to experiences
in the sense of something such as a sensation, he did not deny that there
is a way in which we could speak of an experience of meaning involved
in the use of certain words and phrases. Although he could imagine a
language in which the "soul" of a word played no part, words typically
gain a certain character and identity through usage, and this plays an
important part in understanding (491–527).

He distinguished, however, two uses of "understanding" that "make
up its meaning, make up my *concept* of understanding" or what falls under
this category—one in which a sentence might be replaced by another
and in which the "thought in the sentence" was the "same" (*Gleiche*) and
another in which the sentence was unique and irreplaceable, as in the
case of a musical theme or a poem in which meaning involves feeling
(*empfinden*) in the sense of emotion. When Wittgenstein spoke of the
"thought" in this latter case, it was the thought "*in*" the sentence and not
behind it—it was the use of the words as something grasped in its imme-
diacy like hearing a word or piece of music in a certain manner or seeing
a certain expression on a face and then maybe, because of a change in
"context [*Umgebung*]," experiencing a change of "aspect" that amounts to
a "reinterpretation" (*Umdeutung*). He once again noted that although use
cannot be divorced from the manner or idiom of expression, this should
not be confused with some occult entity standing behind the language.
What he was getting at in these remarks was that "words are also deeds,"

and although we may think that meaning is often a matter of a "feeling" (*Gefühl*) behind words, meaning resides in use, function, expression, and the particular conventions that are invoked and evoked in the application of words. For example, the numeral "1" might be used in saying that something is one meter long, but it might also be used in stating that one person is present, that is, a measure as opposed to a number. As President Clinton insisted, different rules (*Regelen*) govern the use or meaning of "is," such as in the cases of saying that the "rose is red" and "two and two is four." The fact that the notation is the same is "an inessential coincidence," just as some rules in a game may not be essential to the "*point*" of the game. He likened meaning to "a physiognomy," in the sense that words can take on different faces or expressions. He insisted again that "language is an instrument" and its "concepts [*Begriffe*] are instruments," and because the concepts one uses make a difference, "concepts lead us to make investigations" (525–70).

The existence of both mental and physical concepts should not create the idea that "psychology treats of processes in the mental (*psychischen*) sphere, as does physics in the physical. Seeing, hearing, thinking, feeling, willing, are not the subject matter of psychology *in the same sense* as that in which the movements of bodies, the phenomena of electricity, and so forth are the subject matter of physics." The key difference is that the psychologist, like the philosopher or anyone involved in social inquiry, "observes the utterances (the behavior [*Benehmen*]) of the subject," which amount to the subject's thoughts. The grammar of psychological states and the criterion for being in a state such as "expectation" or "being of an opinion, hoping for something, knowing something, being able to do something" are very different from that of physical states and, in some instances (such as in the case of "thinking" and "believing"), from each other. But such "an 'inner process' stands in need of outward criteria" of "significance" (*Bedeutung*), which include both the verbal and nonverbal conventions of human behavior and its "situation" or "surroundings" (*Umbegung*). This is what constitutes a description of a "state of mind" (*Seeleenzustandes*), which one can attribute both to oneself and to others. When one speaks of having an "intention [*Absicht*]" or making a "decision," it is not a locatable phenomenon, but a manifestation of some conventional expression in some particular set of circumstances. He noted that "a main cause of philosophical diseases" is "a one-sided diet: one nourishes one's thinking with only one kind of example" (571–93).

What Wittgenstein was once again calling into question was the persistent notion that in interpreting or understanding speech there is an apprehension of something special, such as "feeling" or an "aura" or "atmosphere," that accompanies speech and that gives it meaning, significance, depth, and so on, as if "thinking were grounded in a thought-schema, as if we were translating from a more primitive mode of thought into our own." In the case of "recognizing" or "remembering" something, we are not comparing it with some "picture" that we carry around with us. It is this kind of view of mental concepts that leads us to puzzle, for example, about what kind of an action is involved in things such as "willing" or "wanting" and how such concepts explain what we "do," but these are not some strange form of causal or even "non-causal bringing about." "When I raise my arm, I have *not* wished it to rise. The voluntary action excludes this wish," and when one raises an arm, the arm rises with nothing intervening. While one may reasonably speak of "predicting" both that a person will follow an order and that a certain chemical reaction will take place, these are two quite different language-games. We might reasonably speak of "the expression of intention" (*Willensaunßerung*) as a cause, but it is not the typical sense of "cause," even though we might predict a person's action from such an expression (594–632).

Wittgenstein stressed that in a case such as a person being interrupted in the course of saying something and then resuming, there is not some residual thought that is being reconstituted; it is simply an instance of remembering, as if consulting "brief notes" but without choosing between "interpretations." There is no inner experience of something such as intending, and, for example, a person is not ashamed of an intention, even if explicitly admitted, as something distinct from what they might do and the circumstances of the action. The typical or "natural expression of an intention" is in actions, not in a performative utterance. Although a person may be said to have memories and feelings of fear, desire, and so on that are not linguistic, linguistic expressions "are not mere threadbare representations of the *real* experiences" and feelings. He suggested that to grasp an intention, one might "look at a cat stalking a bird." His point was not that cats literally have intentions, but that what might be called the intentional stance is our natural way of describing actions. Although "we say a dog is afraid his master will beat him," we do not say that the dog is afraid of being beaten tomorrow—because the dog lacks the concept of tomorrow. Meaning, both intended and understood, is not a matter of "states of mind" and experiences, but one of language and context—"our mistake is to look for an explanation where we ought to regard the facts as 'proto-phenomena' [*Urphänomene*]. That is, where we ought to say: *this is the language-game that is being played*," and where we ought to "regard the language-game as the *primary thing*. And regard the feelings, and so forth, as a way of looking at, interpreting, the language-game." He suggested that "in the use of words, one might distinguish 'surface grammar' from 'depth grammar.'" For example, the way in which the word "mean" (*meinen*) is typically used in a sentence may lead us mistakenly to look for some "process or state" to which it refers and to which one could point, but "a mental attitude doesn't 'accompany' words in the sense that a gesture accompanies them." To say that "'I meant *this* by that word' is a statement which is used differently from one about an affection of the mind." Meaning something is not like aiming at something, "and nothing is more wrong-headed than to call meaning something a mental activity!" (633–93).

Thus the main body of the *Investigations* ended where it began, or we might say that the current of the remarks had run its course. The dominant theme running through the work was the continuous struggle against the myth of the mental as the source of meaning, which could reasonably be construed as framing the most enduring problem in both what is involved in the shared understandings that underlie social interaction and what is involved in interpreting those understandings. And this continued to be the informing concern of much of his subsequent work.

5

CONVENTIONAL OBJECTS, CONCEPTS, & THE PRACTICE OF INTERPRETATION

And this language, like any other, rests on convention. (*PI*, 355)

Concepts lead us to make investigations. (*PI*, 570)

Every interpretation hangs in the air together with what it interprets. (*PI*, 198)

—WITTGENSTEIN

FURTHER REMARKS ON PHILOSOPHICAL PSYCHOLOGY

The intricacies of the use of mental terms that Wittgenstein probed might seem too precious for social scientists to confront, but his remarks relate to conceptual entanglements in which the language of these fields is deeply involved. After the *Investigations*, much of his work continued to be devoted to elaborating his basic claims about meaning, interpretation, and the character of mental concepts. This included an analysis of the concept of emotion and an emphasis on emotions as discursive phenomena peculiar to creatures that can "talk" and have "mastered a language" and participate in the "pattern" of meaning that constitutes "the tapestry" of the human "complicated form of life." He was pointing out that for philosophers, and, we may say, anyone engaged in social inquiry, "emotions" are expressions that are elements of human interaction and not reducible to physiological phenomena. One might speak of experiencing an emotion, but, as in the case of meaning, this is different, for example, than experiencing a sensation such as pain or a "mental image," even though sensations might accompany an emotion. His point was that meaning resides in the conventions informing speech and action, which we attribute to human beings and which humans invoke. We do not begin with the belief that a person may be an "automaton," but with an "attitude towards a soul (mind, *Seele*). I am not of the *opinion* that he has a soul." And "the human body is the best picture of the human soul." There are various ways to look at human "behavior" (*Benehmen*), but there is no sharp break between mind and body, which simply represent different aspects of a human being and the respective grammars and language-games. Wittgenstein claimed that "playing our language-game" of explaining meaning "always rests on a tacit presupposition" about what sort of conventional activity is going on—for example, a play, a psychological experiment, and so on (*PPF*, 1–34).

He also continued to insist that we "cannot explain *intentionality* [*Intention*]" as an "atmosphere" in our "minds" (*Geiste*) surrounding a word—"a 'corona' of faintly indicated uses." Understanding and knowing how to engage in some activity are not explained by referring to some "inner process," any more than meaning is some mystical underlying "experience" (*Erlebnis*) that one has in hearing and uttering words. He again acknowledged, however, that there is a way in which a word may be said to have a different "character" in different "contexts" and yet at the same time to have a single character or "face" (*Gesicht*), because the latter was the consequence of typical use. He also reiterated that equating meaning with use included such things as the form of "expression," as in the case of singing, but that there is no "feeling" or "atmosphere" that goes along with a word and transcends different contexts and forms of expression. Contexts are important for understanding meaning, but "an atmosphere that is inseparable from its object—is no atmosphere." The "picture" that we sometimes have before us of how "the mind can give a word meaning" and the "picture" of humans evolving to a point of the awakening of consciousness "takes us in" and leads us to ask strange questions about what constitutes consciousness, and where it resides, and how it functions. In the case of emotions and feelings, the task is not to conduct an investigation of what they are, as if they referred to some fact in natural science, but rather to illuminate the grammar, and the behavior, related to these concepts. A statement such as "I am afraid" can mean different things in different contexts (*Zusammenhangen*), but if a person wanted to explain or represent it, this might be done by showing how to "*act*" (*spielen*) fearful. "Different concepts touch here and run side by side for a stretch. One does not have to think that all these lines are *circles*" (35–110).

It was at this point that Wittgenstein undertook his extensive, and much discussed, examination of the complicated grammar of seeing (*sehen*), which was a crucial element of his analysis of interpretation and paralleled his discussion of the relationship between understanding and interpretation. This was, however, an elaboration of a brief discussion in the *Tractatus*, and it related to his conception of values. He began by focusing on differences in "uses of the word 'see,'" and particularly the "categorical difference" between seeing an object and seeing a "likeness" or resemblance (*Ähnlichkeit*) between two objects. In the latter case, the object "has not changed; and yet I see it differently. I call this experience 'noticing an aspect.'" While psychologists might be interested in the physiological "*causes*" (*Ursachen*) of such phenomena, his concern was with the concepts involved. He noted how an illustration of a geometrical figure in a book might be seen or understood in different ways, that is, how it could manifest different aspects (e.g, a box or a glass cube) depending on how the text interpreted and described the illustration. Consequently, a person might "*see* the illustration now as one thing, now as another.—So we interpret it, and *see* it as we *interpret* it," that is, interpretations can influence seeing and understanding. He emphasized that an interpretation is not an "indirect description" of some bedrock "visual experience," because there is no such preconceptual experience (111–17).

He famously deployed Jastrow's figure of the "duck-rabbit" to illustrate the difference between what he referred to as a "'continuous seeing' of an aspect and an aspect's 'lighting up.'" An important, but not entirely evident, element of this discussion was that it presumed that a person first saw a picture of an animal's head. This was the basic object and not merely marks on paper or even simply what purported to be a picture that required deciphering. The issue was whether it was to be seen and understood as a duck or as a rabbit. Although one might see only a "picture-rabbit" or only a "picture-duck," one might also see them alternately but not simultaneously. Since such an "expression of change of aspect" has the "form of a report of a new perception" (*Wahrnehmung*), it may seem to be an "expression of a *new* perception and, at the same time, an expression of an unchanged perception." The answer to this puzzle is not to refer to some private "inner picture," because if each aspect were represented by an exact copy, there would be no difference. Therefore, he concluded, "'seeing as . . .' is not part of perception" but rather *conception*. Consequently one might be inclined to say, "it is like seeing, and again not like seeing." He imagined how, on some occasion, a person might be walking through a field and report seeing a rabbit, but in another instance might be surprised by the appearance of the animal and exclaim, "rabbit!" Both instances could be considered as "expressions of perception and visual experience [*Seherlebnisses*]," but even though the exclamation might be viewed as similar to a physical reaction, it involved an "expression of thought" about what is seen and a "description of a perception," which was more an interpretation than a report. "And that's why the lighting up of an aspect seems half visual experience, half thought." The "criterion of a visual experience" is a "representation [*Darstellung*] of what is seen," but this, like "the concept of what is seen," is very "elastic." He concluded that, as in the case of understanding, "the concept of seeing makes a tangled impression," but in describing something such as a landscape, "there is not *one genuine*, proper case of such a description." It is a mistake to seek "fine distinctions" and attempt to come up with a common denominator of "what is really seen," such as sense impressions. It is simply that "the everyday language-game is to be *accepted*" and needs no special justification (118–60).

He went on to explore how a picture of a triangle, for example, could be seen in many ways or viewed in terms of various aspects. But, he asked again, "how is it possible to *see* an object according to an *interpretation*?" His basic answer was that an interpretation is separate from what is seen and can change the aspect in terms of which a triangle is seen—a mountain, a wedge, and so on—and "the aspects in a change of aspects are *those* which, in certain circumstances, the figure could have *permanently* in a picture." All this, as I will point out in chapters 6 and 7, had a great deal to do with the issue of evaluative judgment and matters of persuasion. He noted that in "aesthetics" a person might be told to see or hear things in a certain way, which is really to call attention to an aspect. The word "seeing" might have a number of different applications—such as in the example of a picture of an animal that had been shot with an arrow. One could be said to "see" two protruding parts of an arrow as opposed to "seeing" an arrow piercing the animal. What is involved in such an instance is a conceptual rather than a physiological or perceptual difference. "What forces itself on one is a *concept*" that determines one's "attitude" toward a picture. Wittgenstein maintained that he was not, at this point, attempting to classify and elucidate all the psychological concepts, but only to demonstrate how "conceptual unclarities" about a word such as "see" might arise. He had pointed out earlier that we do not normally see familiar objects *as* these objects; we simply see them. We do not, for example, see a knife *as* a knife or a lion *as* a lion. But one might possibly see an "F" *as* a "gallows," and this would be a case of noticing an aspect and interpreting, just as a child at play might "interpret" a chest as a house. The "lighting up of an aspect" can be expressed in various ways. It is not the same for all objects, but some require more "imagination" (161–219).

One kind of aspect is "organizational," such as in the case of how different parts of a picture might be seen as belonging together, which might, as he had said about understanding, involve "mastery of a technique." He again noted that although there is no experience of meaning in the sense, for example, that the sensation of pain is an experience, one could speak of seeing in a particular manner as an experience of meaning. Two different concepts are involved, or, we might say, the word "experience" has two different, but related, aspects. One can experience the sounds of music but also hear a "plaintive melody" or see or hear "sadness." These are conceptual differences rather than perceptual, like the difference between "aspect- blindness" and poor eyesight. While the latter is a physiological problem, the former is a logical problem and involves questions about the meaning of a concept. He again related an aspect to "physiognomy" as he had in the case of elucidating the meaning of a word. He remarked that "according to the fiction with which I surround" some figure, "I can see it in various aspects. And here there is a close kinship with 'experiencing' the meaning of a word." Aspects can come and go as a consequence of conceptual and contextual shifts. For example, "'thinking' and 'talking in the imagination'—I do not say 'talking to oneself'—are different concepts" (220–46).

He argued that "what I perceive in the lighting up of an aspect is not a property of the object, but an internal relation between it and other objects"; but there is the question of whether "I really see something different each time, or do I only interpret what I see in a different way?" Although both ways of speaking might be intelligible, he was "inclined to say the former," because while "to interpret is to think, to do something, seeing is a state." He claimed that "it is easy to recognize those cases in which we are *interpreting*. When we interpret, we form hypotheses, which may prove false." His point in all of this was to stress that "we find certain things about seeing puzzling, because we do not find the whole business of seeing puzzling enough." He emphasized again that "the concept of an aspect is related to the concept of imagination" and can involve a matter of "will," which, again, makes it similar to interpretation. There may, however, in varying degrees, be cases of "aspect-blindness," which are "*akin* to the lack of a 'musical ear'" or the inability to grasp the meaning of a certain word. He concluded this discussion by emphasizing once more that "*the importance of this concept lies in the connection between the concepts of seeing an aspect and of experiencing the meaning of a word*" (247–61, emphasis added), and that what was also important was the parallel, on the one hand, between seeing and seeing as and, on the other hand, between understanding and interpretation.

Returning to the general issue of linguistic meaning, Wittgenstein noted once again that meaning is in part a matter of expression and that there may be applications of a word that are not characteristic of typical usage. He stressed, however, that "the figurative use of the word can't come into conflict with the original one," because the former depends on the latter. It is possible to "speak of a 'primary' and 'secondary' meaning of a word," but "only someone for whom the word has the former meaning uses it in the latter." He distinguished, for example, between a language-game involving *the* meaning (*Bedeutung*) *of* a word and one involving meaning *the* word. Although a single word "can seem to carry a particular meaning within itself," apart from its application, he again pointed out that this is somewhat illusory and the result of past associations and that it does not conflict with the basic idea of meaning as use. Similarly, only someone who has learned to calculate either on paper or out loud can, by the use of this concept, make intelligible what is involved in calculating in the head. However, such a "secondary meaning is not a 'metaphorical' meaning" but a derivative meaning (262–78).

He also continued to emphasize that whatever images may accompany or illustrate our speech and action, they "are not the meaning or intending," and "the intention *with which* one acts does not 'accompany' the action any more than thought 'accompanies' speech." "'Talking,' (whether out loud or silently) and 'thinking' are not concepts of a similar kind," but they are connected in that both require reference to language. Words "must surely belong to a language and to a context, in order really to be the expression of the thought," and "if God had looked into our minds, he would not have been able to see there whom we were speaking of." And we might add that neither could a cognitive scientist. To explain what one means by saying what one thought "does not refer to an occurrence at the moment of speaking," and it is different from the language-game of saying that one thought, or was reminded, of something in the course of speaking. "Meaning something is not a process which accompanies a word. For no *process* could have the consequences of meaning something" (279–92).

He noted, still once again, how we can speak of "the familiar face of a word, the feeling that it has assimilated its meaning into itself, that it is a likeness of its meaning," but this is a consequence of the way in which some words are conventionally employed. In certain circumstances, we may ask ourselves how we can "find the 'right' word," but it is not usually the case that we know what we want to say and are looking for the right word—as if translating from one language to another or attempting to put a prosaic statement in poetical form. In most instances, we simply have not actually decided exactly what we want to say. We may, however, conjure up or possess images that we wish to describe and convey and for which we choose various vehicles of expression. What is often involved when we say that we have a thought but are puzzled about how to express it is that we really want a substitute for the expression that has first occurred to us. When we claim that a word or a name is on the tip of our tongue, we are usually simply saying that "the word which belongs here has escaped me." Wittgenstein noted that although William James claimed that in such circumstances something is there yet not quite there, "this is not an experience at all," any more than it is "an intention, interpreted as an accompaniment of action." This is just a manner of speaking in "*certain situations*" and "surrounded by a behavior of a special kind" (293–300).

He suggested that what is often referred to as "silent, 'inner' speech [*Reden*] is not a half hidden phenomenon, seen, as it were, through a veil. It is not hidden *at all*," but the concept gets mistakenly viewed as an inner parallel to "an 'outer' process." "The close relationship between 'inner speech' and 'speech'" reflects the fact that what is said inwardly can be communicated audibly and can "*accompany* outer action," such as in the case of singing inwardly, reading silently, or calculating in the head while gesturing outwardly. So, again, he insisted, "let the use of words teach you their meaning." It is misleading to claim that what people say to themselves is hidden, because the person speaking does not "know" the location. It is simply that third-person doubt does not exist for the person speaking. To say that "I know" what I want, believe, wish, feel, and so on "is either philosophers' nonsense or, at any rate, *not* a judgment a priori." These are just ways of talking. "I can know what someone else is thinking, not what I am thinking," and here "a whole cloud of philosophy condenses into a drop of grammar," a drop that he would further attempt to examine in *On Certainty*. He claimed that "if I were to talk to myself out loud in a language not understood by those present, my thoughts would be hidden from them," but thoughts, as such, are not hidden in the manner of "an unperceived physical process." "If we see someone writhing in pain with evident cause, I do not think: all the same, his feelings are hidden from me." The traditional image of the inner and outer collapses (301–24).

Under various circumstances, however, a person may not be "transparent" to us anymore than "when one comes into a strange country with entirely strange traditions" and, even after having "mastered the country's language," does "not *understand* the people. (And not because of not knowing what they are saying to themselves.) We can't find our feet with them." This is often the case with the social scientist, but the notion of not knowing what is going on inside someone is "a *picture*" that expresses a conviction but does not explain the conviction. The reason that "if a lion could talk, we wouldn't be able to understand it" is because it participates in a different form of life. One can guess another's intentions, thoughts, and future actions, all in the same sense, but to say that "'only he can know what he intends' is nonsense and what he will do, wrong." But while in a particular instance someone may not be able to predict my actions, I can "foresee them in my intention," and this is different from someone else predicting my actions. "The kind of certainty is the kind of language-game," but "we don't notice the enormous variety of all the everyday language-games, because the clothing of our language makes them all alike. What is new (spontaneous, 'specific') is always a language-game" (325–36).

He stressed that discovering motives and discovering (what we typically think of as) causes are two different things. It was in this context that he pointed out that while the term "methodology" may apply both to a physical investigation and to a conceptual one, it is necessary to distinguish between them. To talk about subjective certainty about someone's state of mind as opposed to objective certainty is to mix up language-games, just as in the case of using mathematical certainty as a paradigm. "What has to be accepted, the given [*Gegebene*], is—one might say—*forms of life.*" Agreements about matters such as color and mathematics are conventional judgments, and one learns correct judgments in many matters, including something such as genuineness of feeling, but not by a technique or system of rules. "A child has much to learn before it can pretend. (A dog can't be a hypocrite, but neither can it be sincere)" (337–64).

Wittgenstein reached the core of the difference between the natural and human or social sciences when he asked, "if concept formation can be explained by the facts of nature, shouldn't we be interested, not in grammar, but rather what is its basis in nature?" He maintained that "we are, indeed, also interested in the correspondence between concepts and very general facts of nature. (Such facts as mostly do not strike us because of their generality.) But our interest is not thereby thrown back on to those possible causes of concept formation; we are not doing natural science; nor yet natural history—since we can also invent fictitious natural history for our purposes." He stressed that he was "not saying: if such-and-such facts of nature were different, people would have different concepts (in the sense of a hypothesis). Rather: if anyone believes that certain concepts are absolutely the correct ones, and that having different ones would mean not realizing something that we realize—then let him imagine certain very general facts of nature to be different from what we are used to, and the formation of concepts different from the usual ones will become intelligible to him." He suggested that we "compare a concept with a style of painting," which may in some sense be arbitrary but not without criteria (365–67).

As in the case of meaning and other mental concepts, remembering is not an experience and has no "experiential content," but certain experiences and feelings might go along with remembering. The "*idea of memory content*" comes from confusing language-games, but this points to the manner in which "the confusion and barrenness of psychology is not to be explained by its being a 'young science'; its state is not comparable with that of physics, for instance, in its beginnings. . . . For in psychology, there are experimental methods *and conceptual confusion*. . . . The existence of the experimental method makes us think that we have the means of getting rid of the problems which trouble us; but the problem and method pass one another by." He noted that "an investigation entirely analogous to our investigations of psychology is possible also for mathematics. It is just as little a *mathematical* investigation as ours is a psychological one. It will *not* contain calculations, and so it is not, for example, formal logic. It might deserve the name of an investigation of the 'foundation of mathematics,'" which would be a conceptual investigation (368–72).

THE LANGUAGE OF EMOTION

Among mental concepts, maybe the most difficult to conceive in Wittgensteinian terms is emotion, because, for many philosophers and social theorists, from James to the present, the term "emotion" seems to demand a physical state as its reference and a naturalistic form of inquiry that would explain what emotions really are. It might seem that surely emotion is something physical that may be expressed in language but belongs to a different ontological realm. Wittgenstein, however, consistently stressed the discursive and conventional character of emotions, and when, in some of his last work, he undertook a yet more detailed account of psychological concepts, the concept of emotion remained prominent. He noted that "in science it is usual to make phenomena that allow of exact measurement into defining criteria for an expression; and then one is inclined to think that the proper meaning has been *found*" (Z, 438). This often results, however, in quite arbitrarily assuming that some physical correlate of an expression of emotion is the meaning of "emotion." But not only the general concept of emotion itself but types of emotion such as fear, anger, and so on are very generic family-resemblance concepts, and it is important to resist reifying the terms and applying the paradigm of a physical state and assuming that we can explain emotions by specifying some physical event, either internal or external, as a cause of an emotion or as the emotion itself. To ask about the nature of emotion is first of all a conceptual query and not an empirical question, and the latter presupposes an answer to the former. Wittgenstein was quite unequivocal about what can be the bearer of an emotion. He again asked if one could imagine an animal angry, frightened, unhappy, or happy, and he found no real difficulty with these attributions, because they were descriptions framed in terms of the paradigm of behavior, which we typically describe in terms of conventions that belong to human activity. It is difficult to conceive of emotions as really applying to animals, because these are elements of the form of life that we associate with linguistic and symbolic capacities. His basic point was that professing or otherwise expressing something such as hope required possessing the concept of hope.

In the *Investigations*, Wittgenstein tended to use the term "feeling" (*Gefühl*) generically to include most of what we would typically refer to as emotions. Only twice did he use the more singular term *Gemütsbewegung*, which may be the best equivalent for the English word "emotion." His change in strategy is significant in several respects. It reflected his increasing concern with differentiating more clearly between the grammars of mental terms such as "sensations," "feelings," and "emotions," but he continued to emphasize that it is a mistake to seek a physiological answer to the meaning of psychological terms. Much of this later work was devoted to demonstrating further that the difference between the "inner," or mental, realm and the "outer," or physical, realm is a matter of grammar and logic rather than a fundamental dualism regarding what is invisible and visible or nonphysical and physical. He maintained that "the difficulty is to know one's way about among the concepts of 'psychological phenomena'" and to realize that "thinking in terms of physiological processes is extremely dangerous in connexion with the clarification of conceptual problems in psychology." He suggested that maybe "the best prophylactic against this is the thought that I don't know at all whether the humans I am acquainted with actually have a nervous system" (*PP*, 1:1054, 1063). The problem was that there had developed a picture of something going on inside a person that was accessible only to that person and that "psychology was now the theory of this inner thing." What are involved, however, are in fact two language-games that bear a complicated relationship to each other rather than the problem of finding the physiological referents of psychological phenomena. To question the existence of such referents was, again, not to fall back on the assumption of "a mind *alongside* the body, a ghostly mental nature," and he also once again suggested that the whole "human being is the best picture of the human mind" (281, 289, 692)

In the case of emotion, the problems revolved around such things as mistakenly assuming, like James, that because people might say they "feel depressed," depression is a "bodily feeling" known by introspection (135, 321). He noted that if we saw an ape tearing things up we might wonder what was going on "inside" him, but this manner of speaking would not be much different than wondering about how much grief was in our heart (325, 347, 439). Grief, joy, and hope are no more events we inwardly observe than belief is; rather, they are matters of what we say and how we behave and in what circumstances (446, 450, 460). We might choose not to speak and act in a particular manner that expresses emotion, but that presupposes that we could in fact speak and act in that manner. He posed the question of why we treat fear or hope as an emotion but do not do so in the case of belief, and his basic answer was that the former is, somewhat like pain, in its first-person use, a concept for the expression of an experience (*Erlebnisbegriffe*), while beliefs, as well as intentions, have no particular characteristic form of expression. Although emotions might reasonably be broadly spoken of as experiences, they are not something that physically "happens" to one or what in that sense one "undergoes" (596, 836).

He said that he "would like to speak of a genealogical tree of psychological concepts" (*PP*, 1:722), and he undertook a quite extended "classification" (2, 63, 148) in which he distinguished emotions, that is, *Gemütsbewegungen*, from dispositions, moods, and sensations (*Empfindungen*) such as pain. His purpose was not to achieve "completeness" or to find some common essence, but rather to demonstrate how a limited examination "casts light on the correct treatment of *all*" (311). What he was doing was not categorizing and describing objects but clarifying the grammar or application of words. He claimed that what are common among emotions (such as joy, fear, and depression) are "duration" and often a tendency to follow a "course" involving appearing, abating, and so on. Unlike sensations, emotions "do not give us any information about the external world," and despite metaphorical phrases such as "sick at heart" and "the darkness of depression," they are neither "localized" nor "diffuse." Like sensations, however, emotions are often accompanied by characteristic behavioral and facial expression, and although they may also be accompanied by certain sensations, he stressed again that "sensations are not emotions. (In the sense in which the numeral 2 is not the number 2)." Among emotions, it is important to distinguish those that are typically "directed," such as fear, from those, such as anxiety, that tend to be "undirected." For Wittgenstein, these respective language-games were not insulated from each other, but he characterized love and hate as "emotional dispositions" and "attitudes," which could be distinguished by features such as the capability of being "put to the test," and which could also in some cases, such as fear, be referred to as "chronic" as opposed to "acute." But, he again pointed out, "fear is not a sensation" even though sensations may accompany it (148).

He claimed that it was cogent to speak about how emotions such as sadness, hope, or fear might *"colour* thoughts," or even constitute thoughts, such as those that we might categorize as "misgivings," but this is not the case with sensations. It would not make much sense to speak of something such as "toothachey thoughts" (*PP*, 2:153). He claimed that most emotions represent "mental states" (*Seelenzuständen*), which a subject can report much as they report pain, but unlike James, who viewed emotion as comprising sensations, Wittgenstein argued that although a sensation such as pain resembles an emotion in that it is expressed in facial expressions, gestures, noises, and the like, "it did not follow from this that our bodily feeling" is the emotion (177, 321, 499). In most cases, "we *see* emotions," and it is "essential to what we call emotion" that we do not simply observe physical changes such as "facial contortions" from which we *"make the inference* of grief, joy, etc.," but immediately perceive a face as expressing an emotion. If people were brought up not to register emotion by either expression or report, we would have to say, "I have no idea of what is going on inside them," but that would only really be a statement of an "external fact" and not a failure to penetrate some hidden space (568, 570). "We do not see facial contortions and make inferences from them (like a doctor framing a diagnosis) to joy, grief, boredom. We describe a face immediately as sad, radiant, bored, even when we are unable to give any other description of the features.—Grief, one would like to say, is personified in the face" (*Z*, 225).

The discussion of emotion was a central element of his attempt to cast light on the issue of what creatures are the appropriate bearers of typical mental concepts. The question of whether animals other than humans can think was actually not for Wittgenstein a complicated matter once we understand that "thinking" is, in his words, a very "erratic" term. He claimed, however, that "there is nothing that astonishing about a certain concept only being applicable to a being that, e.g., possesses a language." Thinking is, in terms of theoretical content, no different than doing, but what makes humans different is that they are doing things symbolically, however "primitive" a particular human language and mode of thinking may be. As already noted, we do not find it difficult or odd to refer to animals as thinking, knowing, and so on, because these are the terms we typically use to describe behavior, but conventional behavior is a special class. We often use these "everyday" concepts for such scientific purposes as describing the cognitive processes of various creatures, but the paradigm case of the concept of "'thinking' refers to human life, not to that of grasshoppers," simply because grasshoppers cannot read or write. He noted that monkeys learning through trial and error how to use a stick to reach a piece of food can be said to be thinking, but that does not entail that much of what we typically mean by "thinking" can apply to monkeys. It is a mistake to assume that when used in some operationally defined sense, the real meaning of psychological or mental concepts has been discovered. The natural scientist deals with physical phenomena, while the social investigator deals with conceptual phenomena (*PP*, 2:23, 62, 130, 194, 205, 224, 310).

He again confronted the common assumption that a person's thoughts are hidden from an observer. He said that "the picture 'He knows—I don't know'" is like that of looking for an object that we believe could never really be found, like a needle in a haystack, and that looking for where the experience of grief is felt, in the mind or some place in the body, is equally futile. Such pictures are "the worst enemy of our understanding" and distract us from paying attention to what someone says and does and to the context of speech and action. People can describe their thoughts and express them or not express them or pretend to be thinking something that they are not, but it is not the case that only the person knows what the person is thinking in the sense that the person has access to some private mental event. It is simply the logical difference between a first-person report and a third-person claim. We are not faced with finding something that is psychologically or physiologically impossible to discover, but simply with two different language-games. "The comparison of thinking to a process that goes on in secret is a misleading one" (*PP*, 1:139, 439, 449, 498, 580–81). Although "'thinking' is not behavior," it would not "be completely wrong to call speaking 'the instrument of thinking,' but it would be wrong to conceive of speaking as an 'instrument' or carrier of thought." The real point is that "what happens inside is no more important than what can happen outside, through speaking, drawing etc. (From which you can learn how the word 'thinking' is used)," and when we do speak of a "thought-process" it is something like operating (in writing or orally) with signs. Even things such as "hope, belief, etc." are "embedded in human life," which is a life of convention (*PP*, 2:6–8, 12, 16).

For Wittgenstein, the notion of "non-verbal thinking" was mistakenly based on the model of being able to do one thing without simultaneously doing something else, such as to "read without moving one's lips." The fact that someone can calculate without speaking or writing is not evidence for a capacity to calculate without signs, and James's claims about the deaf-mute "cannot convince one that it is possible to think without a language. Indeed, where no language is used, why should one speak of 'thinking'?" (*PP*, 1:213–14). This whole issue arises from the assumption that there is some inaccessible place in which thinking takes place. Thoughts, however, are not hidden, as if they were written down in a secreted diary and not revealed. Really "nothing is hidden," except possibly some physical process, and to claim that they are in principle hidden because they take place in the mind is only a "pleonasm." When we think silently our thoughts are only hidden in the sense that someone might not be able to guess what the thoughts are—not because they cannot be perceived because they exist in the "soul." The body does not function as a "façade" hiding the workings of the mind. He claimed that "instinct comes first, reasoning second. Not until there is a language-game are there reasons," but the conventional world is autonomous (*PP*, 2:689). The mistake about the soul and body is basically the same as that of assuming that the meaning of a word is something invisible that is parallel to the object or process to which the word refers (*LPP*, 1:127–28). A thought is hidden only in the sense that another person is doing the thinking. What is involved is, again, simply the logical "asymmetry" of "inner" and "outer" concepts and not something metaphysical. We might not understand what someone says or does, and in this sense we might speak of it as hidden, but although thinking and doing may be considered as different kinds of facts, that is, inner and outer, they are not different in the sense that "species" are different. They are more like aspects of the same thing (*LPP*, 2:28, 32, 36, 62–63). There are many things that we can think but probably cannot do, but probably we can think most things that we are capable of doing.

Much of his discussion of inner and outer continued to focus on demonstrating that emotions are not subliminal phenomena of which we see the traces in what people say and do, but rather are an essential part of their conventional repertoire, which like other aspects of human behavior that we sometimes locate as belonging to an "inner" dimension gain "meaning only in the stream of life," the "bustle" of conventional human activity. He noted that in many instances what is involved in saying that the "'inner is hidden' would be as if one said: 'All that you *see* in a multiplication is the outer movement of the figures; the multiplication is hidden from us,'" and as in the case of people speaking to themselves, the "words only have meaning as elements of a language-game." In most cases, "there is an *unmistakable* expression of joy and its opposite," and when an emotion is hidden, "it is not hidden because it is inner" but because it is not expressed. Emotions are part of "the whole swirl [*Gewimmal*] of human actions" along with concepts, judgments, and the like. We are sometimes uncertain about these things, but "we don't need the concept 'mental' (etc.) to justify some of our conclusions that are undetermined, etc. Rather this indeterminacy, etc., explains the use of the word 'mental'" as well as how uncertainty about the "outer" corresponds to uncertainty about the "inner." It is simply the comparison of the language-games dealing respectively with mental and behavioral concepts that lead to the false picture of something more than a logical account of an inner and outer dualism. He once again insisted that "I presuppose the *inner* in so far as I presuppose a *human being*," and that, for example, is the creature that smiles, not a body or an inner face. In the end, he concluded that what we often refer to as "the 'inner' is a delusion. That is, the whole complex of ideas alluded to by the word is like a painted curtain drawn in front of the scene of the actual word use" (*PP*, 1:625, 687; *LPP*, 1:28, 30, 32, 33, 35, 36, 62, 63, 66, 69, 78, 79, 84).

If emotions are conceived in the manner suggested by Wittgenstein, it is necessary to confront the issue of how we access these phenomena. If they are not like the objects of natural science, but rather conventional or discursive phenomena, they are objects of interpretation. The recognition of the importance of emotion and the rise of cognitive science have once more pulled social theory back in the direction of amalgamating the social and natural sciences, but Wittgenstein's work provides the basis of a more unified and autonomous vision of social inquiry as an interpretive endeavor. And if philosophical investigations are, as he claimed, conceptual investigations, it is necessary first of all to confront the concept of a concept.

WORDS AND CONCEPTS

Although Wittgenstein insisted that "grammar" referred to both an object of analysis and a form of analysis, it is important to emphasize once more that this did not imply that language is unrelated to the world. Much of the meaning of language is in its application to the world, and "the connection between 'language and reality' is made by definitions of words, and these belong to grammar, so that language remains self-contained and autonomous." Grammar could be considered "arbitrary" in that it is "not accountable to any reality. It is grammatical rules that determine meaning (constitute it)." He suggested that the rules of cookery are not arbitrary, because cooking, unlike language, has a particular goal or end, but in the case of grammar if you do not follow a particular rule, you are simply playing a different game and subscribing to different conventions (*PG*, 35, 55, 88, 112, 133; *Z*, 320). He spoke of philosophy as grammatical investigation, but also, especially, as conceptual investigation, because concepts are what principally tie together thought, language, and the world. There is, however, no more nebulous term in the human sciences, including philosophy, than "concept," which is often conflated with "word." Words are signs, but specifying the nature of a concept seems much more elusive.

When social scientists speak of concepts such as power, representation, and so on, they often imply that these are objects, with various facets, on which a person could have different perspectives and impose different interpretations. What is really going on in such discussions is sometimes difficult to determine, but what is often involved are different concepts to which a word such as "power" is applied, often with some degree of ambiguity about what kind of concepts are in question, whether these are concepts specifying some theoretically distinct thing or analytical or family-resemblance concepts for generalizing about various attributes or particulars. Wittgenstein stressed that while metaphysics blurs the distinction between factual and conceptual investigations, philosophical investigations, properly conceived, are conceptual investigations. But he also stressed not only that many concepts are "vague," but that "'concept' is a vague concept" and that "the word 'concept' is by far too vague" (*RFM*, 412). He did not offer an explicit answer to the problem or explain exactly what he meant when he said in the *Investigations* that certain concepts could have "blurred edges" and might be "akin" to one another. But when he said that if people did not understand a concept he could teach them to use the words, he was indicating that words and concepts are not the same thing, even though they are related. He said that *"when language-games change, then there is a change in concepts, and with the concepts the meaning of words change"* (*OC*, 65, emphasis added). Philosophers and social scientists sometimes speak of concepts as elastic, developing, or even "essentially contestable" (Gallie 1955–56), but in many such instances we are actually talking about the same word applied to different concepts. There certainly can be change *within* a concept without a change of basic identity, but, as Wittgenstein said, "you can vary the concept, but then you might change it beyond recognition," which is when it becomes another concept with the same name (*PP*, 2:691).

What Wittgenstein spoke of in *The Blue and Brown Books* as a "substantive," or thing to which a word is taken as referring, he spoke of in the *Philosophical Grammar* as a "concept-word." This again indicated that not all words refer to concepts and that there is not necessarily a special word for each concept. There is a difference between words and concepts, because "it is not in every language-game that there occurs something that one would call a concept. A concept is something like a picture with which one compares objects." In his "builders" game, the key words did not refer to concepts, but he noted that "it would be easy to add to it in such a way that 'slab,' 'block' etc. became concepts. For example, by means of a technique of describing or portraying those objects. There is of course no sharp dividing line between language-games which work with concepts and those that do not. What is important is that the word 'concept' refers to one kind of expedient in the mechanism of language-games" (*RFM*, 435). Words are often ambiguous or indefinite, because a particular "pattern of life" may not be rigid and because it may not be clear whether or not the words refer to concepts and to what concepts they may refer (*PP*, 2:211). So the question is that of what concepts are and what concept-words do.

Concepts are not expressions of ideas or representations in the mind, and they are not the linguistic reflections of natural kinds. They are grammatical, but, again, this is not to say that they are unrelated to the "world," and consequently "an education quite different from ours might also be the foundation for quite different concepts" (*PP*, 2:707; *Z*, 387). Philosophical inquiry, however, deals with meaning and not directly with the world. This is the difference, for example, as we will see in the next chapter, between science and the philosophy of science. Even though the question of the correspondence between concepts and the facts of nature is relevant, philosophical inquiry is directed toward concepts, because "the limit of the empirical is—*concept-formation*" (*RFM*, 12, 387), where the essence, or what kind of thing an object is, is expressed. The best short answer to the question of what constitutes concepts is to say, as Kuhn would stress, that they stand for the *kinds of things* that populate the world and that are usually designated and discriminated by various forms of linguistic usage. It is instructive that the word "concept" (*conceptus*) means, literally, the thing conceived. But if what characterizes concept-words is that they refer to things and to kinds of things, there are, so to speak, different kinds of kinds. As we shall see in chapter 7, normative concepts are a special class, and, as already stressed, a distinction that often appeared in Wittgenstein's work was the difference between what we might call theoretical concepts, which are more typical of natural science, and family-resemblance, analytical, and categorical concepts, which are particularly important when speaking of meaning, language, and other instances of conventional phenomena. It would be possible to construct a whole taxonomy of concepts, but one of the main problems in social inquiry is distinguishing between concepts that correspond to things and those that designate a class of things. This is the case with a word such as "meaning," which is a family-resemblance concept, but which is often mistaken for the name of a theoretically independent object that occupies a special location. And it is important not to use one kind of concept as a paradigm for assessing the other. Wittgenstein noted, for example, that "'heap of sand' is a concept without sharp boundaries—but why isn't one with sharp boundaries used instead of it?—Is the reason to be found in the nature of the heaps? What is the phenomenon whose nature is definitive for our concept?" (*Z*, 392). Heap may be a useful concept, but it is a concept of a very different kind than, for example, the concept of an atom. Wittgenstein referred to how "Socrates pulls up the pupil who when asked what knowledge is enumerates cases of knowledge. And Socrates doesn't regard that as even a preliminary step to answering the question. But our answer consists in giving such an enumeration and a few analogies" (*PG*, 76), such as in the case of talking about thinking, understanding, meaning, and similar mental concepts. So concepts are one of the types of instruments in the tool-kit of language, but we have still not reached the theoretical core of language and human practices. That core is *convention*, and the question is, what are conventions and what are we doing when we explain conventions?

CONVENTIONS

When we say that a green light means "go," we are not referring to the mind of the city planner or to the interpretation of a driver, but to the convention that is instantiated in the use of the light and to which a driver may or may not conform. This may be obvious, but a mistake that arises from our manner of speaking, and then is often given an imprimatur by philosophy, is to perpetuate the notion that there is something outside the use of the signs that animates the signs and resides either in the world or in the mind. What is at stake is identifying the conventions in terms of which the signs are used. We tend to ask what the driver intended or meant to do, as if there were some place in which the explanation could be found that was different than what was done or said and the context in which it took place. We might reasonably ask instead about when a convention originated, how it evolved, where it is situated in the weave of life, and to what extent a person was instantiating it or conforming to it. But the explanation is not a matter of knowing a person's mind in the sense that one might know the source of steam coming from the spout of a teakettle. In social theory, there are continuing problems related to choosing between ideational and behavioral explanations of social phenomena, between agency and structure, between mind and interpretation as the source of meaning, and between an individualist and a collectivist ontology. One way to deal with such issues has been to suggest that we should somehow combine such social ontologies and, for example, look at the interaction between agency and structure. Another strategy has been to claim that social phenomena consist of practices, institutions, rules, and so on; but although this may appear to resolve some of these dilemmas, and even find support in Wittgenstein's work, practices are not theoretical objects but a category of such objects. There cannot be a theory of practices if we take theories to signify claims about what exists and the manner of its existence. "Practice," for example, is distinctly a family-resemblance term and not a theoretical term. Wittgenstein often spoke of practices, but he did not view them, any more than language-games, as ontologically primitive. "Practice" refers to a concept that serves to designate a range of social phenomena. It does not answer the question of the nature of social phenomena.

Wittgenstein maintained that what is "given" are the "forms of life," and although this is a somewhat open concept, he continually stressed that forms of life and language-games consist of concepts, rules, customs, norms, and so on, which, as he said, in the end, comes down to conventions. These are manifest in the language and action of individuals, groups, practices, and so on. What I will call *conventional realism* is the key to a theoretical account of social phenomena. Thought, speech, and action are different aspects or modes of conventionality, but they are theoretically identical. It is neither that thought, as such, is the explanation of speech and institutions, nor vice versa. These have the same content and can be treated in a similar manner, such as Austin did in analyzing speech-acts, which, as Wittgenstein also stressed, are examples of doing things with words in accordance with a range of syntactical, grammatical, and performative conventions. And thinking, as well, is doing conventional things with signs, only maybe without, for example, expression on paper or in behavior. Sometimes thinking involves actually picturing signs, as when playing music according to a score when the physical score is not present or as in the case of literally talking to oneself. But it may involve simply performing conventional games such as calculating or puzzle-solving. There is no special medium of thought.

Wittgenstein's theory of conventions can be modeled in various ways (see, e.g, Gunnell 1998), but what is more important is to make the theory clear. Although he denied that machines and animals can think, because they cannot talk, the question of what can be the bearer of convention is an interesting issue, and whether, for example, IBM's Watson qualifies is debatable. But what is certain is that conventions informing symbolization characterize and explain the human form of life. What Wittgenstein maintained from the beginning was the necessity to forget the notion of agency and a "subject that thinks and entertains ideas" (*TL*,

5.631) or to forget choosing between agency and structure as independent variables, since in both cases we are really talking about conventions and the different mediums in which they are manifest. And, as Wittgenstein argued, conventions are acquired by training, which in turn provides the platform for infinite forms of innovation. Once we have gotten down to conventionality as the theoretical bedrock of social reality, distinguished between words and concepts, explored the concept of meaning, and differentiated between understanding and interpretation, it is important to clarify yet more fully the concept of interpretation and to take up the issue of interpretation as a practice of inquiry and as the defining task of the human sciences.

THE PRACTICE OF INTERPRETATION

As I have already emphasized, Wittgenstein consistently stressed the difference between interpretation and understanding. An interpretation is something given in signs, an argument, and an account of a conventional object. It is an explanation of meaning and not the source. A symbol can be endlessly interpreted, but in many cases "I do no interpreting. I do not interpret, because I feel at home in the present picture. When I interpret, I step from one level of thought to another" (Z, 229, 234, 287). In many places, including *The Big Typescript*, where much of his final work was adumbrated, he continued to point out that "an interpretation is a supplementation of the interpreted sign with another sign." Although we may have occasion to interpret something, such as an order, we do not normally interpret it—we hear or grasp it or understand it (BT, 16). Understanding involves the capacity to act in a language and have mastery of a technique. It is not an act that one performs or some process that takes place between an order and its execution. Understanding a sentence, he suggested, is not unlike understanding a picture or a musical theme, and normally understanding does not require choosing between interpretations. In typical cases of communication, it is usually sufficient to give the signs, but if there is misunderstanding, it may be necessary to invoke an interpretation. The issue is not what word should be used; it is distinguishing between two different concepts. He stressed that to interpret is to do something, while seeing and understanding are states. He noted that when we interpret, we advance hypotheses, and interpretations are claims and arguments that are defeasible. The language-game that is the object of inquiry is one thing, and an interpretation is another thing. The latter is the product of a perspective on the language-game. He conceived of philosophy as a distinctly interpretive practice, but one that sometimes went awry. When a person hears an explanation of something, the person may not understand it, and this might trigger an interpretation or a variety of interpretations.

In some of his last work, Wittgenstein continued to pursue a clarification of the concept of interpretation. Returning to his example of the ambiguous duck-rabbit figure, he asked, do I "see" something different or "only interpret what I see in a different way"? He was again "inclined" to conclude that in most cases it was an instance of the former, because "interpreting is an action," which would include, for example, descriptions of one's visual experience. "When we interpret, we make a conjecture," which might be right or wrong, while we would not typically speak of seeing as true or false. An interpretation, on the other hand, "becomes an expression of the experience" of seeing. He even allowed for "involuntary interpretation," which "forces itself on us" in certain circumstances, and this seemed very close to the case of "seeing as" or the dawning of "an aspect" where, optically, what is seen remains the same but where there is a change in "conception" whereby one might "clothe" what one sees in an "interpretation." One can see, hear, and understand a meaning yet "not interpret it *at* all," but in answering a question about it, one "might interpret," which would involve "a thought" and an act of "will." A change of aspect, that is, "seeing as," such as in the case of shifting from specifying a figure as duck or as rabbit, is very akin to an interpretation, because even though an aspect may "dawn" on one, changing an aspect often involves "more thinking than seeing." It is "to do something" and thus involves interpretation (*PP*, 2:1, 8, 9, 20, 22, 31, 33, 378, 482).

At one point, Wittgenstein offered the example of "someone watching the sun and suddenly having the *feeling* that it is not the sun that moves—but we that move past it. Now he wants to say he has seen a new state of motion that we are in; imagine him showing by gestures which movement he means, and that it is not the sun's movement.— We should here be dealing with two different applications of the word 'movement.'" He initially suggested that "we see, not change of aspect, but change of interpretation" (Z, 215–16), but he would eventually conclude that change of aspect and interpretation are basically similar. He suggested that images and imaginations are like interpretations, because they involve a "creative act, that is, as opposed to visual impressions, we make them up" (*PP*, 2:111). He continued with the same point in his last remarks on psychology, where he stressed again that "interpreting is a kind of thinking; and often it brings about a sudden change of aspect," and often "astonishment," whereby there is change of "perception" that is the result of a "conceptual" change and "thinking" (*LPP*, 1:179, 518, 565).

The human sciences are necessarily interpretive practices, but there is still the question of what this entails with respect to how to go about it. There is no single necessary approach to interpretation, but the core of any answer must address the issue of how the language of the interpreter can provide an account of the conventions that are interpreted. Much of the answer to this is suggested in Wittgenstein's discussion of philosophy and its method. His particular account of method need not be taken as definitive, but it points up some important aspects of what is relevant for the social and human sciences. Clearly, in Wittgenstein's view, a person could understand without interpreting and could interpret without understanding, but at the same time, one might reasonably suppose that the best, or most just, interpretation, as he indicated in his comments on *The Golden Bough* and as Kuhn would maintain, is one based on first gaining an understanding of the language and vision of the world that was manifest in the object of inquiry. One might argue that someone such as Kuhn was a better historian and philosopher of science because he was initially trained as a scientist, but this may not always be the case. One could understand a ritual without participating in it, and consequently it is important to distinguish between understanding *in* a practice and the understanding *of* a practice, even though the former is not necessarily the key to the latter and could even be inhibitive. What distinguishes understanding from interpretation is that an interpretation is, so to speak, another text, and although it might be a contribution to the understanding of a human practice, either by participants or by observers, it is another, albeit entwined, concept. Since meaning is, at least in the first instance, a matter of use and *understanding* within a language-game, encountering something such as a foreign culture, or even an ambiguous signpost, requires *interpretation*. This involves not only some sort of entry into the realm of understanding that defines the practice under investigation, but a rendering of that realm in the language of the interpreter. The appropriate questions, then, are those of what constitutes interpretation, what forms of inquiry belong to the genre of interpretive practices, and how one goes about the task of interpretation. Here we must return to Wittgenstein's account of a "perspicuous representation" (*übersichtliche Darstellung*).

This is a difficult phrase to translate, and some commentators have suggested "presentation" rather than "representation." But, as already noted, *Darstellung* typically presupposes the autonomy of what is represented, and it implies both interpretation and explanation. It is very important to note that it was in the remark preceding his statement about philosophy leaving everything as it is that Wittgenstein first introduced this concept, which he claimed was fundamental and characterized his approach. What was necessary was to overcome the "craving for generality" (*BB*, 17) that was associated with traditional philosophy, and which has characterized the social sciences and led to the attempt to emulate the natural sciences. This entailed a disdain for the particular, but it is precisely particularity that characterizes social phenomena, even though there is a certain generality in conventions and even though the goal of philosophy and human inquiry as a whole is to go beyond a mere description of particulars. The perspicuous representation, or what Wittgenstein referred to as his "mode of representation," was an interpretive device for reconciling the dual demands of particularity and generality and for resisting the tendency to reify the means of representation and confuse the means with what was represented. He claimed that "nothing is more important for teaching us to understand the concepts we have than constructing fictitious ones" (*PP*, 2:19; *CV*, 74). These constructed language-games are best described as ideal typifications, and although they are widely employed in the social sciences, they are often not recognized as such and are often presented as theories or models of inquiry and projected onto the object of inquiry rather than functioning as vehicles of representation and communication.

Although in the *Investigations* he had concluded that a perspicuous representation was a *Weltanschauung* because it constituted a perspective on the subject matter, he later took pains to distinguish his position from that of Oswald Spengler and Goethe, who both sought to locate some essence underlying what an investigator might from some perspective construe as similar phenomena. For Wittgenstein, the perspicuous representation was a constructed heuristic. He had suggested that what was required in giving an account of a *Lebensform* and *Weltbild* were "sketches" that produced the kind of understanding that illuminated connections. He eventually became dubious about referring to this as a *Weltanschauung*, because although the term refers to a particular way of looking at things, it usually implies an ideology or worldview that is embraced within a certain community. He claimed, however, that "the philosopher is not a citizen of any community of ideas. That is what makes him into a philosopher" (Z, 455). What Wittgenstein was talking about was a particular perspective or external way of seeing, an interpretive frame that would serve to represent and communicate the nature of a particular indigenous *Weltanschauung*, in a manner that at once allowed some generalization while capturing the historical particularity and its context. This was very similar to what Max Weber had attempted to do in his account of something such as the Protestant ethic. This "ethic" did not actually name a phenomenon, but was a term of art for characterizing a range of phenomena. It was a way of reaching an understanding and conveying that understanding. The kind of representation that Wittgenstein sought would be accomplished by what he referred to as inventing intermediate cases. He claimed that "the only way for us namely to avoid prejudice—or vacuity in our claims, is to posit the ideal as what it is, *namely* as an object of comparison—a measuring rod as it were—*within our way of looking at things*, & not as a preconception to which everything *must* conform. This namely is the dogmatism into which philosophy can so easily degenerate" (*CV*, 30), and into which social inquiry has so often degenerated.

Although there seems to be no evidence that Wittgenstein was familiar with the work of Weber, there is a remarkable similarity between Weber's conception of the ideal-type and Wittgenstein's philosophical method, and both individuals developed their approaches partly in response to the propensity of philosophers and social theorists to adopt the model of natural science and impose external generalizations on the particularities of social phenomena. Both were also intrigued with, but critical of, Spengler. Weber had engaged in a personal disputation with Spengler, which included their respective views of Marx and Nietzsche as cultural critics and inquirers. Weber's and Wittgenstein's interest in Spengler reflected in part the latter's pessimistic views regarding the condition of modern Western civilization, but also in part Spengler's mode of studying civilization. Weber and Wittgenstein were, however, ultimately concerned about the manner in which Spengler had projected his prototypes into his subject matter, and this was at the heart of Wittgenstein's critique of metaphysics, which would certainly apply to the social philosophy of someone such as Hegel. This was what Wittgenstein referred to as "injustice in Spengler." Although Spengler saw the necessity for ideal typification, he, like Goethe, believed that the ideal must be immanent in what it typified. Wittgenstein claimed that "the ideal loses none of its dignity if it is posited as the principle determining the form of one's approach. A good unit of measurement." Spengler's projection of the ideal into reality and tendency to mistake family resemblances for essences allowed "prejudices to constantly slip into the discussion" and "willy nilly ascribe what is true of the prototype of the approach to the object to which we are applying the approach as well; & we claim 'it *must always be* . . .'" In this way, we "confuse prototype & object" and "we find ourselves dogmatically conferring on the object properties that only the prototype necessarily possesses." What is at the root of this mistake is the worry that "the approach will lack the generality we want to give it if it really holds only of the one case." The prototype, however, belongs to the approach and form of inquiry and is not useful "by virtue of a claim that everything which is true only of it holds for all the objects to which the approach is applied." This error is the source of "exaggerated dogmatic claims" that obscure the object of inquiry (*CV*, 21, 31). He noted that "our investigation does not try to *find* the real, exact meaning of words; though we do often *give* words exact meanings in the course of our investigation" for the purpose of creating a model that would illuminate the object of inquiry, but the paradigm is in the scheme of inquiry and not the object (Z, 467). In the case of the basic facts of natural science, which are presented and determined by the theoretical language of science, there is not an endemic problem of imposing a prototype, even though somewhat similar methodological issues may arise.

There is often confusion in reading Wittgenstein, because he claimed that the task is to describe and explain language use, but at the same time he claimed that he rejected empirical hypotheses. The answer to what might seem a conflict is that, by "describing," he was referring to discerning the conventions that are manifest in the use of language, not to describing in the manner in which a grammar book states rules of usage. Even Winch seemed at times to project Wittgenstein's concept of a rule into the practices that were the object of inquiry, but the rules to which Wittgenstein referred were also basically ideal-types for describing and explaining the conventions that were expressed in social phenomena. As he often noted, no game has all the rules written down, and not everything that takes place in a game is governed by rules. What is involved is something like the difference between what we might call knowing *about* language use, which has its own language and mode of description, and knowing *how* to use language. His image of investigation was not empirical in the sense of natural science, but in the sense of any interpretive enterprise, which he also spoke about at times as a matter of making hypotheses. Even his account of linguistic meaning as use was less an empirical claim than an ideal-type designed to illuminate how language functioned. Interpretation is always a matter of attempting to make sense of something and often to convey that sense to someone else, and it is often necessary to resort to familiar examples. The danger, however, is to allow the examples, the means of representation, to become confused with what they seek to clarify. Anthropologists, from Frazer to Clifford Geertz, have used kings, priests, and other figures as paradigms, but it is always necessary to assess the extent to which such paradigms do justice to the subject matter, that is, whether they produced clarity or obfuscation, that is, whether the reader of such an interpretation might gain the false sense that this was more than an analogy.

In discussing interpretation, it is difficult to avoid confronting the concept of a context. Thinking, no more than speaking, can be detached from the "system" of conventions in which they gain meaning (*Z*, 101, 146). Wittgenstein's focus on meaning as use, on the holistic character of language, on the manner in which words gain meaning by their role in sentences and speech-acts, and on the place that these acts have in language-games and forms of life has contributed to making him a candidate for the title of "arch-contextualist"—and even relativist. He insisted that "only in the system has the sign any life" and that it is not possible to separate thinking from the activity in which it takes place (*Z*, 101, 146). But the details and implications of his contextualism require considerable unpacking. He emphasized that linguistic meaning is largely a function of the general "context" (*Zusammenhang*) of an utterance and that actions, facial expressions, observations, and intentions all gain significance in terms of their surroundings (*Umbegung*) and circumstances (*Umständen*). Even the solution of mathematical problems depends on the context of their formulation. He noted that many familiar paths may lead off from

hearing or seeing any set of words, and consequently if we do not immediately understand the words, it becomes necessary to invent or guess at
a context. Such an invention, however, is an interpretive act, and since
positing such an "atmosphere" is a specific interpretive task, it can be done
well or badly. There is, then, so to speak, an art to contextualizing.

Wittgenstein noted that there were countless kinds of sentences,
and that these are not fixed. They change with changes in the practices,
the language-games, and the forms of life that constitute discursive
regimes. What can be said of linguistic performances in this respect can
be said of actions and events as a whole, which also have material or
behavioral conditions and a comparable grammatical, syntactical, and
performative context. So there is no doubt that contextual sensitivity was
essential to Wittgenstein's concept of interpretation, but he nevertheless
noted that contextual enthusiasm should be constrained. Contexts are
neither causal explanations of what they contextualize nor clues that aid
in determining a subjective meaning behind verbal expressions, any more
than the meaning of a musical phrase is something behind the score or
than numbers are mathematical objects that are represented by numerals. And this warning may be appropriate in certain cases of the practice
of intellectual history, where it sometimes seems as if reconstructing a
context takes precedence over the object that is contextualized. He cautioned, for example, that although an identity is in part ascribed to an
object in terms of its context, interpreters can become so caught up in
their fascination with a context and its explanatory power that they lose
sight of the object of inquiry. "People who are constantly asking 'why' are
like tourists who stand in front of a building reading Baedeker and are so
busy reading the history of its construction, etc., that they are prevented
from seeing the building" (*CV*, 46). There is, however, a further difficulty,
and that is the issue of what kind of thing constitutes a context.

Wittgenstein had indicated that contexts can be both discovered
and imposed. There are (what might be called) indigenous or "natural"
contexts, which are logically comparable and empirically connected to
the object that is the subject of interpretation. Such contexts are, like
the claims about the object of inquiry itself, *reconstructions* and interpretations. What historians and other interpreters often advance as an
explanatory context, however, is a *construction* of the interpreter, which
is often derived from other work that itself is open to interpretation. A
context such as "modernity" is a construct of the interpreter and very

different from positing a context such as the "Cold War" that has an intrinsic historical identity, but the former can sometimes masquerade as the latter. Wittgenstein did not object to constructing or inventing contexts as a way of achieving clarity about an object of inquiry, but, as in the case of any interpretive device, he was concerned about the possibility of reifying such a context. His allusions to the similarity between philosophy and anthropology went beyond what even Winch had suggested in "Understanding a Primitive Society" (1964). Wittgenstein had said at one point that "savages have games . . . for which there are no written rules. Now let's imagine the activity of an explorer traveling throughout the countries of these peoples and setting up lists of rules for their games. This is completely analogous to what the philosopher does" (*BT*, 313). This should leave little doubt about his view of the epistemological symmetry between philosophy and social inquiry and what he spoke of as the necessity of taking an ethnological point of view, which not only enhanced objectivity but placed the object of inquiry in context.

The question that finally must be posed is if it really makes any difference in the conduct of the practice of interpretation whether we embrace mentalism, interpretism, or what I have referred to as Wittgenstein's conventional realism. There are many instances in which philosophical accounts of a practice, such as the philosophy of natural science, have little significance for participating in the practice that is the object of analysis, but, for a variety of reasons, both logical and historical, this is often not the case with respect to the relationship between philosophy and the social sciences. Philosophical accounts of interpretation have consistently infiltrated or, for example, as in the case of deconstruction and Foucault's genealogical method, even given birth to interpretive practices. Consequently, philosophical remediation may be required. The basic problem with both mentalism and interpretism as metatheories of interpretation is, first of all, that they tend to be treated as methods or approaches when they are actually theoretically detached epistemological claims; in practice they tend to lead to a neglect of texts and other discursive phenomena, that is, they distract us from the particularity of the objects that they claim to illuminate as well as from undertaking a theoretical account of those objects. The ideas both of "original meaning" and of interpretation "going all the way down" involve the displacement of texts and social phenomena. Just as meaning in the first case recedes into the nebulous world of mental intention, it recedes, in the second case, into the interpretation and leads to confusion between what is represented and the means of representation. Conventional realism entails the theoretical autonomy of both the object and the practice of inquiry.

Many intellectual historians as well as others in the human sciences profess great theoretical concern with texts, but in practice, texts often actually receive short shrift in favor of speculation about the ideas behind them or the contexts in which they are situated. Some are so intent on narrowing down the context in order to reveal the meaning behind the text that the actual works fade from view, and often the explanatory context adduced is a retrospectively imposed drama, which is a construction of the interpreter. Postmodernists are so convinced of the indeterminacy of meaning that they often feel quite free to invent it and seem so overwhelmed by all the interpretive frames that might be imposed on a text that, as in the case of Jacques Derrida's repetitive reinterpretation of *The Postcard* (1987), the object of inquiry loses all identity. To focus on the text is neither to dismiss the very idea of authorial intention nor to deny that it is only through interpretation that meaning becomes an object of inquiry. It is only to recognize that the locus of meaning is the object of investigation and that interpretation defines the character of all authentically representative endeavors. There is nowhere else to find an intention except in the conventions of speech and action. It is as fruitless to assume a "black box" of nondiscursive original intentionality as it is to believe that interpretations are the source of meaning.

If we wish to exemplify Wittgenstein's approach to meaning, understanding, and the practice of interpretation, Kuhn's struggle to come to grips with what was involved in the practice of the philosophy and history of science offers an edifying case, which is significant for thinking about any form of social inquiry.

6

INTERPRETING SCIENCE
Kuhn as a Social Theorist

> It is a fact of experience that human beings alter their concepts,
> exchange them for others. (*PP*, 2:727)
> Not empiricism and yet realism in philosophy, that is the hardest
> thing. (*RFM*, 325)
>
> —WITTGENSTEIN
>
> History, if viewed as a repository for more than an anecdote or
> chronology, could produce a decisive transformation in the image
> of science by which we are now possessed.
>
> —KUHN
>
> Philosophers deal with a never-never land that has hardly any
> point of contact with the actual lives of scientists, politicians,
> people like you and me.
>
> —FEYERABEND

ALTHOUGH KUHN's *Structure of Scientific Revolutions* has been justly interpreted as a challenge to the logical positivist/empiricist philosophy of science, his critique of what he referred to as "the image of science by which we are now possessed" was less that account of scientific explanation itself than its reflection in popular views of science and particularly, by the 1950s, its residue in the self-image and aspirations of the social sciences. In the last major interview before his death, he acknowledged that at the point that he wrote *Structure* he was not well read in logical empiricism and that "it was against that sort of everyday image of logical empiricism—I didn't even think of it as logical empiricism for a while"— that he was reacting (1997). He noted that much of his initial formulation of the arguments of *Structure* had been developed in the context of discussions with social scientists and that he believed that it was less the fluidity of the subject matter of social science than the particular contentious character of social-scientific communities that explained the absence of the patterns of paradigmatic shift that he claimed to discern in the history of natural science. He did not, however, ever investigate the degree to which there were such shifts in the history of the social sciences (Gunnell 2004c). He doubted that the conservative character of "normal" natural science, in contrast to the typical "number and extent of the overt disagreements between social scientists about the nature of legitimate scientific problems and methods," was because "practitioners of the natural sciences possess firmer or more permanent answers to such questions" (1970c, viii). He also noted that he "gradually realized that a lot of the response was coming from social scientists" (1997). It was because social scientists had become so dependent on philosophy for their vision of science, rather than on any direct contact with the actual practice of science, that they responded to Kuhn's work by first embracing it but then by rejecting it after recognizing and fearing its implications for what had become their ideology of science.

Kuhn's road to *Structure* was indeed long, and the period at the University of California at Berkeley was an important part of that journey. It was here that he began to formulate more reflectively his approach to the philosophy of natural science as a form of social and historical inquiry, and this was in part a consequence of his exposure to Wittgenstein, which was in turn related, in a complicated manner, to his contact with Paul Feyerabend.

FEYERABEND

Two years after Kuhn arrived in Berkeley, and four years before the publication of *Structure*, Feyerabend joined the philosophy department. It is safe to assume that there was more interchange between Kuhn and Feyerabend than Kuhn ever publicly acknowledged, but they were distinctly different, although contentious and passionate, personalities. Kuhn's publications, however, were seldom polemical, while Feyerabend was consistently on the attack, with often florid rhetoric, against a variety of philosophical doctrines and positions, which initially included Kuhn's argument. Both, however, were physicists before they were professional philosophers, which distinguished them from many of their contemporaries who, even in the case of the philosophy of science, were trained as philosophers and tended to project their philosophical schemes onto their image of the practice of science. What has in part led to the misinterpretation of Kuhn is the fact that unlike those of many of his predecessors, including both Popper and the positivists, his account of science was not an attempt either to underwrite or to displace the self-understanding, let alone the behavior, of scientists. This was a position that Feyerabend eventually came to understand, endorse, and propagate, but his eventual acquiescence was grounded in his early exposure to Wittgenstein. Although Kuhn was personally and intellectually closer to Cavell than to Feyerabend, the latter's acquaintance with Wittgenstein's work was, as opposed to Cavell's in the early 1960s, considerably less "tentative." Feyerabend was initially best known as a follower of Popper, but later he became identified as a defector from what he then referred to as the Popperian "church" (Feyerabend 1994, 164). The beginning and end of his philosophical career were, however, marked by an involvement with Wittgenstein's work, and the development of his own philosophy pivoted on the tension between the ideas of Popper and Wittgenstein. Toward the end of his life, he noted that although when he had been a student he had believed in the positivist dictum that scientific knowledge is the only real knowledge, he had subsequently never subscribed to any orthodox "philosophical position." An interviewer suggested that this was because he had become "an anarchist," but Feyerabend answered, "No. Then I read Wittgenstein" (1991, 489).

Feyerabend was, like both Wittgenstein and Popper, a Viennese. He was drafted into the German army during World War II, and, while fighting on the Russian front, was severely wounded and permanently partially disabled. He was in many ways a romantic, Byronic figure. He had a lifelong involvement with acting and singing, and when he returned to Vienna in 1947, he dabbled in the humanities and social science before taking up theoretical physics and embracing logical positivism. He joined the Austrian College Society, which had originally been founded by resistance fighters, and it was within this group that he organized the Kraft Circle in honor of Victor Kraft, his dissertation director, who was the last member of the Vienna Circle to remain in Vienna. Like some of the positivists, he associated with Marxist intellectuals, and he later regretted that he had passed up the opportunity to work with Bertolt Brecht. He first encountered Popper in 1949 at the Society's Alpbach forum, where Popper conducted the philosophy seminar. Although intrigued by Popper, it was also at this point that he was introduced to the work of Wittgenstein, who had finished the manuscript of the *Investigations* in the summer of 1949, just before a visit to the United States. There were deep personal and intellectual tensions between Popper and Wittgenstein, and their divergent careers and perspectives had been already pointedly manifest in their confrontation at Cambridge in 1946 (Edmonds and Eidinow 2001). After returning to England in the late fall and receiving a diagnosis of terminal prostate cancer, Wittgenstein moved to Vienna, where his sister was also close to death, and where the English philosopher Elizabeth Anscombe had come to meet with him, as well as improve her facility with the German language, in preparation for translating the manuscript of the *Investigations*.

Feyerabend was one of the first individuals to have access to the final form of the manuscript. He had met Anscombe, who he described as "powerful and to some people forbidding," at Alpbach, and she participated in some of the meetings of the College Society. During the course of her regular discussions with Wittgenstein, she allowed Feyerabend to read the manuscript, which they discussed and which, he noted, had a "profound influence" on his thought (1978, 114). He also succeeded in convincing the normally reclusive Wittgenstein, who at that point was working on what would become the manuscript of *On Certainty*, to make a presentation to the Society. Although appearing an hour late, Feyerabend reported that he gave a "spirited performance and seemed to prefer our disrespectful attitude to the fawning admiration he encountered elsewhere" (1978, 109). This exposure to Wittgenstein led to Feyerabend's earliest formulation of what would later be referred to as the concept of incommensurability, which was substantially the same as the concept that Kuhn later applied to the relationship between successive scientific theories. Feyerabend recognized the tension between Wittgenstein's ideas and various forms of philosophical rationalism, such as that manifest in both positivism and the work of Popper, and after completing his doctorate at Vienna in 1951, he applied to study with Wittgenstein at Cambridge. Wittgenstein died before Feyerabend arrived, and he then enrolled at the London School of Economics, where, somewhat by default, he selected Popper as his supervisor. He was inducted into Popper's philosophical entourage and even became Popper's assistant. His early exposure to Popper left him with the impression that the ideas of Popper and Wittgenstein were similar, but the deeper he became involved with Popper's circle, the more he began to sense fundamental differences—particularly with respect to the issue of the relationship between philosophy and its subject matter. Although his involvement with Popper was to a large extent based on pragmatic decisions, he did find Popper's approach "seductive" and initially "fell for it," but he eventually came to see it "as an excellent demonstration of the dangers of abstract reasoning" and various forms of philosophical rationalism, "whether dogmatic or critical" (1995, 89).

In England, Feyerabend also resumed his discussions with Anscombe and began to elaborate his emerging belief, inspired by his reading of Wittgenstein, that universal criteria for assessing the verisimilitude of a scientific theory could not be adduced by philosophy. Popper was ultimately unsympathetic, because the idea of incommensurability was, in his view, not compatible with his commitment to philosophical realism, his claim that the logic of falsification was the key to scientific judgment and the catalyst of scientific progress, and his belief that philosophy held the answer to improving scientific practice. It was at this point that Feyerabend undertook a detailed reconstruction of the *Investigations*. The long essay, arguably the first of its kind, was eventually translated from German by Anscombe and published in 1955. It was in many respects a remarkable piece of work, which captured the basic flavor of Wittgenstein's treatise in a comprehensive but analytically precise manner. He later stated that he had studied Wittgenstein's work more "thoroughly than anything from the Popperian inventory, though there are still some people who regard me as a Popperian apostate" (1991, 489). There were, from the beginning, deep ideological as well as latent philosophical differences between Feyerabend and Popper, as well as Popper's followers, and, by the 1960s, this would become more pronounced.

Feyerabend struggled to re-present the *Investigations* as a philosophical theory and as a response to various forms of philosophical realism and essentialism, as well as to the kind of position that Wittgenstein had advanced in the *Tractatus*. He nevertheless explicitly recognized, and grappled with, the fact that the creation of a formal philosophical theory was not Wittgenstein's goal. The work was, he claimed, a therapeutic "means of getting rid of our philosophical troubles" rather than of establishing new philosophical doctrines. He noted that, compared with the positivists, Wittgenstein's strong distinction between philosophy and its object of analysis, such as science, was novel, and, in seeking to label Wittgenstein's position, he suggested that it might be construed as "instrumentalist" or "pragmatist," but concluded, without elaboration, "that Wittgenstein's theory of language can be understood as a constructivist theory of meaning" (1955, 462, 482). In retrospect, he realized that he agreed with what he took to be Wittgenstein's "debunking of pure theory" in philosophy, which was in part what finally led him to define himself as "a Wittgensteinian."

One of Popper's most faithful acolytes, or, as Feyerabend put it, his "pit bull," was John Watkins, who, along with William Bartley and others, was among those who were eventually "excommunicated" from Popper's circle for failing, in the end, to adhere sufficiently to the ideas of the master. Watkins, Joseph Agassi, and Imre Lakatos had, however, urged Feyerabend to become an even more enthusiastic and "faithful Popperian," and, despite his reservations, he undertook the translation of *The Open Society*, which Popper later referred to as his "war effort." With Popper's support, he gained a position at Bristol, in the same year that he published what he referred to as his "Wittgensteinian monster." Three years later, however, when he took the permanent post at Berkeley, he encountered Kuhn and first read—at that point in what he later referred to as a "rather old-fashioned way"—an early draft of the manuscript of *Structure* (Feyerabend 1995, 89–100, 109). What Feyerabend meant by "old-fashioned" was that he initially, like so many others, viewed the work as an attack on the idea of objectivity and truth in science, when, as he would later recognize and argue, it was, in effect, a defense of the autonomy of scientific practices and a new perspective on how to practice the philosophy of science.

By the early 1960s, Feyerabend had rejected the core doctrines of logical positivism. Although he was moving in the direction of Kuhn's position, he still maintained an allegiance to some of the general tenets of Popper's philosophy, which Kuhn himself had acknowledged as influencing his own work. There was a persistent and deep ambivalence in Popper's argument. While he claimed that there were no theoretically or conceptually independent facts, he still maintained that scientific explanation, and scientific progress, depended, as the positivists had argued, upon some form of comparison between theory and the "world" as well as upon conformity to a universal deductive logical form. The basic issue dividing Popper and Kuhn would be less a distinct epistemological disagreement, or even a different view of the history of science, than their respective claims about the relationship between philosophy and science.

It was also this issue that, in the end, precipitated Feyerabend's intellectual and personal break with Popper. Whether Popper, as he claimed in his autobiography, was responsible for the death of logical positivism or whether, as many of his critics have charged, he persisted in holding on to the remnants of its basic assumptions and philosophical attitude, he never relinquished a belief in the capacity of philosophy to specify what he believed was the underlying logic of scientific explanation and the criteria of scientific judgment and progress, whether or not this always accorded with actual scientific practices.

In a series of publications, Feyerabend (1962, 1963, 1964, 1965, 1970a, 1970b, 1970c, 1970d) dismissed the ontological distinction between theory and fact and concluded that theoretical terms determined the meaning of observational ones and that there was only a pragmatic difference between the two; he rejected the instrumentalist account of theories as constructed tools for organizing and explaining given facts; he first used the term "incommensurable" and argued for the incommensurability of scientific theories; he claimed that logical empiricists, in their attempt to provide a formal normative account of scientific explanation, were "dogmatists" who were bereft of an understanding of scientific practice and the history of science; and he claimed that the whole rationalist project of the philosophy of science was obsolete. Elements of these arguments coincided with the position of Kuhn. Feyerabend still assumed, however, that philosophy could, in some manner, speak to the practice of science in a critical and enlightening fashion and that the proliferation of and competition between theories explained the progress of science. In the same year that Kuhn published what Feyerabend came to refer to as his "revolutionary" book, Popper was a visitor at Berkeley, but by this point Feyerabend not only had begun a pointed dissent from what had become the "received position" in the philosophy of science represented by individuals such as Carl Hempel and Ernest Nagel but had expressed explicit disagreements with Popper's position. Like Kuhn, Feyerabend stressed that formal philosophical accounts of scientific explanation were not in accord with actual scientific practice, but despite what he later referred to as Kuhn's "magnificent book" and despite how Kuhn had studied history "while I was still enmeshed in abstract speculation," he had not fully extricated himself from the spell of Popper's ideas (1991, 506).

This ambivalence was very evident in a volume (Lakatos and Musgrave 1970) that was the product of a 1956 colloquium in London. The meeting had originally been planned around a confrontation between Popper and Kuhn and around issues that arose in discussions of Kuhn's work in Popper's LSE seminar. Although Feyerabend and Lakatos did not actually attend, a third of the volume was devoted to Lakatos's agonizing attempt to find a middle way between his attachment to Popper and the impact that Kuhn's work had begun to exercise on him. Kuhn's contribution to the book had originally been intended as part of a Festschrift for Popper, and Kuhn noted that although their views on many problems were "very nearly identical," their "intentions" were radically divergent. Kuhn claimed that while he was devoted to giving an account of the actual practice of science and distinguishing its "normal" and "revolutionary" stages, Popper reversed the relationship between these stages and advanced an "ideology" of science and a set of "procedural maxims" derived from images of revolutionary change, which he presented as a standard for all authentic scientific practice. Kuhn claimed that Popper conceived of past theories as outdated "mistakes" and "consistently sought evaluation procedures" that could "be applied to theories with the apodictic assurance," when the answer to why science progresses must in the end "be psychological or sociological" (1970a, 3–21). Popper's response was to elaborate at length what he considered to be the "dangers of normal science" for the "growth of knowledge," even though he later acknowledged that his criticism applied less to Kuhn's actual argument than to how others had interpreted it.

Feyerabend later noted that since his discussions with Kuhn in the early 1960s, he, as well as Lakatos, had "looked at science in a new way," but, like Lakatos, he was, at that point, still unable to accept what he took to be Kuhn's "general ideology which I thought formed the background of his thinking" and which, if embraced, would "inhibit the advancement of knowledge" and reinforce "anti-humanitarian tendencies." Despite what he believed to be Kuhn's "intended" ambiguity about whether his work was descriptive or normative, Feyerabend, like so many others, still interpreted it as having normative implications, which, in effect, he claimed seemed to render "normal science" not much different than "organized crime" (1970a, 197–98). But, after voicing these reservations, he concluded that "science is, and should be, more irrational than Lakatos and Feyerabend, the erstwhile student of Popper, had been prepared to admit." Feyerabend began to criticize Popper directly and noted that, with respect to the issue of incommensurability, he "wholeheartedly" agreed with Kuhn. Furthermore, he claimed that the concept of a "scientific method, as softened up by Lakatos," was but "an ornament which makes us forget that a position of 'anything goes' has in fact been adopted" and that there is "trouble in the third world" of transcendental ideas propounded by Popper. All this, he claimed, "changes science from a stern and demanding mistress into an attractive and yielding courtesan who tries to anticipate every wish of her lover."

While Lakatos wished to construct a normative image of scientific rationality that was based on Popper's formulation, he also attempted to construct a descriptive and historical account of scientific practices that allowed for a certain element of the kind of "dogma" that characterized what Kuhn referred to as "normal science." A significant aspect of all this was, however, ideological. Lakatos, like Popper and many of his followers such as Gellner, viewed Kuhn through the lens of their interpretation of Wittgenstein's work and as a threat to the very idea of scientific truth. Lakatos claimed that "the clash between Popper and Kuhn . . . concerns our central intellectual values, and has implications not only for theoretical physics but also for the underdeveloped social sciences and even for moral and political philosophy." He argued that Kuhn's position had "authoritarian and irrational overtones" which suggested that "truth lies in power" and "vindicates . . . the political credo of contemporary religious maniacs (student revolutionaries)" and that scientific change is a matter of "mob psychology." Although Lakatos had come to accept Kuhn's criticism of Popper's criterion of falsification, he claimed that there was implicitly a "stronger Popperian position," which implied "rational progress" and deserved to be elaborated in a more "sophisticated version." This was the first statement of what became Lakatos's popular account of how the "history of science has been and should be a history of competing research programmes (or, if you wish, 'paradigms') but it has not been and must not become a succession of periods of normal science: the sooner competition starts, the better for progress." This was conceived as deviating from what he took to be Kuhn's "psychological" approach, because "the—rationally reconstructed—growth of science takes place essentially in the world of ideas, in Plato's and Popper's 'third-world,' in the world of articulated knowledge which is independent of the knowing subject" or practicing scientist (1970). Lakatos's formulation gained a considerable following in the social sciences, because it seemed to fit more readily the kind of work in which many social scientists were engaged and because it

offered a halfway house for the tension between historicity and rationalism that social scientists were beginning to experience, and attempting to
reconcile, in their continuing search for philosophical authority.

In the Lakatos and Musgrave volume, Kuhn took the opportunity
to reply to his critics and particularly to those who still believed that
the "problem of theory choice can be resolved by techniques that are
semantically neutral." He was not willing to go as far as Feyerabend in
proclaiming the "intrinsic irrationality of theory-choice," because he
believed that there were good reasons that were indigenous to a paradigmatic context, but he maintained that the philosophy of science was
not up to date with respect to the issue of how "language fits the world"
(1970b, 234–35). Kuhn seemed to have some difficulty pinpointing exactly
what was agitating his critics and precipitating such strong criticism,
when all he was saying was that in a debate about the status of a theory
there is no neutral philosophically determinable basis of choice. But he
cut closer to the bone when he said that "'truth' may, like 'proof,' be a term
with only intra-theoretic applications." He and Feyerabend had come
to agree that theories are "incommensurable" and that words become
attached to nature only within scientific practice, where there is less any
strict "theory-choice" than a "conversion." Feyerabend claimed that it
was actually the "great merit" of Wittgenstein to have discovered the
incommensurability of theoretical paradigms and that what Kuhn had
done in his historical narrative was to rediscover this fact and make the
point more "concrete" (1978, 66). Whether Kuhn actually rediscovered it
in Wittgenstein's work is more difficult to determine.

After Kuhn left Berkeley in 1964, Feyerabend was also often in
other locations, but by the point that Kuhn published the second edition
of *Structure*, their basic positions were hardly distinguishable. Feyerabend, however, was beginning to take an even more definite and radical
stand than Kuhn with respect to the relationship between philosophy
and science. While Lakatos's argument was in part a consequence of his
worry that recent events, such as the student uprisings that characterized the 1960s, were a threat to truth and rationality, the political and
cultural atmosphere at Berkeley during this period inspired, or at least
reinforced, Feyerabend's antirationalist sentiments. The first version of
his "anarchistic theory of knowledge" (1970a) might be interpreted as an
exaggerated version of Popper's argument about the evolution of science
as the survival of the fittest theories, but he would soon pointedly dis-

tance himself from any lingering connection with Popper's ideas. While lecturing in London in 1968, Feyerabend had, however, become more closely acquainted with Lakatos, who, he noted, eventually became "one of the best friends I ever had" and who was at this point beginning to drift even further away from a strict Popperian position. Feyerabend said that Lakatos "genuinely admired Popper and wanted to form a movement around Popper's philosophy. Eventually, however, he became disillusioned," and despite his continued attempt to hold on to vestiges of the Popperian model, he was finally deemed heretical by his mentor. Feyerabend had intended to incorporate a version of his essay "Against Method" from 1970 into a book (*For and Against Method*) in which Lakatos would present an opposing view. Lakatos, however, died in 1974, and Feyerabend revised his own contribution as an independent volume.

Although Feyerabend's animadversions "against method" have often been interpreted as advancing the normative claim that scientists, in order to ensure the progress of their enterprise, should adopt an unconstrained research stance, his actual argument was, like that of Wittgenstein, against *philosophical* theories of science as a description of and guide to scientific practice as well as an arbiter of scientific truth. What he was rebelling against were not methods *in* science but philosophical accounts *of* scientific method. His adage "anything goes" was his recognition that there was no formula that explained scientific discovery and change and that it was this openness and variation that was the key to scientific progress. Such progress was not the result of testing theories against given facts, the logic of falsification, or any other such precept, but rather the lack of a consistent and dogmatic method or logic. The very idea of a scientific method was, he claimed, an invention of philosophy, and scientists would be ill advised to subscribe to it. The reception of *Against Method* had certainly contributed to the growing critique of logical empiricism, but there was still a general lack of understanding regarding the central message, despite the fact that Feyerabend explicitly stated that "anything goes" was not a "principle" he was recommending for scientific practice, but an account of the history of scientific practice. He argued that the formulation of principles governing scientific inquiry belong to science rather than philosophy. His phrase was, he stated, "the terrified exclamation of a rationalist who takes a closer look at history." His conclusion was that "science can stand on its own two feet and does not need any help from rationalists, secular humanists, Marxists and similar religious movements; and, secondly, that non-scientific cultures, procedures and assumptions can also stand on their own two feet and should be allowed to do so" (1988, vii–viii). He had come to recognize, however, that in their search for scientific identity and authority, "representatives of the so-called 'soft' sciences lack methodological imagination and, naturally, adore the simple-minded caricatures they find in philosophy books" (1991, 507). By the point of the third edition of *Against Method*, Feyerabend believed that the situation in the philosophy of science had gotten a great deal better because of what he referred to as Kuhn's "masterpiece" and that his views and those of Kuhn had become virtually "identical" (1992, 213).

By 1978, when Feyerabend published *Science in a Free Society*, he, like Kuhn, claimed that theoretical transformations in science constituted an ontological change in the concept to which the word "world" referred, and he recommended that science should be studied much in the same manner that anthropologists study various cultures. Different practices entailed different criteria of reason, and it was not the task, or within the capacity, of philosophy to legislate the logic of science. His argument sounded a great deal like that of Winch, but it was certainly, as in the case of Wittgenstein, an argument against epistemology and metaphysics as a philosophical project, and he recommended that philosophy focus on a description of what constituted knowledge in different scientific contexts. Philosophical methodologies were simply abstract idealizations of certain points in the history of science. Epistemology, he claimed, was "sick," and "anarchism," or the acceptance of the relativity of judgments regarding the criteria of knowledge, was the remedy.

He began to turn even more broadly against the whole enterprise of the philosophy of science as it had been typically practiced, and particularly against the assumption that there was any philosophical basis for claiming that science, including Western science, exemplified any superior form of rationality. But he also began to discuss more directly the issue of the relationship between "reason and practice," that is, the philosophy of science and the conduct of science, which he concluded were simply "*two different types of practices.*" There was no escape from "traditions" and history. He was even willing to embrace a kind of "Protagorean relativism," if that entailed accepting the "pluralism of traditions and values" (1978, 28), but he really dismissed the "spectre of relativism" as a bogeyman invented by rationalism and, understandably, feared by elites who worry about "democratic judgment" and diversity. These same themes were pursued in *Farewell to Reason* (1987).

Through his acquaintance with J. L. Austin in England, which in many respects reinforced the ideas he had derived from Wittgenstein, Feyerabend was led to conclude that "there were two types of tumors to be removed—philosophy of science and general philosophy (ethics, epistemology, etc.)—and two areas of human activity that could survive without them—science and common sense" (1995, 142). It was not merely a matter of properly understanding the practice of science, but of clarifying the relationship between philosophy and science. He argued that "many philosophers are so far removed from the details of scientific research or of political action that their advice becomes an exercise in low comedy" and "rings hollow when addressing important scientific and moral issues" (1991, 508). This embrace of what many, and often he, took to be "relativism," which extended beyond the incommensurability of scientific theories to the claim that cultures are more or less autonomous entities with their own criteria of truth and modes of judgment, represented the final break with Popper and his followers. But, as he noted, one of his "motives for writing *Against Method* was to free people from the tyranny of philosophical obfuscators and abstract concepts such as 'truth,' 'reality,' or 'objectivity'" as well as from what is sometimes called "relativism" and from more recent "obfuscators" such as Derrida, who also in their own way believed it possible for philosophy to speak about the nature of truth, or the lack thereof, in either science or everyday life (1995, 180). He recognized that the issue of relativism was still tied to the quest for philosophical privilege and that what many referred to as relativism was largely simply the negative reflection of rationalism. Those who attacked it claimed access to transcendental truth, and those who could be construed as embracing it often believed it was the basis of a critical capacity to deconstruct claims to truth.

Feyerabend ended up much more estranged from the philosophy of science profession than Kuhn, who, to the end, struggled to make his claims intelligible and acceptable to scholars in the philosophy and history of science. Although Feyerabend eventually backed away from what he had referred to as his "Protagorean relativism," while still admitting to being a "fervent relativist in some senses," he reiterated once more that the whole issue of relativism "is as much a chimera as absolutism" and that the charge of relativism was really rooted in the problem of the relationship between philosophy and science. He claimed that "one should let the sciences speak for themselves and that their message cannot be summarized in a theory or methodological system." In response to criticisms, such as that of Noam Chomsky, that he had made "any standpoint as good as any other," he insisted that he had never said or believed anything of the sort, and he stressed once again that "anything goes" was not a recommendation for the practice of science, but a rebuke of the "principles proposed by leading philosophers of science." Although he came to accept nearly all that Kuhn had said, he claimed that Kuhn did "not permit history to speak unrehearsed; he wants to bundle it up in theoretical ropes" (1991, 503, 507, 495). He found it difficult to say what would be involved in writing what he referred to as philosophically "unrehearsed" history, but his point was that Kuhn's historical work not only reflected but purposely exemplified a philosophical viewpoint about language and the world and about the relationship between philosophy and its subject matter. And a close look at Kuhn's career reveals that he was in fact pursuing history from a philosophical perspective and for a philosophical purpose.

THE PHILOSOPHY OF SCIENCE AS SOCIAL INQUIRY

Kuhn had a significant, and transformational, impact on Feyerabend, but it would be a mistake to assume that the relationship was one-directional. And at Berkeley, during the late 1950s and early 1960s, Wittgenstein's ideas were beginning to permeate the intellectual atmosphere. As I have already indicated, it is more difficult to establish precisely Kuhn's connection to Wittgenstein's work than in the cases of Winch and Feyerabend. Kuhn explicitly refers to Wittgenstein only once in *Structure*, with respect to the manner in which Wittgenstein's account of games and family resemblances illustrates how paradigms function (1970c, 44–45). And in his later work, in which he paid much more attention to issues of linguistic meaning and sounded even more Wittgensteinian in some of his phrasing, there is no explicit reference. Kuhn was not always unambiguous and consistent about specifying his intellectual identity, but to the extent that he was a historian, he, from the beginning, pursued history because of philosophical concerns. Although some of his philosophical conclusions were the consequence of his historical research, his narrative was designed to illustrate certain critical philosophical theses as well as exemplify a way of practicing philosophy that he increasingly identified as a form of social inquiry. Although Kuhn's philosophical "ropes" were not the kind that Feyerabend had initially supposed, Kuhn's "internalist" historical method, in pursuit of his argument about the "essential tension" between "tradition and innovation" in the evolution of the natural sciences, was philosophically informed.

One of the difficulties in achieving clarity about Kuhn's argument is that readers and commentators, particularly social scientists, have tended to reify some of the key concepts, such as "theory," "paradigm," "anomaly," "crisis," "revolution," and "normal science," and treat them as if they were designations of elements of scientific practice, which social scientists could either find in their own practices or, if lacking, construct. These were, however, Kuhn's ideal-types, his perspicuous representations, and it is important to heed Wittgenstein's admonition and not confuse his means of representation with what was represented. These were concepts for representing and describing the family resemblances between certain patterns that he discerned in the history of science. The similarities that he noted by the use of terms such as "paradigm" were viewed at a high level of abstraction, which sometimes led interpreters to neglect that his actual emphasis, like Feyerabend's, was on the wide range of historical particularities that were involved in various paradigmatic shifts. Although his initial ambiguity about the use of the term "paradigm," so famously pointed out by Margaret Masterson (1970), and taken seriously by Kuhn, may have created some confusion, it was actually the kind of concept that Wittgenstein had insisted on treating as elastic and having "blurred edges."

Shortly before his death in 1996, Kuhn engaged in an extended discussion about his intellectual development (1997; for further biographical information, see Heilbron 1998; Andresen 1999). He had been an undergraduate physics major at Harvard (1940–43), but he also took a course in the history of philosophy, in which he became especially interested in Kant. After graduation, he received a draft deferment while working on radar projects related to the war, which, during the last days of the European liberation, eventually took him to England and France. He returned to Harvard for graduate work in 1944, where he had intended to pursue theoretical physics but petitioned to take half of his courses in philosophy, even though he finally settled down in the standard but, because of the war, limited physics curriculum. Partly as a consequence of his earlier editorial work on the *Crimson* and various other honors, he was recommended to President James Conant to assist in Conant's history of science program, where Kuhn was asked to do a case study of the history of mechanics. His "ambitions," however, were philosophical, and he was less interested in history itself than in what it might reveal about what it meant for something to be true in science and how this might undergo a change. The germ of his argument in *Structure* emerged from his work in the Conant course, but, from the beginning, he conceived of *Structure* as a "book for philosophers" (1977, 4). When he asked Conant to recommend him for a three-year appointment to the Society of Fellows at Harvard, it was to pursue his philosophical concerns, even though he had begun to look more carefully at the literature in history and sociology of science (such as the work of Robert Merton, Jean Piaget, Karl Polanyi, and Alexandre Koyré) before, in his words, he "let the cat out of the bag." In 1951, he was invited to give the Lowell Lectures at the Boston Public Library, and it was in this series that he presented the core of the argument that would be fully developed in *Structure*, but he did not return directly to the project until after he left Harvard. He had some (unsatisfactory) contact with George Sarton at Harvard, and during his last year as a Fellow, while in England and France, he encountered individuals such as Gaston Bachelard and Mary Hesse and also became acquainted with Fleck's book. He had met Popper, who delivered the James Lectures at Harvard, and although he did not agree with Popper's views about scientific change, he was influenced by Popper's claim that there were no conceptually untainted observations. Popper recommended that he read the work of Émile Meyerson, which Kuhn found helpful. Although there were some who took Kuhn to be advocating a sociological approach to the study of science, his actual view of history was, from the beginning, distinctly internalist, which was evident in his first book, *The Copernican Revolution* (1957). It had been his initial reading of Aristotle in the Conant course, and the stark difference between Aristotle and Newton, that was pivotal in his becoming interested in what was involved in changing scientific conceptions of the world. When he returned to Harvard, where he and Leonard Nash took over Conant's program, he developed the course on the history of mechanics, which, as in the case of his analysis of Galileo, was in some respects a prototype of *Structure*. He remained at Harvard until 1956, and during his last two years, he held a Guggenheim fellowship.

Harvard did not offer him a position, but the philosophy department at Berkeley wanted to hire a historian of science (even though, as Kuhn put it, "they didn't know they didn't want one"). He came to Berkeley with a joint appointment in the history department, even though, to his dismay, the courses could not be cross-listed. Shortly after settling in Berkeley, he was offered a year at the Advanced Center for the Study of the Behavioral Sciences at Stanford, which he devoted to working on *Structure* and where he formulated his basic concepts and such terminology as that of a Gestalt switch. The latter concept was in part influenced by Polanyi's visit and his discussion of "tacit knowledge" as well as by Toulmin's *Foresight and Understanding* (1961), but he conceived it in terms of optical differences, rather than, as he would later stress, conceptual changes. He finished the monograph after returning to Berkeley.

Although Kuhn mentioned Feyerabend as one of four people whose "contributions were most far-reaching and decisive," he did not elaborate on the relationship. He did not believe that they communicated well, even after Feyerabend read the manuscript and despite their common understanding of the concept of incommensurability. His "creative sounding board and more," as he had made clear in the book, became Cavell, who was "*extraordinarily* important. . . . My interactions with him taught me a lot, encouraged me a lot, gave me certain ways of thinking about my problems, that were of a lot of importance." Kuhn had originally derived the concept of incommensurability from mathematics, and he also associated it with the use of scientific models. He later admitted that he used the term "paradigm" too loosely and that he had been unaware of Wittgenstein's use of the term, but he also expressed surprise that he had not had his "nose dragged through Wittgenstein's use of it." It would seem that no one but Cavell would likely have taken up that task, but it is doubtful that at that point Cavell was especially familiar with Wittgenstein's frequent employment of the term. Although Kuhn accepted Charles Morris's invitation to publish the monograph in the *International Encyclopedia of Unified Science*, he was hesitant about this as an exclusive venue, partly because of its positivist heritage. He contacted the editor at the University of Chicago Press, who agreed to publish it separately in its entirety as a book. At this point, he was offered a full professorship at Hopkins; but although both the philosophy and history departments at Berkeley voted to make him a full professor in history, the philosophers viewed him as a historian rather than a philosopher and would not approve a joint appointment. Although he remained at Berkeley on those terms, he was deeply disappointed, which, along with more personal reasons, led to his move to Princeton in 1964.

After finishing *Structure*, Kuhn largely stopped reading work in the history of science and instead focused on philosophical issues, but he hoped that work in the history of science would help bridge the gap that had led the philosophy of science to neglect the actual practice of science. At Princeton, he found that his work had made an impression on Hempel, who had begun to moderate his defense of the theory/fact dichotomy, but Kuhn continued to believe that logical empiricism and work such as that of Hempel was "more likely to mislead than to illuminate historical research." He noted that this kind of philosophy of science was "almost unique among recognized philosophical specialties" with regard to the "distance separating it from its subject matter" and with respect to the manner in which its problems were "generated by the field itself" rather than by a study of the scientific practices. But, at the same time, historians and sociologists had tended to focus on external factors such as the "social milieu" and to display a "resistance to disciplinary history" and to an investigation of the internal dynamics of conceptual change (1977, 11–13, 160). While Kuhn has often been linked to the sociology of knowledge and other contextualist modes of historiography, he actually consistently stressed his commitment to an internalist conceptual approach, which he believed was particularly essential in the study of a "highly disciplined science." There was an important connection between Kuhn's basic philosophical argument about incommensurability and his specification of the basic problem facing a historian of science. He saw a close correspondence between, on the one hand, his account of the conceptual distance between successive paradigms within the practice of science and, on the other hand, the problem of "the fundamental conceptual readjustment required of the historian to recapture the past" and provide an account of earlier scientific practice from the linguistic and theoretical standpoint of the present (1977, xiv), which was the basic problem facing any form of social inquiry.

One of the problems involved in understanding Kuhn has been the assumption that when speaking of theories he was referring to something like hypotheses, that is, potentially contested empirical claims, or to conceptual frameworks for analyzing some realm of data. Both hypotheses and analytical frameworks allow questions about the adequacy of representation and the relationship between such constructs and "reality," but there is no such distinction between basic scientific theories and what counts as reality or the world. The idea of a generic or metaphysical reality that underlies successive paradigms flows from the category mistake of raising talk about theory, conceived as an empirical conjecture or an analytical scheme for organizing given facts, to a metaphysical level, that is, the mistake of confusing presentation with representation. Although the term "theory" varies in everyday use and is philosophically contested, what Kuhn referred to as theories were largely not *claims about reality* but rather *reality claims*, that is, irreducible propositions about the kinds of things that exist and the manner of their existence. Although the word "theory" belongs to the language of philosophical talk about science as well as to the vocabulary of science itself, this definition accords well with what are often designated, both in the natural sciences and in popular parlance, as scientific theories, such as the theory of evolution, the special theory of relativity, Newton's theory of motion, the theory of DNA, atomic theory, and so on. There may not be such reflectively apportioned dimensions of many practices, but what are functionally theories, as Winch had pointed out, belong to, or are implicated in, all discourses and forms of human practice. And both Winch and Kuhn, who were writing at approximately the same point, recognized that there must be, on the part of the social scientist or historian, what we may be inclined to call a theory of theory. The idealist image of theory had carried over into the formulations of positivism and its conception of theories as analytical instruments as well as into many everyday uses of the term, and what Kuhn was challenging was this interpretation of theories as hypothetical claims about some separately specifiable realm of facts or state of affairs.

The problem that, at the beginning of the twentieth century, gave rise to and defined the philosophy of science as an emerging distinct discourse, and eventually a practice, was the dissolution of Newtonian physics as a realistic description of the world and its relegation to the status of a "theory," a term that, since the late nineteenth century, carried the somewhat negative connotation of a speculative claim that was the opposite of "fact." Once theory and fact were conceived as detached from each other, the issue became, as exemplified in the literature of positivism and subsequent work in the philosophy of science, how theories and facts are related to each other. The conclusion was that facts, whether in a phenomenal or physicalist domain, are grounded in some form of observation and immediate experience, while theories are mental constructs and calculi for apprehending them. Once given an empirical interpretation and content through some bridging device such as correspondence rules or operational definitions, theories were viewed as capable of generating verifiable or testable empirical generalizations. This basic image of theory dominated the literature for a large part of the century and found its way into the images of science and the applications of scientific method embraced by social science. Despite the virtual collapse of this philosophical account by the last quarter of the twentieth century, the residue of that interpretation of theory has continued, in many ways, to shape conversations in the philosophy of science and claims such as that of scientific realism, notwithstanding the latter's rejection of many aspects of traditional empiricism.

Despite, or maybe because of, the widespread attention to Kuhn's second-order concepts for interpreting the history of science, the philosophical core of his message has often been obscured. It is, however, more significant than the details of his historical argument, which like most histories of science is still an extrapolation of a philosophical premise. First of all, although Kuhn, like Wittgenstein, is often labeled, or accused of being, an idealist, his position is best designated as representing what I will refer to as *theoretical realism*, which should not be confused with the typical "realisms" in philosophy, which are quite the opposite. What Kuhn's formulation amounted to in some respects was the rehabilitation of an earlier, and even ancient, concept of *theoria*, which referred to seeing something directly and was identified with the perceived object. But, even more important, that rehabilitation entailed a transformation in the idea of philosophy and its relationship to science. If theories created their own sense and reference, philosophy could no longer make authoritative supra-scientific judgments about the criteria of scientific truth—any more than, as Wittgenstein and Winch argued, an anthropologist could neutrally determine what social actions were rational.

At the core of what Kuhn abstracted and designated as revolutions in the history of science were theories that constituted what he referred to as "incommensurable ways of seeing the world and practicing science within it" and that entailed different accounts of "the fundamental entities of which the universe is composed" (1970c, 4–5). This kind of radical paradigmatic shift, despite what might be viewed as a lingering "family resemblance" between old and new theories, involved something tantamount to a "conversion" on the part of scientists and what Kuhn at that point characterized as a "change in visual gestalt," a "switch" whereby "scientists do not see something as something else; they simply see it," but within a "different universe of discourse" (4–5, 14, 19, 85–86, 151–52). Here, Kuhn suggested, was a "picture" governed by "a broadened sense of the term 'rule,'" which amounted to an "established viewpoint" or "pre-conception." None of the shifts described by Kuhn resembled "the methodological stereotype of falsification by direct comparison with nature," and, he claimed, "science students accept theories on the authority of teacher and text, not because of evidence," which was always defined in terms of the accepted theories (38–39, 44–45, 77, 80). It is difficult to miss how closely this formulation corresponded to Wittgenstein's account of language acquisition and rule-following.

Although Kuhn took pains to show typical patterns in past revolutions, his main point was that there was no necessary pattern and that the parallel with political revolutions was not simply metaphorical but had a "genetic aspect" grounded in the fact that what was ultimately involved was "persuasion" and "a choice between incompatible modes of community life," where there was no "standard higher than the assent of the relevant community" (1970c, 92–94). To interpret this as saying that scientific truth is what these communities decide is, however, as Wittgenstein had pointed out, misleading. What constitutes a community is a sharing of beliefs and judgments. It is a matter of the beliefs to which they attach the word "true" and that they accept as how the world is constituted and behaves. Changes in theory bring about different accounts of some dimension of the "population of the universe" and "that population's behavior"— a different conception of some element of "nature" and, consequently, a "redefinition of the corresponding science." Kuhn maintained that theories are "constitutive" of both science and nature, that is, the concepts to which the words "science" and "nature" refer, and that "when paradigms change, the world changes with them," and, in effect, a "different world" emerges much like the manner in which pictures such as Jastrow's duck-rabbit are seen in alternate but incommensurable ways. The "scientist sees differently than he had seen before." What takes place is not a "reinterpretation" of "stable data," but a new vision of the world, which is not "corrigible" by any neutral form of observation (103, 110–15, 122–23).

Kuhn noted that while his historical studies had originally sprung from an "avocational" interest in philosophy, "myths" about science had devolved from philosophy into textbooks and common images of the "accumulation" of scientific knowledge and of the "progress" of science, which hindered a full "treatment of the philosophical implications" of his research. His historical investigation, however, revealed how the "view of science-as-accumulation is entangled with a dominant epistemology that takes knowledge to be a construction placed directly on raw sense-data by the mind"—a view "closely associated with early logical positivism and often not categorically rejected by its successors." What Kuhn defended was what he termed a "theory-determined" account of phenomena (96–98), which challenged the assumption that "sensory experience" was "fixed and neutral" and that theories were simply "man-made interpretations of given data." It was, he claimed, impossible to posit, philosophically, "any neutral language of observations" or "pure precepts" (126–27). What Kuhn was suggesting was that the philosophy of science had become a kind of "theology" of science, which tended to sustain the "dogma" of a reigning scientific paradigm. One might say that it had fallen into the very metaphysical trap that Wittgenstein had warned about. Textbooks provided the "authority" for scientific practice, and then "the popularizations and philosophical works modeled on them," and their entailed histories of science written from the perspective of the present, told a story of cumulative knowledge tracing a progressively better access to "reality." In this context, past revolutions became historically "invisible" (136).

There is a clue to the similarity between Kuhn and Wittgenstein in Kuhn's remark that "I go round explaining my own position to say I am a Kantian with moveable categories." This, however, can be misleading, because despite the fact that Kuhn acknowledged his debt to Hanson's (1958) critique of the positivist theory/fact dichotomy, he never accepted Hanson's image of observations as "theory-laden." Kuhn's Kantianism is better captured in his remark that his early exposure to Kant was a "revelation" that led him to take seriously the idea of the "synthetic a priori" (1997), which is very close to how Wittgenstein conceived the character of grammatical propositions that constituted the grounds of certainty. Davidson's critique of the "third dogma of empiricism" (1984) incorrectly attributed to Kuhn a kind of Kantian "scheme/content" position, when in fact Kuhn rejected any ontological distinction between theory and fact or scheme and content. What theoretical realism, as embraced by Kuhn, entailed was neither the notion of facts as "theory-laden" nor, as Quine put it, that theories are "underdetermined" by facts. Such phrasings still implied a binary relationship between theory and fact. Kuhn, still embedded in the profession of the philosophy of science, did, understandably, not entirely free himself from the language of the earlier formulations. He realized, however, that like revolutions in science, revolutions in philosophy remain to some extent, at least initially, bound to the language of the conceptual regime against which they are revolting.

The whole language of theory and fact is otiose. There is no general problem to be solved. It is not that the concepts of theory and fact and questions about the relationship between them have no place in scientific practice, or in a philosophical account of that practice, but there is no actual philosophical problem or solution. A philosophical account of science might involve the assertion that science posits domains of facticity that amount to particularized instances of theoretical claims or nascent theories and that what scientists often refer to as theories are, among a number of things, generalized claims about a factual domain or inflated factual statements. In practices such as science, the very use of the terms and distinctions between them are, as Feyerabend insisted, pragmatic. Any statement of a fact requires a conceptual identity, and such concepts are derived from a theoretical repertoire. The philosophical notion of testing theories against an empirical background is a false extrapolation from the internal paradigmatic practices of normal or everyday science. Theories are neither revelations nor mere commitments but arguments, and testing is in the end a matter, within any community of knowledge, of surviving other claims. One might wish to say that theories are tested by their ability to be sustained in the face of alternative or contradictory claims, but at the level of theory, even this language is misleading. For example, while the theory of evolution and creationism (or claims about intelligent design) are often juxtaposed and viewed as contradictory theories, even by someone such as Stephen Jay Gould, they are better viewed as incommensurable, since there is nothing in common between the kinds of things subjected to comparative claims, any more than there is in the case of the duck-rabbit figure. The change is conceptual. To say that creationism and evolution offer different accounts of the origin of human beings is misleading, because the term "human being" in this case refers to two different, incommensurable theoretical concepts. It is not at all like saying that there are contradictory claims about how, historically, the Grand Canyon was formed, when everyone basically agrees, geologically, about what kind of thing the Grand Canyon is. It is somewhat ironic that at the very point at which Kuhn's book was published, a relatively sudden but truly fundamental shift in the history of science was taking place, which was as dramatic and sudden as any related in Kuhn's book. This was the revolution in the concepts of continents and mountains, and the earth as a whole, that was a consequence of the theory of continental drift and the advent of plate tectonics. This transformation of both geology and the "world" offers a graphic illustration of how Kuhn's argument and attending concepts apply.

Many individuals, including Francis Bacon and Benjamin Franklin, had noted that the contours of the earth's continents might indicate that they had once been contiguous. As early as 1900, observations of similarities between the fossil record on different continents as well as evidence of matching geological formations had led some geologists to speculate that the continents had formerly composed one large landmass. By the middle of the twentieth century, however, the idea that the continents may have somehow "drifted," and that a collision had given rise to some of the major mountain chains, was almost unanimously rejected by the normal scientific establishment, particularly in the United States, where data suggesting such drift was less obvious and available. The reigning theory of geological science had been formulated in 1857 by the paleontologist James Hall and presented at the annual meeting of the American Association for the Advancement of Science. This theory, later strongly supported by J. D. Dana, a prominent geologist, mineralogist, and textbook author, claimed that while there were vertical up and down movements of land and sea, there were no horizontal movements. The emergence of major mountain chains was the result of huge depressions, labeled "geosynclines," filling with sediment and exerting downward pressure and, supplemented by heat from the core of the earth, folding and elevating portions of the earth's crust.

In 1858, Antonio Snider-Pelligrini, a French geographer, proposed a specific theory of continental drift based on his maps indicating what might appear as a jigsaw puzzle relationship between the continents of Africa and South America. A more elaborate theory of continental drift was first proposed in 1912 by the German geophysicist and meteorologist Alfred Wegener at a meeting of the German Geological Association. This theory, published in book form in 1915 and translated into English in 1922, claimed that the continents had all been part of what he called

Pangaea, a supercontinent, but that they had *somehow* broken apart and "plowed" through the ocean floor. Neither he nor supporters, such as the eminent geologist Arthur Holmes (who among other things had determined how to estimate the age of the earth by radioactive dating), developed a convincing account of what forces could propel such a movement. And various physics experiments appeared to falsify the speculation. Although the theory was vigorously debated briefly in the 1920s, it was generally criticized strongly and often even ridiculed. When discussed at a meeting of the American Association of Petroleum Geologists in 1926, a professor from the University of Chicago asked, "Can we call geology a science when it [is] possible for such a theory to run wild?" In 1941, a widely used textbook asked "what would furnish the motive power for the breaking up and transporting continental masses," and the authors concluded that "it must be admitted that the cause of crustal deformation is one of the great mysteries of science and can only be discussed in a speculative way" (Longwell et al. 1941, 314). Although the theory of continental movement had gained some favor in Great Britain by the early 1950s, it was largely absent from American journals and especially from textbooks and curricula, and if mentioned at all in classrooms, it was referred to as naïve. As late as 1949, the section "From Geosynclines to Mountains" in a major text noted that the idea that "the first stage in the making of a great mountain system is the development of a geosyncline seems paradoxical. Yet the Appalachian and Rocky Mountain systems, as well as most other great mountain systems of the Earth, began in this way" (Holmes 1949, 102). Despite obvious anomalies, geosyncline theory, as late as 1960, was still presented as "one of the great unifying principles in geology. In many ways its role in geology is similar to that of the theory of evolution which serves to integrate the many branches of biological science. . . . Just as the doctrine of evolution is universally accepted among biologists, so also the geosynclinal origin of the major mountain systems is an established principle in geology" (Clark and Stern 1960, 2). It was well into the 1960s before there was serious reconsideration of the theory, and although a leading textbook published in 1971 acknowledged that the "arguments pro and con are inconclusive," geosyncline theory was still deemed the most persuasive (Foster 1971, 414). However, by 1965, a visible crisis had been emerging in geology, and by the mid-1970s, the "conversion" had begun to take place, and the general weight of opinion had quite dramatically turned in support of the claim that "although not absolutely conclusive, evidence for the theory of continental drift [global tectonics, tectonism] is compelling" (CRM Books 1973, 174). Even though, for another decade, there would still be instances of equivocation, plate tectonics became the preferred concept, and continental motion and the upward thrusting of mountains were explained by volcanic intrusions that spread the ocean floor. In the edition from 1978, Clark and Stern completely reversed themselves and concluded that "the basic principles of the new global tectonics are widely accepted" and "form the basis of what might be called the 'new' historical geology" (v). The basic paradigm shift had occurred with a decade.

If we apply Kuhn's perspective to this case, it certainly fits his account of a transition from normal to revolutionary and back to a new form of normal science and of what it means to speak of scientists seeing, and living in, different worlds. The kind of factual "anomaly" that he posited was evident, for example, in the treatment of the fossil record and the manner in which it was explained away by ad hoc hypotheses such as the possibility of land bridges. But such anomalous facts, which Kuhn had focused on, can begin to call into question another and more important type of fact. Between paradigms there is continuity of many things that we can speak of as facts, but at least two classes of facts are involved. For example, the significance of fossils changed, but a trilobite was still a trilobite. What did change, however, were what we might call theoretical facts. One might say that, after the acceptance of plate tectonics, mountains and continents were in various senses still the same kind of thing for everyday observers and mountain climbers, but for geologists there was a more fundamental sense in which although the words remained the same, both mountains and continents were conceived as different concepts and kinds of things, and consequently what was meant by the "world" had changed. But if you ask a geologist what happened, the answer would likely be that a progressively greater understanding of the world had been achieved. And as Kuhn emphasized, it would be perfectly correct for the scientist to say this within the context of scientific practice, but philosophically, as an interpretation of the practice of science, it did not mean much. There is no need to equivocate with respect to the idea of scientists seeing "different worlds." The world of plate tectonics is not the same as the world of geosynclines.

In his "Postscript" to the second edition of *Structure*, Kuhn focused on narrowing his use of the paradigm concept, but this actually had little to do with the main force of his argument. The core claim was still that the instances in which "scientists themselves would say they share a theory or set of theories," or what Kuhn now preferred to refer to as a "disciplinary matrix," involve "incommensurable viewpoints" representing "different language communities" constituted by "practitioners of a scientific specialty." At the core of these communities are "metaphysical" commitments, beliefs, and values "shared by such groups" who nevertheless can gain access to one another's beliefs through "translation" (1970c, 175, 178.) He now reserved the term "paradigm" for what he had earlier termed "accepted examples" but now referred to as "exemplars" into which students are initiated and trained as they become practitioners and which give concrete meaning to the more general theories and laws that are deemed constitutive of "nature" and that provide criteria of "sameness" in specifying kinds of phenomena. This account of paradigm was even more similar to Wittgenstein's frequent use of the term (*Paradigma* or *Vorbild*) in talking about such things as how children learn colors and the use of color words. Kuhn claimed that this is the heart of the shared "tacit" or "intuitive" knowledge that constitutes scientific practice and that, as Wittgenstein had said, cannot be reduced to or replaced by abstract rules (182–94). He stressed that part of what he was doing in advancing his image of theory was defending the "integrity of perception," or seeing and understanding, as opposed to the dominant philosophical "attempt to analyze perception as an interpretive process, as an unconscious version of what we do after we have perceived" (195). This was, as in the case of Wittgenstein, positing the effective unity of seeing and what is seen and emphasizing that "interpretation begins where perception ends" (198).

Kuhn continued to stress the incommensurability of theories, and paradigms, and the manner in which transitions were a matter of persuasion and conversion, but he also emphasized that this did not imply the impossibility of some communication through translation, but only that there is no "neutral language" and no "neutral algorithm for theory-choice," which is ultimately a "community" affair. In many respects, communication across paradigms is, he suggested, similar to what "the historian of science regularly does (or should) when dealing with out-of-date scientific theories" (198–200). This, however, is a matter of interpretation and is therefore something "parasitic" and different from what it would mean to understand in the sense that one might "go native" and "make it one's own." Philosophy has "no theory-independent way to reconstruct phrases like 'really there'; the notion of a match between the ontology of the theory and its 'real' counterpart in nature" (204, 206). Much of Kuhn's later work involved a continuing struggle with the concept of incommensurability, which he, like Feyerabend, explicitly recognized as at the heart of his argument.

Kuhn's first account of incommensurability was simply that there is no common measure of two things. This did not mean, however, that they were incomparable. Despite what the proverb says, apples and oranges can in fact be compared, but we might say that they are incommensurable. His point was that there is no scientific method for assessing competing theories, as there might be for assessing competing hypotheses within a certain theoretical structure, but his stronger point was that there is no neutral observation language that transcends theoretical paradigms. What his early formative encounter with Aristotle's work had suggested was that although Aristotle used (what could be translated as) the same words as Newton, such as "motion," the concepts to which the words referred were different. This is what led him to conclude, "in a sense I am unable to explicate further, that the proponents of competing paradigms practice their trades in different worlds" and "see different things" (1970c, 150). Kuhn never offered a perfectly clear statement of how scientists could live in and see different worlds, but it was partly a problem of the language with which he was struggling. He spoke of a change in paradigms as involving a "displacement of the conceptual network through which scientists view the world" (102), but this kind of statement still seemed to imply that a theory was a perspective on given phenomena, which was exactly the kind of claim he ultimately wanted to avoid. His point was better stated when he said that theories told "the scientist about entities that nature does and does not contain and about the ways in which those entities behave," and thus not only are they constitutive of scientific practice, but there is a "sense in which they are constitutive of nature as well," that is, how the scientist conceives of nature (109–110). He claimed that scientists come to "see the world differently" and thus are "responding to a different world," but this statement could still be construed as ambiguous and even contradictory. He suggested that "the historian of science may be tempted to exclaim that when paradigms change, the world changes with them," and that "we may want to say that after a revolution scientists are responding to a different world" (111). Referring to Jastrow (or Wittgenstein), he said that it was similar to the manner in which ducks become rabbits. But there was actually no need for him to qualify his point. In science, the world, in the first instance, is not represented and interpreted, but seen and presented. But at times, however, he continued to suggest that there was a separation between seeing and the kind of thing that was seen and that "the scientist sees differently from the way he had seen before" (115). This implied more an interpretation than a "perception," but, like Wittgenstein, Kuhn wanted to distinguish between observations and "interpretations of observations." Some data become reinterpreted, but interpretations presuppose a paradigm, and some things, like phlogiston, simply disappeared and were replaced by other facts that "had not existed at all." After a "conversion," "the data themselves had changed" and that is "one of the senses in which we may want to say that after a revolution scientists work in a different world" (135, 141).

Part of the difficulty here, which made Kuhn sensitive to charges of relativism, was one of sorting out the uses of the word "world." When we talk abstractly about the relationship between language and the world, we are really not talking about anything unless we place the term "world" in some first-order discursive context such as natural science or common sense. Unless we privilege some discourse as a basic observation language, it is meaningless to say that the world remains the same between scientific revolutions. The philosopher/historian is not in the business of science, but in the business of clarifying the meaning of what the scientist says, and when scientific theories change, what scientists mean by the "world" changes. Wittgenstein noted that the only difference between the idealist and realist in teaching a child the meaning of "chair" is the "battle cry" (*PP*, 2:339; *Z*, 414), and the same is true with respect to a choice between saying (with respect to a transition between paradigms) that the world changed and saying that it did not. Kuhn, like Wittgenstein, viewed language and the world as autonomous. Kuhn said that "the world is not invented nor constructed" (*RSS*, 101–2). The working scientist may be inclined to say that the world had not changed, but rather that new discoveries about the nature of the world had been achieved; but that is the difference in the perspectives of the scientist and the philosopher, which accounts for why scientists and other practitioners often have trouble understanding and coming to grips with Kuhn's work. There is a fundamental difference between engaging in science (religion, politics, everyday life, and so on) and describing and explaining it, and it would in fact be odd for those engaged in such practices to attempt to readjust themselves in light of philosophical claims, just as it would be odd for the philosopher or any social inquirer to attempt to give an account of a practice in the language of the practice. Winch had sorted out this issue in detail, and Michael Oakeshott (1975) had emphasized the differences, and the practical as well as cognitive relationship, between the language of "doing" and the language of interpreting a "doing" (Gunnell 2011, ch. 2). After *Structure*, Kuhn began to devote less time to talking about science than to talking about the problems of what is involved in a philosophical inquiry into such a language region and about such things as the nature of concepts and the difference between understanding and interpretation.

Although language and the world are different, and autonomous, concepts, the world only appears in linguistic presentations of the world. As Wittgenstein said, "the limit of language manifests itself in the impossibility of describing the fact that corresponds to (is the translation of) a sentence without simply repeating the sentence" (*CV*, 3). Kuhn argued that there is no formula that could explain the "conversion" involved in moving from one paradigm to another. It might be precipitated by a person such as Galileo, Newton, or Einstein, but, as in the case of continental drift, it might not be associated with any single individual. In his later work he did attempt further explication. He claimed that such change in meaning involved, as he had already emphasized in *Structure*, not simply one concept but, as Wittgenstein stressed in *On Certainty*, its place in a system of concepts that constituted the theoretical context and the disciplinary matrix.

The fact that Kuhn had few philosophy graduate students may speak to his personality, but it also may speak to the state of philosophy at that time. While at Princeton, he was invited to be a member of the Institute of Advanced Studies, where he had contact with individuals such as Clifford Geertz and where Quentin Skinner was a visiting scholar. This prompted a deeper inquiry into conceptual and historiographical issues, which he attempted to apply in his study of *Black-Body Theory and Quantum Discontinuity, 1894–1912* (1978). This was in part an attempt to demonstrate that Max Planck viewed his work as a contribution to classical physics rather than, as Kuhn argued, the revolution that it actually entailed, indicating how, from the perspective of scientists as well as many historians of science, revolutions remain "invisible." Kuhn moved to MIT in 1979, and, in 1980, he critically reviewed a volume of essays from 1976 on methodology revolving around Lakatos's formulation. In earlier comments on Lakatos's project, he had said that "what Lakatos conceives as history is not history at all but philosophy fabricating examples," and he recognized that sometimes "history done for the sake of philosophy is often scarcely history at all" (1980, 183). What he was getting at was not that there was not a philosophical purpose for pursuing history. The purpose, as in the case of Wittgenstein, was to achieve clarity about the past, which entailed that the philosopher looking at the past of science was in fact a historian and engaged in that form of inquiry. The volume under review concluded with remarks on the essays by Feyerabend. Kuhn judged Feyerabend's comments as sometimes "brilliant" but unrelievedly negative and amounting to an argument for the "impossibility" of the "entire enterprise" of constructing a "theory of science" (191). But while Feyerabend had once misunderstood Kuhn, Kuhn now misunderstood Feyerabend. The type of "method" that Feyerabend was criticizing was precisely what Kuhn was also arguing against. What Kuhn meant by a "theory" in this instance was a historical generalization about the character of scientific change. It did not resemble the normative methodology that Lakatos wished to impose as a framework for rationally reconstructing research programs. If there was a difference between Kuhn and Feyerabend at this point, it really amounted to little more than the fact that Feyerabend, in his own excursions into the history of science and his emphasis on the myth of a scientific method, had become even more particularistic than Kuhn, who still wanted to say something general about the character of scientific change. Kuhn's "theory" consisted of little more than Wittgensteinian or Weberian ideal-types for representing scientific practice, and it was never offered as an image of how science evolves, or should evolve, in some philosophically rational manner.

From 1980 to the early 1990s, Kuhn devoted himself to refining certain aspects of his argument, but his basic claims did not change. He began to stress the "holistic" character of changes in meaning and the "way in which words and phrases attach to nature" in terms of not simply the criteria of application but "the set of objects and situations to which those words and phrases" refer and the difference in "taxonomic categories" (2000, 28–32). He also began to emphasize that incommensurability did not entail the impossibility of translation, as well as the difference between translation and interpretation and how the latter involved conceiving of the "historian as an interpreter and language teacher."

Although he valued the perspective of Charles Taylor on interpretation and the human sciences, he maintained that Taylor made a mistake in assuming that the language of natural science was fixed and neutral and could serve as a contrast model for thinking about social phenomena. He concluded that "traditional meaning theory is bankrupt" and that his concern now was more with "language change" than with models of normal and revolutionary science (2000, 37, 43, 45, 57). He noted that early on his reading of the works of individuals such as Max Weber and Ernst Cassirer on the social and human sciences had provided him with a sense of what he had hoped to do in describing natural science. They, however, as in the case of Winch and Taylor, had viewed natural science from the perspective of the positivist image. He began to talk about a projected book in which he would deal with this range of issues and with how the problem with the history and philosophy of science continued to be the persistence of the old image of science and how the emerging change in the image of science had been effected by philosophy rather than the study of history.

In 1984, Kuhn, reflecting on his book on Planck, said that it was the "most fully realized illustration of the concept of history of science basic to my historical publications" (231). He claimed that his method of reconstructing the past was based on a general neo-Kantian approach and the work of Koyré. What he meant by "neo-Kantian" was, again, not a return to a scheme/content distinction, but accepting an important difference between the language of the investigation and the language of the subject matter and avoiding, insofar as possible, confusing what was represented with the mode of representation. In this case, it meant not reading the history of science from the standpoint of the present state of science, but instead recovering past concepts and modes of thought and, in the case of Planck, demonstrating how different those modes might be from the ideas to which they gave rise. The continuing historiographical problem, however, was how to achieve clarity about such ideas. His general view was that one "must approach the generation that held them as the anthropologist approaches an alien culture," which requires finding the "categories" to "map experience" that are different than those the investigator might typically possess, that is, avoiding "Whig" history or the kind of "ethnocentric" attitude that leads to a "suppression" of a proper understanding of the subject matter on its own terms but yet may make it possible, as in the case of his study of Planck, to understand the subject matter better than it understood itself (246). There is nothing to suggest that at this point Kuhn was reading Wittgenstein, but he was certainly on the same wavelength with respect to the concepts of understanding, interpretation, and critical assessment.

While Kuhn attempted to explicate the concept of incommensurability further in terms of a taxonomic difference, he did not relinquish the claim that different taxonomies yield different conceptions of the world, as opposed to the arguments of Kripke and, at that point, Putnam, who propounded the idea of essential natural kinds that would remain rigidly designated despite changes in terminology, which was a type of argument that Wittgenstein had also specifically challenged. He argued that the difference in "lexicons" in the course of the history of science ultimately bars mutual access to different possible worlds. For Kuhn, taxonomic reclassification was at the heart of revolutions and the incommensurability of paradigms, but it was at this point that he made very explicit that the role of the philosopher/historian was both to understand and to interpret a paradigm. This required penetrating the "lexicon" of a past paradigm and understanding and learning it in order to clarify it and render it in the language of the interpreter. Although incommensurability, as Kuhn had always argued, did not entail that some degree of translation between theories was impossible, the possibility of such translation was limited. Different world-visions or presentations are involved in different cultures as well as in different configurations of normal science. When there is a revolution in science, there is a "redubbing" and a new taxonomy that is more than a change in words. It is a conceptual change and a reordering of the kinds of things that are believed to constitute the world and their relationship to one another (2000).

During the last years of his life, Kuhn continued to accentuate the fact that "philosophical goals prompted my move to history," and it was on philosophy that he focused. This was in part to address what he saw as an unwelcome "byproduct" of what was becoming the new image of science based on an investigation of "scientific life," which his approach had contributed to initiating. What had begun to engage his attention was exactly how a consensus in science was both achieved and transformed by "negotiation" and how this could be conceived in a manner that was compatible with the assumption that science could reach "true or probable conclusions about the nature of reality." What he specifically wanted to combat was the claim of some, such as proponents of the "strong pro-

gram" in the sociology of knowledge, that scientific knowledge was simply a product of interest, power, and authority, and amounted to little
more than the "belief of the winners" (1992, 4, 8–9). His answer was very
similar to Wittgenstein's argument in *On Certainty*. He argued that there
was what might be considered an "Archimedean platform" of judgment,
but that it "moves with time and changes with community and sub-com-
munity, with culture and subculture." This did not mean that there was a
lack of reasoned discussion. General values and criteria, such as simplic-
ity and scope, remain operative, but the criteria of application differed as
theories changed. The philosophical idea of coming closer to the truth
or reality had no real content, and "the Archimedean platform outside
of history, outside of time and space, is gone beyond recall." A process of
"comparative evaluation is all there is," and scientific development is like
"Darwinian evolution" (12–14). He suggested that, like biology, scientific
development involves "speciation" and an "evolutionary tree" of changing rational belief punctuated by revolutions (15–19). Kuhn's increased
emphasis on meaning seemed closely related to Wittgenstein, but he
did not directly specify any such connection. It is reasonable to assume
that this work reflected to some extent the conversations at Princeton
with individuals such as Skinner and his partial sympathy with Taylor's
argument, but it is interesting that Kuhn did not adopt the mentalistic
view of meaning embraced by individuals such as Skinner and Taylor.
He never speculated, or even raised the issue, of what was in a scientist's
"mind" apart from what the scientist said and did.

What Kuhn focused on was what he came to speak of as "kind-
concepts," which were very similar to what Wittgenstein spoke of as
"concept-words" typically represented by nouns, but yet very different
from the natural kinds posited by Kripke and Putnam. His "theory of
meaning" assumed, however, that humans have neural capacities for dis-
criminating kinds of things and consequently come to possess a "lexicon"
or what could be spoken of as a "mental module" or linguistic domain
"in which members of a speech community store their kind terms." He
pointedly distinguished between words and concepts and noted that
"kind-concepts need not have names, but in linguistically endowed
populations they mostly do." In instances of scientific change, there is
"change in concepts and their names," and consequently there is a change
in the scientific lexicon. In many respects, this was an extension of his
earlier discussion of exemplars. A person is taught kind-terms, which

are also "learned in use," and in this process one not only gains knowledge of concepts and the properties to which they apply but learns how they are "projectable" and allow generalizations of various types. Kuhn stressed that this is a matter of "convention rather than fact." Individuals may share the same kind-terms yet diverge with respect the particulars of usage. This may be a matter of "polysemy," or applying a "name to different concepts," which can be resolved semantically, but there may also be a conceptual divergence that requires resolution with respect to what a word actually refers to and what will survive in the lexicon of the scientific community. In the case of a conflict regarding what concept a word will refer to, either one concept replaces the other or "speciation" results in different scientific specialties and communities. He continued to suggest that it is not "inappropriate to say that the members of the two communities live in different worlds" and that the task of the historian is to describe those worlds, which requires that the historian must be, in effect, bilingual, that is, must be involved in both understanding and interpretation (1993, 315–16).

Kuhn continued to warn of the danger of confusing what was represented with the means of representation and claimed that the historian is less a translator than a language learner, because full translation between lexicons is often not possible. He noted again that in order to interpret and communicate, the historian must become a "language teacher" with respect to conveying the meaning of kind-terms and constructing a narrative. The great danger was that of using the names characteristic of a contemporary field when talking about concepts from the past—and this included even the names of the sciences themselves—because what can be expressed in one language may not be possible in another (1993, 318–21). Although a lexicon need not create the same "expectations" among individual members of a community, the "*structure*" must be shared or communication will break down, and without a "common culture," incommensurability will result. He suggested that the relationship between the individual and the group is similar to the difference in evolutionary biology between an individual organism and the species. He claimed that "science is intrinsically a community activity" and that the community is, like a gene pool, an autonomous entity and not a mere aggregate of individuals (1993, 326–29). This was in many respects much like Wittgenstein's account of what was involved in sharing conventions.

Kuhn never relinquished sensitivity to the question of how he could believe in scientific truth, but at the same time write a history of how scientific truth varies historically. His answer, as he had implied earlier, was rooted in the difference between the perspectives of the scientist and the historian. He insisted that science is cognitive and gains knowledge of nature, but he denied "all meaning to claims that successive scientific beliefs become more and more probable or better and better approxima-tions to the truth" and that "truth" refers to a "relation between beliefs and a putatively mind-independent or 'external' world." There is, for example, no metric for comparing Aristotle and Newton. A lexicon is a product of "tribal experience," and its "logical status, like that of word-meanings in general, is that of convention. Each lexicon makes possible a correspond-ing form of life within which the truth or falsity of propositions may be both claimed and rationally justified, but the justification of lexicons or of lexical change can only be pragmatic," that is, its foundations are inter-nal to the lexicon. Kuhn again described himself as working within "rela-tivized Kantian categories," but he believed it was useful to replace what he had referred to as "theoretical terms" with Hempel's reformulated des-ignation of those that were "antecedently available," which would help clarify, for example, how lexicons are learned and transmitted and how kind-concepts and exemplars come to constitute the "world in which members of a culture live." He continued to maintain that scientific prac-tice is best described as how "puzzle-solving" within an accepted lexicon leads to knowledge of nature, but that because this involves an impor-tant sociological dimension, "those who proclaim that no interest-driven practice can properly be identified as the rational pursuit of knowledge make a profound and consequential mistake" (1993, 330–31, 333–34, 339).

Although challenges to Kuhn's arguments are often based on claims about continuities between scientific theories, they typically miss the point. Kuhn was not claiming that the shift between paradigms lacked continuity at all levels of description. Kuhn maintained that he was a "convinced believer in scientific progress" and in what scientists believed to be true about the world. This is not really such a schizophrenic posi-tion as one might assume. Certainly people potentially have the capac-ity to reflect on their own beliefs and to find a language in which to do so. His perspective fitted the extent to which science can be construed, like biological evolution, as a "unidirectional and irreversible process" in which later theories reflected their capacity to survive and do better in the operative "puzzle-solving" environment of normal science. But it is another thing to claim that theories could philosophically be construed as "somehow a better representation of what nature is really like" in the sense, for example, that we evaluate an advance in the cartography of a particular region of the world (1970a, 206). He remained, however, somewhat circumspect about the practical relationship between his enterprise and the conduct of scientific inquiry. He claimed that in some respects "the normative and descriptive are inextricably mixed" and that while what he had presented was "a theory about the nature of science, the theory has consequences for the way in which scientists should behave if their enterprise is to succeed" as well as for how other parallel historical and philosophical enterprises might be approached. He did, however, give short shrift to these issues and to what exactly this might involve (208–9). And it was appropriate to give it minimal attention, because there is no philosophical answer.

Although he specifically mentioned his interest in Benjamin Whorf's account of the "effect of language on world view" (vi), the Wittgensteinian character of Kuhn's analysis is much more pronounced. Even Whorf's much maligned and misinterpreted position is not best stated in terms of an idealist account of language determining the world, but rather as language embodying an ontology, which accords well with Wittgenstein's position. Just how difficult it was to characterize Kuhn's book and judge its place in terms of the issue of the relationship between the philosophy and practice of science is evident in the commendatory blurb on the revised edition. The commentator stated that "since Kuhn does not permit truth to be a criterion of scientific theories, he would presumably not claim his own theory to be true." This statement, however, represents the persistent tendency to misconstrue Kuhn's argument, still so evident in Errol Morris's rendition. These were, significantly, the comments of a scientific journalist who was reading Kuhn as if Kuhn were a participant observer attempting to describe the activity of science from the perspective of the scientist. For Kuhn, truth is not a criterion or object, but an evaluative term with wide-ranging criteria of application. The criteria for judging scientific theories are the claims that scientists deem as worthy of being referred to as true. The statement also reflects the fallacy of assuming that to claim that the criteria of truth differ in various contexts and that theories are incommensurable is somehow self-refuting, such as what is putatively the case with what is much discussed

by philosophers as the liar's paradox. But as Wittgenstein pointed out
in several instances, this so-called paradox or contradiction does not
take into account how and where the words are used. In his remarks
on the foundations of mathematics, Wittgenstein continually stressed
the difference between how mathematicians might treat a contradiction
and how it might be treated from the standpoint of an anthropologist
(e.g., *RFM*, 192). In the case of Kuhn, we are dealing with the difference
between the claim of a scientist and the claim of the historian of science.
If Kuhn can be construed as offering a theory about scientific change,
it is certainly not a "theory" in the sense that Kuhn used the term when
describing the practice of science, although such a theory was involved
in what he took to be the nature of social phenomena, such as those
involved in the practice of science. If one considered his claims to be
true, it would be in the sense that any historian might claim to describe
a historical pattern in some human practice, but what Kuhn did was, like
Wittgenstein, to return the criteria of scientific truth to the practices in
which there were criteria for its application and take it away from the
province of philosophical abstraction.

The truth-claims that Kuhn advanced were about science and not
the world. In doing so, he, as well as Winch and Feyerabend, exemplified Wittgenstein's dictum that, in an important sense, philosophy leaves
everything as it is. But even though philosophizing, or any kind of social
inquiry, does not, as such, transform its object, this, as Kuhn recognized,
does not mean that they cannot make judgments about that object and
even have an impact upon it. This, however, raises the question of judgments, and this requires confronting the difference between judgments
in a practice and judgments about a practice, which brings us back to
the issue of commensurability—and to the concept of certainty. If one
wished to seek a philosophical explication of the argument that Kuhn
struggled so hard to make in support of his philosophy of science, it
would be Wittgenstein's account of meaning and interpretation, and
especially the treatment of conceptual change in *On Certainty*.

WITTGENSTEIN ON THE MOON
Certainty, Truth, & Value

> A characteristic of theorists of the past cultural era was wanting to find the a-priori where there wasn't one. (*PPO*, 89)
> You cannot lead people to the good; you can only lead them to some place or other. (*CV*, 5)
> Our motto might be: "Let us not be bewitched." (*Z*, 690)
>
> —WITTGENSTEIN

KNOWLEDGE AND CERTAINTY

The reason that so many commentators still believe that the work of Wittgenstein and Kuhn inhibits inquiry is because these commentators are, for various reasons, in search of certainty. But this is not simply the certainty that scientists profess regarding the results of their research, the certainty that religious advocates proclaim, the certainty of the values and ideologies pursued by political actors, or the vast number of certainties in terms of which we conduct our daily lives. The worries about certainty as a general proposition arise from within philosophy and its search for a form of certainty that both exceeds and grounds the actual practices of life and provides a basis for assessing them. But these worries sometimes spill over into the activities of individuals such as Errol Morris and into fields such as the social sciences, which turn to philosophy in search of the authority to gain purchase either within their field or for a basis of

judging their subject matter. Wittgenstein believed that the proper ethical stance is to reject these metaphysical images of certainty, because such
a rejection forces us both to deal with the particularities of judgment in
various contexts and to avoid searching for a mythical certainty beyond
doubt and experiencing the debilitating fear of a doubt beyond certainty.
Both Wittgenstein and Kuhn argued that the foundations of our practices reside in the practices themselves, but that these foundations tend
to change—and can be changed. What, to a contemporary reader, might
first appear as Wittgenstein's poor choice of a claim that was certain and
indubitable, that is, that no one had ever been, or could be, on the moon,
actually demonstrates his principal argument: that even our most basic
concepts and beliefs, which form the structure of our *Weltbild*, are subject
to alteration and that the only common feature among such transitions
is, as Kuhn also recognized, some type of persuasion. There are, and have
been, many ways to characterize and approach Wittgenstein's *On Certainty*—as a new form of foundationalism, as an epistemological treatise,
and so on, but such general characterizations distract from the comprehensive thematic character of the text.

At the core of Wittgenstein's remarks was the claim that it is only
"within a language-game" and a particular practice that certainty and
doubt are meaningful concepts. His argument, in effect, abolishes the
metaphysics of realism, idealism, and skepticism. These are the "propositions that one comes back to again and again as if bewitched," but that we
should "expunge from philosophical language." Claims such as "there are
physical objects" masquerade as hypothetical empirical propositions for
which philosophy claims to provide, or deny, support. He urged that we
"forget this transcendent certainty," such as that sometimes attributed to
formal logic, because "everything descriptive of a language-game is part
of logic." Even the "meaning of a word is a kind of employment of it,"
that is, a matter of "what we learn when the word is incorporated into our
language." These uses change, and when "we imagine the facts otherwise
than as they are, certain language-games lose some of their importance,
while others become important." In this way "there is an alteration—a
gradual one" and "when language-games change, then there is a change
in concepts, and with the concepts the meaning of words change."

We can say that the "test of a statement belongs to logic," but only
in the sense that the "*truth* of certain empirical propositions belongs to
our frame of reference [*Besugssystem*]." When one uses words such as

"certain," "know," "see," and "doubt," there is typically no question about their general connotation, meaning, or function, but there can be a great deal of ambiguity, difference, and conflict, with respect to the criteria of application. Wittgenstein argued that when G. E. Moore claimed indisputable knowledge of the reality of his hands or of the fact that the earth existed before he was born, he was only stating his "unshakeable conviction" and did not prove anything about what is real. Wittgenstein recognized, however, that in calling attention to such affirmations, Moore was, at least inadvertently, making an important point. What in many cases might appear as a "hypothesis" is really often a claim that functions as "a foundation for research and action" and that is "isolated from doubt" and normally "lies apart from the route travelled by inquiry." A person might, as Cavell pointed out to Morris, be able, through persuasion or even intimidation, to "convert" someone to such a foundational belief, but this "would be a conversion of a special kind," which is unlike convincing an individual of the truth of a particular factual claim. The individual "would be brought to look at the world in a different way," or, maybe more accurately stated, to see a different world (1–92).

At the time Wittgenstein was writing, it seemed reasonable to suggest that experience and learning would incorporate the basic belief that no one had ever been on the moon (just as it was assumed at that time that the continents were fixed on the earth's crust), but such an aspect of a general "picture of the world" (*Weltbild*) is not like a proposition gained by an assessment of its empirical accuracy. It is instead part of "the inherited background against which I distinguish between true and false." Such a picture of the world might even be construed as a "mythology" or as similar to the "rules of a game learned in the course of playing it rather than learning explicit rules." It would be as if some propositions, which might take "the form of empirical propositions, were hardened and functioned as channels" which contained others that were more "fluid." But the relationship might be altered, and what was once hardened might become fluid. Although "the mythology may change back into a state of flux, the river-bed of thoughts may shift," it is necessary to "distinguish between the movement of the waters on the river-bed and the shifts of the bed itself; though there is not a sharp division of the one from the other." A "proposition may be treated at one time as something to test by experience, at another time as a rule of testing," just as "the bank of that river consists partly of hard rock, subject to no alternation or only an imperceptible one, partly of sand, which now in one place now in another gets washed away, or deposited." What Wittgenstein continually stressed was that a person's "convictions do form a system, a structure" that is "so anchored that I cannot touch it" and in which "all testing, all confirmation and disconfirmation of a hypothesis takes place." It is the "system" that is the "essence of what we call an argument," and it is "not so much the point of departure, as the element in which arguments have their life" (93–105).

The revision of such basic assumptions is not unusual, and only philosophers or practices influenced by philosophy would likely be led to ask whether there is any such thing as "objective truth" and similar questions posed outside any context. Wittgenstein claimed that what counts as objective truth is based on "an ungrounded way of acting," which "is as sure a thing for me as any grounds I could give for it." Moore's claim to know various things with certainty was simply a reflection of the fact "that some of these propositions must be solid for us," just as the rules of arithmetic are. Even "the game of doubting itself presupposes certainty" about something that "stands fast for me," and "we use judgments as principles of judgment." When Moore claimed that he knew various things without doubt, he was "really enumerating a lot of empirical propositions which we affirm without special testing" and which have "a peculiar logical role in the system of our empirical propositions" and are typically learned but not arrived at "as a result of investigation" (106–38).

Wittgenstein claimed that at the heart of a practice are not simply general rules, which are always porous, but "examples" in which the "practice has to speak for itself." What one is taught are "*judgments* and their connection with other judgments," and it is "a *totality* of judgments" and "a whole system of propositions" that we take as obvious and come to believe and in which "consequences and premises give one another *mutual* support." A child, for example, is initiated into a "system" of "facts and beliefs" that are "held fast by what lies around" and that are prior to particular doubts. Such "judgments themselves characterize the way I judge, characterize the nature of judgment," and "not-doubting" is "part of judging" and forms "part of our *method* of doubt and enquiry." It is only in retrospect that one may come to "*discover*," and reflect upon, the foundational propositions, which are the "axis" on which particular judgments turn. "In order to make a mistake," a person "must already judge in conformity" with others, and, in a similar manner, "doubt comes *after* belief." One initially learns and accepts a great deal on the basis of various forms of "human authority," and this "world-picture" is the "substratum of all my inquiring and asserting" and not really "subject to testing." Although "the difficulty is to realize the groundlessness of our believing," even in science, some of our "empirical propositions" actually function as "a norm of description" and constitute our "world-picture," which is not a "hypothesis" to be tested by the "facts" of science, but rather is the basis on which one comes to "*learn* the sciences" and in terms of which one acts "with *complete* certainty" (139–74).

The problem with the use of phrase "I know," in the case of Moore's assertions, was that it was spoken as if it were a report that is no more subject to doubt than the statement "I am in pain." There are, however, claims for which one has justified belief, and "at some point one has to pass from explanation to mere description" of how things are or what we assume is certain and conforms to "reality" and the "facts." At such a point, "justification comes to an end." As opposed to a claim to know something, which is defeasible, a claim of certainty expresses "complete conviction, the total absence of doubt, and thereby we seek to convince other people." To be "objectively certain" is to possess evidence that "we *accept* as sure" in the course of "acting without doubt," but outside some particular context, the concepts of objectivity and subjectivity have little meaning. We use terms such as "true" and "false" to refer to what does or does not correspond to the "facts," but what is involved in such correspondence is simply that what is true is what we cannot find any reason to speak against. Although justification and "giving grounds" come to an end, that end is not propositions based on a special kind of "*seeing*," but on "our *acting*, which lies at the bottom of the language-game" and which provides a "picture" that is beyond true and false. It is this that "seems to be fixed, and it is removed from the traffic. It is shunted onto an unused siding" that "gives us our way of looking at things, and our researches their form," and constitutes what belongs to "the *scaffolding* of our thoughts" (175–212).

Although holistic, "our 'empirical propositions' do not form a homogeneous mass." In the case of our foundational propositions, despite their linguistic form, "the idea of 'agreement with reality' does not have any clear application," because they function as the standard of reality. And what a person holds fast to "is not *one* proposition but a nest of propositions." In 1950, it was assumed that no one had "ever been on the moon" and that the continents did not move. These were part of the common "manner of judging, and therefore of acting." These were not things about which it made sense to say that one "knew" in the sense in which that term is often used, because it was simply, for whatever reason or training, what one believed and what provided the basis for other specific claims to knowledge, which might prove wrong. It was in the case of such propositions that one could say, "I have arrived at the rock bottom of my convictions. And one might almost say that these foundation-walls are carried by the whole house." It is simply that "at the foundation of well-founded belief lies belief that is not founded." Our empirical propositions may form a hierarchy, but in the end, it is a matter of propositions all the way down (213–53).

Wittgenstein once again stressed, however, that, despite what might seem to be the solidity of various systems of belief, "a language-game does change with time," but changing a person's *Weltbild*, that is, what one has learned in school or what people of a different culture might believe, "would happen through a kind of *persuasion*" (*Überredung*) and might happen dramatically and quickly. Although many such beliefs are incommensurable, and consequently experiments and experience often can never really "*give the lie*" to a system of belief, it is quite possible that we "may change our whole way of looking at things." This amounts to a new "'empirical foundation' for our assumptions" and illustrates the fact that "we belong to a community which is bound together by science and education" (254–98).

Sometimes he spoke of foundational assumptions as basic empirical propositions, but sometimes he was "inclined to believe that not everything that has the form of an empirical proposition *is* one," by which he again meant that it is not a hypothesis for which there are criteria for testing and that in such an instance "rule and empirical proposition merge into one another." He claimed that "the lack of sharpness *is* that of the boundary between *rule* and empirical proposition," between a "norm of description" and a particular description, but this is in part because, as opposed to what he had said in the *Tractatus*, "the concept 'proposition' itself is not a sharp one." He now claimed that the word "proposition" can stand for quite different kinds of concepts. Although at any particular time and place there are, in practical situations, criteria for what it is reasonable to believe, what people ultimately "consider reasonable or unreasonable alters."

What haunted these remarks, however, was not simply the question of whether there were philosophical grounds for assessing judgments within a practice, but whether there were grounds for one practice judging another, for judging from, so to speak, the outside. He asked if there is any "objective" basis for deciding, for example, between those who believe the creation story in the Bible and those who believe that it has been proven false by science. What is involved in such instances is not a contradiction, which requires some common ground of dispute, but a conflict between different propositions that "meet" but are respectively held "exempt from doubt." There is no philosophical basis for adjudicating such an issue. He noted that it even "belongs to the logic of our scientific investigations that certain things are *in deed* not doubted," because they are "the hinges" on which other propositions turn, and "if I want the door to turn, the hinges must stay put." There is "doubting and non-doubting behavior," but, he reiterated, "there is the first only if there is the second." To say that "I know" is usually to express certainty that is *"comfortable,"* as opposed to "struggling" to reach the point of comfort associated with a "form of life" in which there is "something that lies beyond justified or unjustified; as it were, as something animal." Wittgenstein asked if this ultimately entailed that "knowledge is related to decision" and if our social and moral values are simply matters of choice. His answer was that these are less a matter of decision, in the typical use of that term, than the fact that the "absence of doubt belongs to the essence of the language-game" and that "knowledge is in the end based on acknowledgement." He noted that "it might interest a philosopher," or at least "one who can think for himself," to read what he had said, because even if his remarks had "hit the mark only rarely, a philosopher would recognize the targets" (299–388). So we might ask at this point, what, exactly, were these targets?

The basic targets were metaphysical doctrines, but what is often misunderstood in reading his remarks and what has led to the charge of relativism is the assumption that he was claiming that judgment is without grounds or foundations. His point was, however, really quite the opposite. Most judgments are not fragile but deeply entrenched. The problem is that both within a practice and between practices there are occasionally competing but incommensurable grounds of judgment, which philosophy, or any other form of social inquiry, cannot arbitrate by fiat. His target was the dogmas of metaphysics that professed to establish such grounds. If we take his argument as confronting us with the problem of relativism, it is a distinctly philosophical problem with little practical import. It is a problem generated by the fear of losing what metaphysics had promised. It is not a problem *in* science or any other concrete practice. Despite internal conflicts and transformation in belief in a field such as science, practitioners are not driven to seek a standard of truth that lies beyond that which characterizes their practice. It is philosophers and social theorists who are agitated, and the problem arises from philosophy's relationship to these practices. The foundations that Wittgenstein was denying were those that lie outside any concrete realm of discourse. He was not denying that philosophy could or should add its voice to the discussion, and he was not at all reticent to add his voice to, for example, the conversations of mathematics, psychology, and anthropology. Beyond enhancing clarity, it was not, however, clear what philosophy could contribute, but philosophy, or any other form of social inquiry, is seldom in a position to exercise persuasion. This is precisely what drives the search for the transcendental and spawns attempts to move beyond persuasion—and beyond language. Such seductive hopes underlie whole academic enterprises such as scientific realism and critical social theory. Maybe someone such as Plato or Marx was also seduced by the transcendental siren, but in such cases, there may have been more reason to believe in the persuasive force of such claims. Contemporary academic critical theory or the vestiges of metaphysics in the philosophy of science may seek to assure us that there is a "real world" out there and that even if we cannot immediately see it, its existence is demonstrated by the success of science in manipulating nature. But it is clear that the manipulation of both nature and society has often been accomplished on the basis of what we might today consider to be false beliefs.

Wittgenstein's constant point was simply that "our knowledge forms an enormous system. And only within this system has a particular bit the value we give it." And some of those "bits" function as "foundations" of action and thought within the language-game. It would be misleading to describe Wittgenstein as offering a new form of philosophical foundationalism or to characterize him as an immanent foundationalist, even if such phrasing might in some ways be descriptive of his argument. We do not begin by formulating such propositions. We are trained to accept them. As Wittgenstein noted, per Goethe, "in the beginning was the deed." What Moore spoke of as what he knew was, however, not like what "know" means when "used in ordinary life," but instead it was a statement by a philosopher about the general grounds of knowledge. This is what Wittgenstein referred to as "fishy." When a contemporary philosopher such as Searle says that if you do not believe in the correspondence theory of truth and that it is objectively possible to demonstrate the existence of an external world—try falling off a cliff—he is simply doing what Moore did. We tend to be "often bewitched by a word" such as "know" and to assume that such a performative utterance validates what is asserted, but simply to assert or repeat certainties, such as "I have two hands," does not justify claims about the existence of the world any more than "12 x 12 = 144" demonstrates the truth of mathematics. These are moves within a game in which "something must be taught as a foundation." The kind of "doubt that doubted everything would not be a doubt," because "every language-game is based on words 'and objects' being recognized again. We learn with the same inexorability that this is a chair as that 2 x 2 = 4." In the end, "certainty resides in the language-game" rather than in either correspondence with a hypothetical "world" or a state of mind (379–457).

General doubting or skepticism as a basic stance of investigation simply leads to a kind of infinite regress, where one would need to "investigate the investigation" and so on. But no practice is actually based on such a stance. And focusing on a mental state such as belief and other "psychological terms merely distracts from the thing that really matters," that is, understanding the practices at issue. From the very beginning, "when a child learns language it learns at the same time what is to be investigated and what is not," and in general, "we learn first the stability of things as the norm, which is then subject to alteration." Language emerged from practices associated with the basic human form of life and "did not emerge from some kind of ratiocination," and children are initiated into language and a conception of the world by doing things and being taught to do things. The language-game does not rest on some kind of special knowledge about, for example, the existence of abstract entities such as "physical objects." And "the possibility of knowledge about physical objects cannot be proved by the protestations of those who believe that they have such knowledge." Our foundational judgments have "the character of a rule." One might ask how, on "specific grounds," doubt is introduced, but there is no general answer. Doubt comes into the picture in particular situations. Children do not enter the world as congenital skeptics but quite the opposite. It is necessary to "look at the practice of language" to see how doubt actually enters, but this presupposes that one already "trusts something" and that "*as a rule* some empirical judgment or other must be beyond doubt" (458–519).

Moore's mistake was to think that he could meet the assertion that one cannot really know, for example, that there is a tree in front of him by simply replying that he did know it. This was not a real issue, but only the shadows of philosophical realism and skepticism confronting each other. When a child learns a language, it learns how, for example, to use color words without doubt. We might be inclined to say that a young child "knows" colors, but it might be more accurate to say that at first the child is only able to *do* certain things such as naming a particular color, even without having actually mastered the concept of what something "*is called.*" The game of "knowing only begins at a later level." Similarly, we might say that a dog that comes when it is called "knows" its name, but it is really only able to respond to the sound of being called. It is not participating in a language-game that involves concepts such as knowing and believing. "The language-game is so to say something unpredictable. I mean: it is not based on grounds. It is not reasonable or unreasonable. It is there—like our life." Although "the concept of knowing is coupled with that of the language-game," there is a great variety in such games. One can even imagine a primitive language-game, such as that of the builders in the *Investigations*, in which our concept of knowledge did not exist. In our system of mathematics, the justification for a claim to know something "is a proof." With respect to the language-game with people's names, it is the case that "everyone knows his name with the greatest certainty." If someone were to conclude, from the fact that people have in some cases changed their minds about what is true or false, that there are really no grounds for believing anything, it would involve a "misunderstanding of the nature of our language-games." And it is also a misunderstanding to seek the meaning of an expression "by contemplating the expression itself, and the frame of mind in which one uses it, instead of always thinking of the practice." We may trust a physicist as opposed to an oracle, but to call the latter wrong is merely to announce one's of own beliefs and grounds. It is a matter of "using our language-game as a base from which to *combat* theirs." When "two principles really do meet which cannot be reconciled with one another," the respective proponents declare "the other a fool and a heretic," and although each may give reasons in such a case, "at the end of reasons come *persuasion*. (Think what happens when missionaries convert natives)." What Wittgenstein was advancing here was not the position that there are no reasons for claiming one *Weltbild* to be better than another, but only that philosophy does not hold any special key, either theoretically or practically, to settling such a conflict. And although in some instance it might seem that "the foundation of all judging would be taken away from me," "would it be *unthinkable* that I would stay in the saddle however much the facts bucked?" His answer was, in effect, that it happens every day in areas ranging from science to politics (520–620).

It would be quite correct for a person to claim to know something that the person has learned, such as some fact about anatomy, even if the person was not an expert on the subject, but it would be meaningless in most cases to say that I know that I am a human being. If such a claim did make sense in some circumstance, maybe as a response to aliens from another planet, it would no longer be "philosophically astonishing" in the sense that Moore intended such a claim. The point of all this was to further demonstrate yet once more that "a doubt without an end is not even a doubt." A person "cannot be making a mistake about 12 x 12 being 144," but "*mathematical* certainty" cannot be contrasted with what some might speak of as the "relative uncertainty of empirical propositions." Two different language-games are involved, and one may be made as exempt from doubt as the other. The difference is that the mathematical proposition operates as if it had "officially been given the stamp of incontestability" and "is a hinge on which your dispute can turn." It has become "fossilized." Individuals might want to say that, in many instances, they cannot be mistaken, as in saying that they know that they were never on the moon, but often the phrase is used rhetorically "with a view to persuasion" and less as a move within a practice than as a defense or critique of a practice (621–76).

After reading Wittgenstein and Kuhn one might still want to ask, like Peggy Lee, "is that all there is?" Is there not something deeper than the conventions in which we operate and to which we can repair in order to justify our claims about the world and about what is true and false? In the social and human sciences, this loss of metaphysical foundations seems particularly disconcerting in the case of values such as justice and the basis on which it can be articulated and prescribed. And if we cannot find a metaphysical basis, we tend to seek a naturalistic source, such as in the case of recent psychological research that claims to have discovered the basic, but conflicting, structures of both morality and its contravention in how babies gravitate toward or reject certain objects. A conception of philosophy as a form of social inquiry opens up not only questions about values as a type of phenomena, but questions about the role of the investigator in not only accessing and assessing but formulating values. Social theorists have often engaged Wittgenstein's work with respect to reflecting on what is often referred to as normative or evaluative inquiry. Some have been motivated by either deriving a substantive message, maybe about some issue such as democracy, or establishing the cognitive authority to mount critical and prescriptive claims about their subject matter. Others, however, have viewed his philosophy as radically deficient because it lacked such resources. Although his later work can be construed as having certain implications for dealing with a variety of substantive value concerns and although it offers critical potential, it is neither the salvation nor the bane of normative purchase. He did not offer any definite answer to the questions of whether or how philosophy could judge its subject matter, and he was ambivalent about whether or not his work could, would, or should have a practical effect. He was largely willing to let the chips fall where they may, but, at the same time, resisted the philosophical propensity to attempt to "shit higher than your arse" (Edmonds and Eidinow 2001, 16). Consequently, among many of those seeking normative validation, Wittgenstein's work has continued to evoke an aporia and spawn worries about relativism, particularly with respect to normative judgment.

It might seem strange that in the *Investigations*, which dealt primarily with the nature of social phenomena and with how to represent social phenomena, Wittgenstein had almost nothing to say about values and ethics, while in the *Tractatus*, which focused on how to represent the "world," he had a great deal to say about these issues. Part of the explanation is that he did not substantially change his mind about the basic nature of values and ethical judgment, but he did increasingly bring them within what Sellars referred to as the "space of reasons."

SHOW AND TELL: ETHICS IN THE *TRACTATUS*

The preface to the *Tractatus* has sometimes been given short shrift, but there is, as Wittgenstein himself stressed, a need to give it close textual attention. He began by stating that the basic problems that have been posed by philosophy stem from the fact that "the logic of our language has been misunderstood" and that "the whole sense [meaning, *Sinn*] of the book" is that "what can be said at all can be said clearly, and what we cannot talk about, we must pass over in silence [*schweigen*]." As Bertrand Russell noted in his introduction to the book, Wittgenstein seemed to say a considerable amount about what could not be said, so it is necessary to be clear about exactly what could, and could not, be talked about and how.

He stated that "the aim of the book is to draw a limit to thought, or rather—not to thought but to the expression of thoughts." At this point, he was assuming a basic difference between thought and language, which he so pointedly rejected in his later work. In another place, he said, "Does a *Gedanke* consist of words? No! But of psychical constituents that have the same sort of relation to reality as words. What those constituents are I don't know." He added that his "main point is the theory of what can be expressed by propositions . . . and what cannot be expressed by propositions, but only shown [*gezeigt*]; which, I believe, is the cardinal problem of philosophy" (*CL*, 124). His assumption was that it would be absurd to attempt to draw a limit to thought, because we cannot think "what cannot be thought." It is "only in language that the limit can be drawn, and what lies on the other side of the limit will simply be nonsense [*Unsinn*]." Although he might seem to have been equating language as a whole with propositions, it would become clear that it was possible to do more with words than state what he defined as propositions. Language was also a vehicle for showing, and it was within language that the distinction between what was and was not propositional was drawn.

The problem with the word "nonsense" is that the typical connotation, in both German and English, is distinctly pejorative and suggests more than simply something lacking what he defined as propositional form. In his work as a whole, he often used "nonsense" to refer to plain nonsense and linguistic muddles, but he once said, "Don't *for heavens sake*, be afraid of talking nonsense! Only don't forget to pay attention to your nonsense" (*CV*, 64), which suggested that nonsense was not necessarily lacking meaning. And he later noted that it is possible to draw "boundaries" between what is "senseless" (*sinnlos*) and what has "sense" or meaning in different ways and for different "reasons" (*PI*, 499–500). So the question is why he wished to draw this boundary. Some commentators have suggested that he was implying that there are different kinds of nonsense and that some kinds are better than others or serve the purpose of communicating something ineffable, but it would be more accurate to say that he was indicating that there are different concepts to which the word "nonsense" can be applied. In the *Tractatus*, he was using "nonsense" in a very specific and restricted, and maybe ironic, manner. Although he seemed to be making a stark distinction between language that is meaningful and language that is not, he fully recognized that what he specified as meaningful was a very narrow dimension of meaning. In the *Investigations*, what he characterized as nonsense was always what lacked intelligibility, and there were instances in which he wanted to demonstrate how "unobvious" nonsense could be made "obvious." But fairy tales and even nonsense poems were considered meaningful, and in the *Tractatus*, he stressed that there is much thinking, and expressing, that is *not propositional* but capable of being meaningfully expressed. The reason for drawing a strict boundary between what could and could not be expressed propositionally was not fully apparent until the end of the book when he began to talk about ethics, which was included among the things that could only be shown, pointed to, demonstrated, presented, made manifest, and so on. Since he claimed that only those thoughts that are pictures of reality and expressed as propositions can be judged true or false, the *Tractatus* itself could not be judged in this manner. Although he admitted that his attempt to express his own thoughts "well" probably did not always "hit the nail on the head," he asserted that "the *truth* of the thoughts communicated here seems to me unassailable and definitive" and provides a "final solution" to the "problems" engaged. So it seems that in an important respect truth and nonsense were not mutually exclusive, and he insisted that, in the end, this emphasis on what can be expressed (*gezagt*) as a proposition indicated "how little had been achieved when these problems are solved."

Wittgenstein's reactions to Frege's work were ambivalent, but reflections of Frege's account of language run through the *Tractatus*. Both Frege and Wittgenstein (in the *Tractatus*) conceived of an intricate relationship between thought and language. Language was necessary to express thoughts as well as reflect on them and put them into words so that they could be measured against the world, and they conceived of thoughts and thinking as ontologically prior to and distinct from language. Although, in the *Tractatus*, it may be difficult to pin down exactly how Wittgenstein conceived of thoughts, it seems that at this time he assumed something like a "language" of thought that consisted of disembodied mental representations. This may have been a step in the direction of his short subsequent flirtation with a phenomenological or "primary" language before he turned toward the argument for the basic unity of thought and language that characterized the later work. In the *Tractatus*, he, like Frege, explicitly conceived of thinking as dressing itself in the sensible language of both science and ordinary life. This facilitated an intersubjective sharing of thoughts and freed them from their private habitat and, by their logical projection in language, made them capable of being judged as either true or false. When he insisted that it is necessary to remain silent about certain things, he was talking about propositional silence, and the grammatical implication was not only that we cannot help but pass over these things in silence but that we should proactively do so. There were certain things that simply did not allow propositional expression, and it was a mistake to try. His reason for this sharp distinction between fact and value or science and other discourses was, however, to make sure that each usage "gets its due" (*CV*, 70). Issues such as the meaning of life and what is good and valuable could not be solved by science. But a central theme of the work was that even the connection between science and reality could not be propositionally expressed and therefore belonged to the category of what can only be shown. It could not be put into propositional form and compared with the "world," which consisted of "atomic facts" composed of "objects" or "things" that constituted various "states of affairs."

The intricate numbering of the remarks in the *Tractatus* might create the illusion that there is an argument that is systematically presented, but the discussion actually jumps all around and appears to involve some striking inconsistencies, which, by any interpretive strategy, are difficult to elide. It is a mistake to approach this work with the aim of making everything fit perfectly together, but, in all fairness, he consistently downplayed the significance of contradictions and paradoxes. The *Tractatus* itself is on the whole more a venture in showing than telling, but what he was attempting to show was not only how the world is represented but what things are not re-presentable—even though they might in some way be *presentable*.

He claimed that thoughts, and their expression in propositions, are pictures of reality and that "what a picture must have in common with reality is its pictorial form." But although a picture can "mirror" reality, it cannot "depict its pictorial form," that is, represent how it represents.

This, however, can be "shown" or "displayed." The concept to which the word *zeigt*, usually translated as "shows," refers plays an important role in the book, but the more than twenty uses of this word, as well as occasionally *weist*, do not always refer to the same concept. Sometimes he used *zeigt* in the manner of pointing to or demonstrating something that could be expressed, even if not propositionally, but the more important uses were those instances when he was talking about the way in which things such as logical form and the internal logical relationship between language and the world are only indirectly manifested. He maintained that the sense of a proposition is "true or false only in virtue of being a picture of reality," but although "the picture is outside its subject," it is "not outside its representational form" (2.17–174, 4.06, 4.061). What a picture represents and what a proposition "shows" is its sense (*Sinn*), which is a thought, "a logical picture of facts," of "how things stand." Consequently, "the totality of true thoughts is a picture of the world," which then can be expressed in propositions (2.221, 3.31, 4, 4.1). And ideally, "the totality of true propositions is the whole of natural science (or the whole corpus of the natural sciences)" (4.11). In the end, however, the logical form that "signs fail to express, their application shows [*zeigt*]" (3.262). He illustrated this logical form by the metaphor of how "a gramophone record, the musical idea, the written notes, and the sound-waves, all stand to one another in the same internal relation of depicting that holds between language and the world" (4.014, 4.022). He hammered home this basic point over and over again: "Propositions can represent the whole of reality, but they cannot represent what they must have in common with reality in order to be able to represent it— logical form. In order to be able to represent logical form, we should have to be able to station ourselves with propositions somewhere outside logic, that is to say outside the world" (4.12, 4.121). "Propositions cannot represent logical form: it is mirrored in them. What finds its reflection in language, language cannot represent. What expresses itself in language, we cannot express by means of language. Propositions show [*zeigt*] the logical form of reality. They display [*weist*] it" (4.12, 4.121). "What can be shown [*geszeigt*], cannot be said" (4.1212).

What constituted the "facts" of the world was, however, not as straightforward as it might have at first seemed. In his brief discussion of the Necker cube, he pointed out that the cube could be seen in two different ways and that "we really see two different facts" (5.5423). One could not, for example, draw a picture of one fact as opposed to the other, and this difference could not be specified propositionally, even though it might be possible to "show" it to someone who might not have at first been capable of seeing it. This provides a clue to what would be his view of ethics. The world is out there, but, for example, "the world of the happy man and the unhappy man are not the same" (6.43). Ethics, too, is aspectical and a matter of attitude, and ethical claims involve showing or presenting rather than making propositional statements about something such as moral facts.

Much of what the *Tractatus* claims to demonstrate is how natural science is possible, but, again, a limitation of these statements of philosophy was that they were among those things that did not fall under the category of statements that could be judged true or false. Such philosophical claims were a form of showing rather than representing. Wittgenstein claimed that if it were possible,

> the correct method in philosophy would really be the following: to say nothing except what can be said, i.e. propositions of natural science—i.e. something that has nothing to do with philosophy—and then, whenever someone else wanted to say something metaphysical, to demonstrate to him that he had failed to give a meaning to certain signs in his propositions. Although it would not be satisfying to the other person—he would not have the feeling that we were teaching him philosophy—this method would be the only strictly correct one. (6.53)

But the truths of philosophy could only be made manifest in the course of doing philosophy. Consequently, he finally concluded dramatically that: "My propositions serve as elucidations in the following way: anyone who understands me eventually recognizes them as nonsensical, when he has used them—as steps—to climb up beyond them. (He must, so to speak, throw away the ladder after he has climbed up it.) He must transcend these propositions, and then he will see the world aright" (654).

He was already using "proposition" in a wider sense than he had initially, but if these philosophical propositions were the rungs of a ladder that led to a clear view of things, one might ask how this squared with his statement, in another context, that if where he wanted to go could only be reached by a ladder, he would not try to go there. In the latter case, however, he was referring to his distaste for traditional metaphysics rather than to how the ladder of philosophy can help one to see the world correctly. This did not mean that all such ladders worked well or that all that was outside propositional form showed something that was valuable. He claimed that "most of the propositions and questions to be found in philosophical works are not false but nonsensical" and arise from "our failure to understand the logic of our language. (They belong to the same class as the question whether the good is more or less identical than the beautiful.) And it is not surprising that the deepest problems are in fact not problems at all" (4.003), that is, not open to philosophical resolution. While many putative solutions to such problems were unintelligible nonsense, his own philosophical claims involved climbing up to a point where he could look on things from a better perspective. After all, Sextus Empiricus, from whom the ladder metaphor may have been drawn, stressed the profundity of philosophical discourse that could be abandoned once it had served its purpose of enlightenment.

Part of what he might seem to have been adumbrating in the *Tractatus* is something that would take center stage in the *Investigations*, that is, that meaning, thought, and the world show themselves in grammar, that is, in the use or application of language, but that we still have to pay attention to the difference between the surface and the depth of grammar. It was not only in the *Investigations* that he stressed the autonomy of ordinary language. In the *Tractatus*, he insisted that "all the propositions of our everyday language [*Umgangssprache*], just as they stand, are in perfect logical order" (5.5563), but that is because

> everyday language is a part of the human organism and is no less complicated than it, it is not humanly possible to gather immediately from it what the logic of language is. Language disguises thought. So much so, that from the outward form of the clothing it is impossible to infer the form of the thought beneath it, because the outward form of the clothing is not designed to reveal the form of the body, but for entirely different purposes.

Because "the tacit conventions on which the understanding of everyday language depends are enormously complicated," it is necessary to expose the logic that lies behind them and allows language to connect with the world (4.002). In some respects, his general view of this issue did not change, but what he meant by logic and where it was located did change. And he would continue to insist that philosophy is not "a body of doctrine" or set of propositions but an "activity," which "aims at the logical clarification of thoughts" and propositions (4.111–12).

Philosophy is like neither psychology nor natural science (4.1121), but, standing either "above or below," it "sets limits to the much disputed sphere of natural science" by showing what is possible in thought and propositions (4.113–16). "All philosophy is a 'critique of language,'" in that it involves "showing that the apparent logical form of a proposition need not be its real one" (4.0031). While propositions "show what they say," the logical tools of philosophy are "formal concepts" and "tautologies and contradictions," which are "not pictures of reality" and "show that they say nothing," that is, are "nonsensical." They are, like mathematics, "part of symbolism" (4.126, 4.461–611, 4.462). "The fact that the propositions of logic are tautologies *shows* the formal-logical-properties of language and the world," and they "describe the scaffolding of the world, or rather they present [show, give, constitute] it. They have no 'subject-matter.'" "Logic is not a body of doctrine, but a mirror image of the world. Logic is transcendental." Mathematics is also a "logical method," and therefore consists of "pseudo-propositions" and tautologies (6.12–6.24). So, at this point, Wittgenstein had specified a great deal that could only be shown and that was not subject to judgments of truth and falsity, but there was more to come.

He claimed that his analysis "shows [*zeigt*] too that there is no such thing as the soul [mind, *Seele*]—the subject, etc.—as it is conceived in the superficial psychology of the present day" (5.5421). "*The limits of my language* mean [signify] the limits of my world," and this is the "truth" about "solipsism," which "cannot be said" in a proposition "but makes itself manifest [*zeigt*]." This statement has been interpreted in a number of ways, but he went on to say that "the world is *my* world" and that "the limits of the language (the language which only I understand) mean the limits of my world. [*Dass die Welt meine Welt ist, das zeigt sich darin, dass die Grenzen der Sprache (der Sprache, die allein ich verstehe) die Grenzen meiner Welt bedeuten*]" (5.6, 5.62). This is a grammatically complex sentence, but a slightly better translation might be: "That the world is *my* world is manifest in the fact that the limits of

speech (the limits of the language that *I alone* understand) signify the
limits of my world." He was not saying that language in general is the
limit of the world, but that *my language* is the limit, the language *I alone*
can understand, that is, a language of thought. It seems reasonable to
suggest, once again, that at this time he believed in something like a
private language, or at least he was saying that one's natural language
is understood in a subjective manner. He would retain the idea that
language was the limit of the world in that there was no way to get
beyond language to a more direct contact with the world, but in the
Tractatus, he stressed that "I am my world. (The microcosm.)" and "the
world and life are one" (5.621, 5.63). He insisted that "no part of our
experience is . . . a priori" and that "there is no a priori order of things"
(5.634). But he also continued to insist that although one's "body" is
part of the world, there is "in an important sense . . . no subject," "no
such thing as the subject that thinks or entertains ideas." To the extent
to which philosophy could speak about a "self," it simply referred to
the fact that "the world is my world," and to the extent that there is a
"metaphysical subject," it "does not belong to the world but is a limit of
the world" just as "nothing *in the visual field* allows you to infer that it
is seen with the eye" (5.61–6333). His views about the human subject did
not substantially change.

Finally, however, there was the question of ethics, which occupied
much of the last portion of the *Tractatus*. A great deal of weight has been
given to Wittgenstein's letter from 1919 to Ludwig von Ficker, a prospec-
tive publisher for the *Tractatus*, in which he stated:

> I once wanted to give a few words in the foreword which now
> actually are not in it, which however, I'll write to you now
> because they might be a key for you: I wanted to write that
> my work consists of two parts: of the one which is here, and of
> everything which I have *not* written. And precisely this second
> part is the important one. For the Ethical is delimited from
> within, as it were, by my book; and I'm convinced that, *strictly*
> speaking, it can ONLY be delimited in this way. In brief, I
> think: All of that which *many* are *babbling* today, I have de-
> fined in my book by remaining silent about it.
> (Monk 1990, 178)

In a letter to Paul Engelmann, he repeated much of this and stated specifically that "the book's point is an ethical one" and that "I would recommend you to read the *preface* and the *conclusion*, because they contain the most direct expression of the point of the book" (Englemann 1967, 35).

Although there have been some extravagant interpretations of these letters, what he seems to have been saying is that matters of ethics are among the things that can only be shown and about which one cannot speak propositionally. But this indicated a limitation of science as much as a limitation of ethics. His aim was to demarcate ethics and science. There was no invidious comparison between the two, but rather recognition of their respective autonomy. But they had more in common than what was at first apparent. If science is conceived in the narrow or "normal" sense of representing facts and engaging in hypothesis-testing, it seems quite different than ethics, but if science is conceived as grounded in theoretical claims, these are as presentational as ethical claims. As I stressed in chapter 2 and in the discussion of Kuhn, the physical world as such is not, in the first instance, *represented* but instead *presented* or "shown."

It is difficult to say whether what he was silent about and his allusion to an ethical purpose were really the "important" part of the book or whether he was saying this because it might have conformed to von Ficker's publishing interests, but he was claiming that ethics belongs to the category of those things that are "delimited," and "shows" by the manner in which it does not correspond to the true/false claims that characterize normal natural science. Ethics comes into view as part of the space delimited by its other, that is, by the material world that surrounds it. Things such as "values" and questions about the "meaning [*Sinn*] of the world," "god," and the "riddle of life" are "outside the world" and apart from statements about "what happens" and "is the case." In the physical world, "no value exists," and "it is impossible for there to be propositions of ethics" or for ethics to "be put into words." "Ethics is transcendental," and "ethics and aesthetics are one and the same" (6.41–6.421. Ethics is "mystical," autonomous, and demarcated by the boundary with "facts," and has nothing to do with physical "events." The factual consequences of ethical commitments, such as "punishment and rewards," lie outside the sphere of the "actions" and the exercise of "will" that falls within the scope of ethics itself (6.422, 6.43–45). Skepticism about such matters does not apply, because there is no actual "problem" about "doubt" that can be answered in the manner of typical scientific problems. So "there are, indeed, things that cannot be put into words. They make themselves manifest. They are mystical." He concluded the *Tractatus* as he began: "what we cannot speak about we must pass over in silence" (6.522, 7), which is to say that an ethical point of the *Tractatus* is the rejection of any form of moral realism.

It is easy to see how the *Tractatus* contributed to inspiring the positivist account of the fact/value dichotomy and an emotive theory of ethics. As late as 1930, in a discussion with Moritz Schlick, Wittgenstein might have seemed to argue for a decisionist account of ethics. He adopted Euthyphro's position that the good is good because it is what God wants—not the Socratic rationalist view that God wants the good because it is good (Rhees 1965). By the end of the 1920s, Wittgenstein had not substantially changed his position on values, but although values remained beyond the "boundaries of language" in the narrow sense that they could not be judged true or false, he set out to talk in more detail about the character of ethical claims.

THE LECTURE ON ETHICS

What is commonly referred to as Wittgenstein's lecture on ethics was delivered in Cambridge sometime between September 1929 and December 1930 and probably at a meeting of the society known as "The Heretics." This was his only such lecture that was ever transcribed, in this case from shorthand notes made by Friedrich Waismann during and after conversations with Wittgenstein and Schlick, but it deserves a careful textual analysis. After finishing the *Tractatus*, Wittgenstein apparently believed that he had done all he could do philosophically, and he left the university to teach elementary school. It was after conversations with Schlick in 1929 that he returned to philosophy, but although he still retained the basic position represented in the *Tractatus*, there was the beginning of some subtle changes.

He introduced his talk (1966) by noting that his reason for choosing such a "difficult subject" was that it was "something which I am keen on communicating." He insisted that the subject was neither a "logical" or "a scientific matter" nor "a popular-scientific lecture" that was "intended to make you believe that you understand a thing which actually you don't understand." He decided to choose a subject that seemed to be of "general importance, hoping that it may help to clear up your thoughts about this subject (even if you should entirely disagree with what I will say about it)." Finally he hoped that, unlike "most lengthy philosophical lectures," the result would be that "in the end you may see both the way" you are being led and "where it leads to."

He began by tentatively accepting G. E. Moore's definition of ethics as "the general enquiry into what is good," but he wanted to suggest a wider sense of "ethics" that would include "what is generally called Aesthetics." He said that in order to make this clear, he would advance a number of "synonymous expressions" that, despite their particular differences, would illustrate the "characteristic features they all have in common." He noted that he could have said that ethics is "the enquiry into what is valuable," "really important," "the meaning of life," "what makes life worth living," or "the right way of living." There were, however, *two* different ways in which these expressions could be used—a "trivial or relative sense" and an "ethical and absolute" sense. This was the beginning of an important step beyond the *Tractatus* to a wider sense of reason in ethics.

In the case of the former sense, he claimed that it would be like talking about something such as a "good chair" in which the word "good" meant or referred to a "predetermined standard," such as serving a particular "purpose," but this, he noted, was, in effect, "a mere statement of facts," and "no statement of fact can ever be, or imply, a judgment of absolute value." He claimed that a description of the "world," by a hypothetical omniscient spectator, would include only true propositions referring to facts, that is, scientific propositions and propositions denoting relative value, and there would be no propositions that, "in any absolute sense, are sublime, important, or trivial." He then raised the issue of whether good and bad, if they are neither things in the world nor properties of those things, could be attributed to "states of mind," as when Hamlet said that "nothing is either good or bad, but thinking makes it so." His response was that a state of mind, even if it were something we could describe, would simply be another fact and "in no ethical sense good or bad" and would not involve any "ethical proposition." Consequently, he concluded that there can be no scientific treatment of ethics, because "our words used as we use them in science . . . are vessels capable only of containing and conveying natural meaning and sense. Ethics, if it is anything, is supernatural and our words will only express facts." A state of affairs that everyone would agree on as "right" is a "chimera," because "no state of affairs has, in itself, what I would like to call the coercive power of an absolute judge." He was once again rejecting any form of moral realism.

He acknowledged that we all have experiences to which we would attribute absolute value, but this is a matter of personal preference. Such experiences might involve something such as "wonder at the existence of the world" or the experience of "feeling absolutely safe, but the verbal expression which we give to these experiences is nonsense!" What happens is that we take expressions from instances in which they make sense, and apply them to what does not make sense. Although it is perfectly reasonable to talk about something such as being safe when there are specific criteria applied, it is not reasonable to talk about safety outside any context. He maintained that "a certain characteristic misuse of our language runs through all ethical and religious expressions." They are really allegories or "similes," but a simile only makes sense if it represents or refers to something factual. There are experiences that we associate with absolute value, but "it is the paradox that an experience, a fact, should seem to have supernatural value." However, "the truth is that the scientific way of looking at a fact," such as the existence of the world, is not the same as looking at it as, for example, "a miracle." He noted that he was "tempted to say that the right expression in language for the miracle of the existence of the world, though it is not any proposition in language, is the existence of language itself," but "all I have said by shifting the expression of the miraculous from an expression by means of language to the expression by the existence of language" is that "we cannot express what we want to express and that all we can say about the absolute miraculous remains nonsense." There is, however, no way to overcome this impasse, because

> these nonsensical expressions were not nonsensical because I had not yet found the correct expressions, but that their non-sensicality was their very essence. For all I wanted to do with them was just to go beyond the world and that is to say beyond significant language. My whole tendency and, I believe, the tendency of all men who ever tried to write or talk Ethics or Religion was to run against the boundaries of language. This running against the walls of our cage is perfectly, absolutely hopeless. Ethics so far as it springs from the desire to

say something about the ultimate meaning of life, the absolute good, the absolutely valuable, can be no science. What it
says does not add to our knowledge in any sense. But it is a
document of a tendency in the human mind which I personally cannot help respecting deeply and I would not for my life
ridicule it.

VALUES AND THE SPACE OF REASONS

Although he seemed to be reaffirming what he had said about ethics
in the *Tractatus*, his analysis did differ. The "mere statement of facts" in
the case of "relative value" was a reason for calling something "good,"
and it was not actually an empirical proposition that could be judged
as true or false by comparing it to the world. It was, as he would later
recognize, to do something different with words than stating facts. And
the lecture appears to confirm that what he meant by "nonsense" was not
something lacking meaning but only what, at this point, he construed as
propositional form, and that he was not depreciating ethics but, again,
distinguishing it from natural science. Furthermore, the status of what he
spoke about as absolute value was similar to the foundational claims that
he would discuss in *On Certainty*. They were part of the bedrock or "scaffolding" on which more specific and concrete judgments rested, and they
hovered in the background of claims of relative value, just as theories in
natural science are the background of the factual claims that Kuhn spoke
of as normal science. What was implicit in all of Wittgenstein's work
was the difference between presentational and representational claims.
The body of the *Tractatus*, the role and language of logic, the remarks
composing the *Investigations*, values and ethical claims, aesthetic judgments, the "hinge" propositions in *On Certainty*, and scientific theories
all belong to what is presented or shown. This is not to say that they
are instances of the same thing, but rather that they are categorically
the same and function in the same way. It is a matter of family resemblance. What they have in common is that they represent nothing and
that there is nothing to which they correspond, because they provide part
of the framework within which representation and correspondence take
place. What they share is also what Wittgenstein referred to as seeing
the world "sub specie aeterni," that is, as a "limited whole" (6.45). While
"the usual way of looking at things is to see objects as it were from the

midst of them, the view *sub specie aeternitatis*" is from "the outside," and this includes "the good life" (*NB*, 83). In the *Investigations*, he was still concerned with capturing the world in this manner, but it was now the world of conceptually preconstituted forms of life.

In the *Investigations*, he noted that "what we call 'proposition,' 'language,' has not the formal unity that I imagined, but is a family of structures more or less akin to one another" (108), and by the point of *On Certainty*, not only was this claim fully developed, but any stark distinction between absolute and relative value had fallen away as well as any sharp line in the web of justification between empirical propositions and other propositions. Value claims, like all other claims, were situated in the space of reasons and were not simply disembodied performances that sought escape from the "cage" of "sensical" language. The idea of absolute value as something outside the realm of justification receded just as surely as the notion that there is an absolute sense of what constitutes a game. All justification, however, both empirical and normative, comes to an end, and there one must stand. What lies beyond that point is persuasion. Persuasion, however, was not some particular method, but might consist of *everything* from reasons to rhetoric. Apart from in *On Certainty*, Wittgenstein did not discuss persuasion, but what he was talking about was very similar to Kuhn's explanation of scientific change.

One of the decisive shifts from the *Tractatus* to the *Investigations* was that in the latter, ethics is only mentioned once and very briefly. One might ask, then, if the *Investigations* lacked an ethical point and why, since he had a considerable amount to say about judgment, ethical judgment was not discussed. Part of the explanation is that his focus was no longer on how language represents the world, but on how philosophy represents language and human conventions as a whole. Normativity, from the rules of language to social values as a whole, infused this subject matter. The world that was now the object of philosophy was a world replete with values. The ethical point of the *Tractatus* had been to establish the autonomy values, but now values were still autonomous but no less grounded than other claims and forms of judgment. What was changing in Wittgenstein's later work was the paradigm of what constituted making sense. The task of philosophy, as he conceived it in the end, was not to justify values but to represent and describe them. This, however, indirectly raised the issue of whether the philosopher had any role as a value-critic and value-presenter. Once we have clarified what was involved in his claim to have rejected theory, there is still the question of how his work might relate to what today is often referred to as normative, moral, or ethical theory. At one point he noted that philosophers "have had the notion of an ethical theory—the idea of finding the true nature of goodness or of duty. Plato wanted to do this—to set ethical inquiry in the direction of finding the true nature of goodness—so as to achieve objectivity and avoid relativity. He thought that relativity must be avoided at all costs, since it would destroy the *imperative* in morality" (Rhees 1965, 23). Wittgenstein claimed, however, that to note various systems of ethics is not to say that they are equally right but only that the philosopher is not ordained to determine which is correct—any more than the philosopher is the arbiter of the correctness of scientific judgments.

NORMATIVE INQUIRY: AFTER WITTGENSTEIN

Despite all the criticism of Wittgenstein as a relativist as well as continuing attempts to tease out of his work either a substantive set of values or a role for the philosopher as an authoritative critic or as a creator of values, he actually ultimately relegated the practical relationship between philosophy and its subject matter to the realm of contingency and circumstance. Just as we can in no way philosophically, for example, justify or criticize theoretically the conventions that determine how we treat concepts of color and therefore can only "portray" them, we are faced with a similar situation in the case of values. Consequently, we might ask what philosophers such as John Rawls (1971) are doing when they advance a "theory of justice" and place it in a lineage reaching from Plato to the present, or what is the status of various claims about moral judgment in analytical philosophy. For example, the Oxford philosopher Derek Parfit's work (2011) reflects two basic dimensions of this kind of enterprise—the fear of epistemic chaos in ethical matters and the presumption that philosophy holds the answer to the problem. He argues that while most moral philosophy has tended, in one way or another, to slide off into nihilism, he has succeeded in arriving at "the supreme moral principle" and a universal answer to ethical judgment. He claims that after carefully consulting the work of his "two masters" (Kant and Sidgwick), and reconciling their different routes in climbing the mountain of moral certainty, he managed to reach the summit where he found that there actually are "true answers" to normative questions about "what

matters" morally and what we should morally do and that these answers
are as defensible as the rules of logic and mathematics. In a strange way,
Wittgenstein might have agreed that they are *as* defensible, that is, that
they belong to a class that is not, in the definitive manner suggested by
Parfit, defensible at all. But just as natural science and metaphysics sublimate the particular, individuals such as Rawls and Parfit seek general
principles that encompass and surpass the particularities and contexts of
political and moral judgment.

Wittgenstein would have surely said that there cannot be a philosophical theory of justice or moral judgment any more than there can
be a theory of truth; there can only be a description, and maybe a therapeutic analysis, of how people use such words as "justice" and "moral."
There is nothing to prevent philosophers and social scientists, any more
than anyone else, from making claims about what is just, but while we
can readily see the grounds on which political actors, judges, religious
leaders, and others might base their conclusions about such matters,
the question of the philosopher's role and authority seems much more
problematical. Wittgenstein had very early on reached the conclusion
that would be apparent in the *Investigations*, that is, to understand "the
use of the word 'good' (in an ethical sense)" would require examining
the "combination of a very large number of interrelated games, each of
them as it were a facet of the use. What makes a single concept here is
precisely the connection, the relationship, between these facets" (*PG*, 17).
What he was saying about words such as "good," which are characteristic
of ethical and aesthetic statements, is that they refer to a certain class of
concepts that are discriminated by their family resemblance rather than
by any common essence. They are very similar to what Stephen Toulmin
(1958) referred to as "modal signifiers," that is, terms that tend to have a
universal performative force but quite different criteria of application in
diverse contexts. What constitutes such criteria is often clear in many
highly structured practices, where the criteria are not contested, but, even
in the case of evaluating an automobile, opinions about the criteria may
differ widely. Wittgenstein said that "Christianity is not a doctrine, not,
I mean, a theory about what has happened & will happen to the human
soul, but a description of something that actually takes place in human
life. For 'recognition of sin' is an actual occurrence & so is despair & so is
redemption through faith. Those who speak of it (like Bunyan), are simply describing what has happened to them; whatever gloss someone may

want to put on it!" (*CV*, 32). Although two religious doctrines, like two scientific theories, may come into opposition, there are no external and neutral reasons for choosing one of them. To borrow from Patrick Henry, we might say that if this be relativism, make the most of it, because philosophical absolutism is an inherently elitist and authoritarian stance that involves an attempt to find reasons that stand outside any particular situation or conception of the world. The significant question about so-called normative theory is the same as one might pose about the philosophy of language, that is, what its function may be in terms of its relationship to its subject matter. Even among the most normatively inclined philosophers of language few would suggest that the primary task is to instruct people in how to speak. So exactly on what basis should social theorists be instructing political and moral actors?

We can play around endlessly with what we think are the implications of Wittgenstein's philosophy for how our social practices should be constructed and arranged, that is, we can find reasons in his work for supporting a number of claims. There is indeed, as so many have pointed out, much to suggest that his work implicitly provides support for valorizing democratic judgment and institutions, but there is, however, one democratic implication that is less often noted. Much of democratic theory not only remains mired in the remnants of philosophical foundationalism (either immanent or transcendental), what we might call democratic metaphysics; it also sustains, at least implicitly, an elitist bias. This is less a bias that intrudes into the image of democracy as a practice than one that emerges from the view of the relationship between philosophy and democratic practices. There has been a tendency for transcendentalism to retreat from an otherworldly location into the nature of social practices themselves, as in the case of Jürgen Habermas and others, but there has been little retrenchment in the idea that the philosopher, the social scientist, the social theorist, or the public intellectual at least occupies a position that in some way stands above or apart from the democratic conversation and provides the terms in which it should be conducted. It is, however, very difficult to draw upon Wittgenstein to support some version of this kind of argument. There is little in his conception of philosophy or its subject matter that suggests an authoritative role for the philosophical judgment, or that such judgment occupies what Naomi Scheman (1996) has referred to as the academician's place of "privileged marginality," in making normative claims about the subject matter. In fact, if anything, the implications seem to speak against such a role or, at the very least, significantly problematize it.

There is nothing to suggest that the philosopher has a special practical role, but it is also a mistake to claim that Wittgenstein, Winch, or Kuhn leave us with a form of relativism that does not allow communication between language-games and that prohibits critical engagement and change. The real issue here cannot be that of the possibility of change within and between language-games—it happens all the time. Once again, the issue that really lies behind all the talk about relativism is whether the philosopher has some special capacity and authority to critically evaluate a practice or prescribe how those practices should be conducted. Wittgenstein and Kuhn do not offer any basis for such authority, but while in one sense their work "leaves everything as it is," it is also the case that when something such as a philosophical account of either natural or social science is set forth in the world, there is an important sense in which the practices of science are not likely to be simply left as they were. Some people, and even scientists, for better or worse, come to see science differently. Whether scientists ought to see it differently is another matter, for which there is no definitive answer. Surely investigations of social practices may lead us to see them differently and suggest the possibility of evaluative and prescriptive conclusions, but for at least the past century, we have been struggling with this intersection, and the answers have ranged from fantasy to efforts directed toward practical engagement.

Wittgenstein did not have a great deal to say about the details of how judgments are justified, because, as in the matter of how doubt is introduced, there is not much to say apart from describing, as Kuhn did, how a particular practice operates or has operated. But he reached the heart of the matter when he recognized that words such as "good," "beautiful," "right," and "just" are adjectives applied in the game of approving. They are first learned by a child as a substitute for gestures, facial expressions, and other symbols of approbation, and they do not really play any significant substantive role in our normative judgments. They function somewhat differently in different cultures, but they are largely ornaments, like grace notes and dynamic accents embellishing a melody, that we attach to the criteria for making such claims within some set of circumstances and to the conventions that govern those circumstances. And when we carry on debates about such matters as justice outside particular contexts, as is often the case in academic discussions, we are thrown back into the dogmas of metaphysics. To say that a particular person is just and another is not is largely, as Wittgenstein noted, an act of "classification" that simply raises the issue of what taxonomic principle is involved. He argued that these are basically expressions of content and discontent, but he was not suggesting that such claims are irrational, because in most instances the persons judging have definite, and often articulate, motives and reasons.

Within practices, ranging from science to religion, there are usually ample and firm foundations of judgment. It would be difficult to conceive of a practice that lacked such grounds. What could be more solid, and more difficult to transform, than the beliefs of practices such as those of natural science and religion? What would firmer foundations look like? The human condition of conventionality is far from a condition of softness and vulnerability. The problem is more likely apt to be one of rigidity. It only seems soft if compared with something too vague to describe, as Wittgenstein noted in the case of philosophers who speak of infinity as if it were actually something comparable to what an actual numeral is used to signify. What is elusive and illusive, and actually nonexistent, is the philosophical grounding of all grounds. It can be misleading, however, to interpret Wittgenstein as saying that in the end everything simply comes down to agreement. This could be construed as true in one sense, but, as he noted, this is not agreement in opinions but in a system of judgments that was never submitted to a referendum. As he put it in another instance, which contradicts interpretations such as Kripke's account of his discussion of rules, he asked, "does human agreement *decide* what is red? Is it decided by appeal to the majority? Were we taught to determine colour in *that* way?" (*Z*, 431). At one point, in the *Nachlass*, Wittgenstein spoke of a *contrat sociale*, but he meant this to be much like Rousseau's account of the conventions that bound individuals together in a democratic polity. It is not an actual agreement but rather what might be called a tacit consensus arising from being initiated into, and participating in, a practice. We are trained in and assimilated into a view of the world and various language-games and activities where we share conventions by participation in the judgments that are constitutive of those activities. Wittgenstein was, in fact, actually willing at one point to call this "relativity," but when he spoke of agreement in judgments, it was not about arbitrary forms of contract, such as a prenuptial agreement, that do not apply to conventionality itself, which, unlike cooking, has no substantive intrinsic end.

Kuhn produced a vivid picture of how change takes place in natural science and what happens when scientific theories clash, and in the case of the controversy surrounding his own work, we can see what happens when different images of philosophy come into conflict. What Kuhn did not address in any detail, however, was the confrontation between arguments in two different practices or the situation in which one practice seeks to evaluate and judge another. This might involve an instance of what could be referred to as the horizontal conflict between the doctrines of biological evolutionism and a religious commitment to intelligent design, but it might also involve the class of more vertical confrontations such as that between social inquiry and its subject matter. The difficulty with the latter is that, unlike the case of the controversy about evolution, such a conflict might not even take place within a common culture. In cases such as the relationship between anthropology and the cultures it studies, or between science and the philosophy of science, there is not likely to be any actual confrontation or significant contact, or at least the conditions and motives (missionary zeal) in which anthropology originated or the philosophy of science (rhetoric of inquiry) took shape have been lost. That original practical spirit, however, is still very much alive in fields such as moral and political philosophy, but the academic cottage industries of arguing about things such as justice and right have largely become exercises in abstracted and dislocated rhetoric that are not unlike the case of some philosophers of science who continue to make normative claims about the criteria of scientific knowledge and explanation.

For Wittgenstein, justice required rendering interpretations that were faithful to the indigenous meaning of the social practices involved and that avoided the reification that was apparent not only in traditional metaphysics and its projection of its schemes onto the world but in the similar tendency of a field such as anthropology to describe and evaluate its subject matter in terms of the *Weltbild* of the interpreter. For Wittgenstein, as for Winch, "doing justice" to the subject matter sometimes entailed giving even "the devil his due" (Winch 1996). This attitude in no way implied an uncritical approach to the subject matter, but only that, in the first instance, it should be fairly represented. Despite the worries of individuals such as Morris, the work of Kuhn has had little actual effect on the practice of science, and it would be difficult to document a significant practical effect of Wittgenstein's work on fields such as mathematics, psychology, and logic. Much of philosophy, as well as much of social theory, remains, however, dedicated to efforts to escape what individuals such as Morris claim to be a dilemma that Wittgenstein and Kuhn have bequeathed to us, but it is only a dilemma when viewed in the context of the tradition of representational philosophy and various forms of transcendental ethics. What Kuhn described was the specific scientific form of life, just as Wittgenstein described the general human form of life. As Hannah Arendt dramatically emphasized at the beginning of her book on the *Human Condition*, the history of Western thought is largely a story of attempting to escape that condition, and we are familiar with her assessment of the consequences of following that path. Actually, however, we might say to Peggy Lee that it is not all there is—we are simply seeking the answer in the wrong place. There is a great deal more if we choose language-games that offer substance. This is why Wittgenstein's concept of philosophy as social inquiry does offer a way forward, because it puts us in contact with the sites in which it is actually meaningful to talk about certainty and doubt and among which the criteria of judgment may fundamentally differ. To wish otherwise is simply a denial of the human condition.

We may feel, like Nietzsche, that when we look into the abyss and see no universal grounds of judgment, the abyss reflects back on us and we somehow lose our capacity to give reasons, but, as Wittgenstein pointed out, we should forget this idea of certainty, recognize that some judgments function as principles of judgment, and confront the fact that justification comes to an end. His point might be construed as not all that far removed from Marx's claim that philosophers have only interpreted the world, when the point is to change it, because Wittgenstein was far from content with things remaining the same in either philosophy or a number of other practices. What separates Wittgenstein from Marx is in part the fact that Marx, like most philosophers before him, believed that interpretation could be made to go all the way down, either through conscious action or through the unfolding of history. Wittgenstein was certainly not happy with modernity and many of the practices that defined it, but he may have been overwhelmed by the complexities he discerned in the contemporary relationship between philosophy and its subject matter and by hesitancies rooted in his own psyche. He did not offer any clear vision of how the vocation of philosophy might alter the social world. Maybe he believed, like Spengler, that it was too late, but it is clear that he believed that there was no particular formula for or explanation of social change and the manner in which theory could be brought to bear on practice. Subsequent attempts to posit general answers have not, in any obvious way, been compelling. There are few instances in which those who wish to evaluate and pass judgment on social practices do not ultimately fall back on what they take to be some transcendental cognitive foundation of either substance or logic. The persuasive force of particular reasons never seems sufficient, but it is in this sentiment, and not the specter of relativism, where the real danger lies.

References

Agassi, Joseph. 1991. "As You Like It." In Munéva, *Beyond Reason*, 379–87.

Andresen, Jensine. 1999. "Crisis and Kuhn." *Isis* 90, supp.: S43–S67.

Austin, J. L. 1962. *How to Do Things with Words*. Cambridge, Mass.: Harvard University Press.

Babich, Babette. 2003. "Kuhn's Paradigm as a Parable for the Cold War: Incommensurability and Its Discontents from Fuller's Tale of Harvard to Fleck's Unsung Lvov." *Social Epistemology* 17:99–109.

Bird, Alexander. 2000. *Thomas Kuhn*. Princeton: Princeton University Press.

Blackburn, Simon. 2005. *Truth: A Guide*. Oxford: Oxford University Press.

Boghossian, Paul. 2006. *Fear of Knowledge: Against Relativism and Constructivism*. New York: Oxford University Press.

Cavell, Stanley. 2010. *Little Did I Know: Excerpts from Memory*. Stanford: Stanford University Press.

Churchland, Paul. 1995. *The Engine of Reason, the Seat of the Soul: A Philosophical Journey Into the Brain*. Cambridge, Mass.: MIT Press.

Clark, T. H., and C. W. Stern. 1960. *Geologic History of North America*. New York: John Wiley and Sons.

———. 1978. *Geologic History of North America*. New York: John Wiley and Sons.

CRM Books. 1973. *Geology Today*. Del Mar, Calif.: CRM Books.

Damasio, Antonio. 1994. *Descartes' Error: Emotion, Reason, and the Human Brain*. New York: Putnam and Sons.

Davidson, Donald. 1980. *Essays on Actions and Events*. New York: Oxford University Press.

———. 1984. *Inquiries Into Truth and Interpretation*. Oxford: Oxford University Press.

———. 2001. *Subjective, Intersubjective, and Objective*. Oxford: Oxford University Press.

Derrida, Jacques. 1987. *The Postcard: From Socrates to Freud and Beyond*. Chicago: University of Chicago Press.

Edmonds, David, and John Eidinow. 2001. *Wittgenstein's Poker*. New York: Ecco.

Englemann, Paul. 1967. *Letters from Wittgenstein with a Memoir*. Edited by Brian McGuinness. Oxford: Blackwell.

Feyerabend, Paul K. 1955. "Wittgenstein's *Philosophical Investigations*." *Philosophical Review* 64:449–83.

———. 1962. "Explanation, Deduction, and Empiricism" In *Minnesota Studies in the Philosophy of Science*, vol. 3, edited by Herbert Feigl and Grover Maxwell. Minneapolis: University of Minnesota Press.

———. 1963. "How to Be a Good Empiricist—A Plea for Tolerance in Matters Epistemological." In *Philosophy of Science: The Delaware Seminar*, vol. 2, edited by Bernard Baumrin. New York: Interscience.

———. 1964. "Realism and Instrumentalism: Comments on the Logic of Factual Support." In *The Critical Approach to Science and Philosophy*, edited by Mario Bunge. Glencoe: Free Press.

———. 1965. "Problems of Empiricism." In *Beyond the Edge of Certainty*, edited by Robert Colodny. Englewood Cliffs: Prentice-Hall.

———. 1970a. "Consolations for the Specialist." In Lakatos and Musgrave, *Criticism and the Growth of Knowledge*.

———. 1970b. "Against Method: Outline of an Anarchistic Theory of Knowledge." In *Minnesota Studies in the Philosophy of Science*, vol. 4, edited by Michael Radner and Stephen Winokur. Minneapolis: University of Minnesota Press.

———. 1970c. "Philosophy of Science: A Subject with a Great Past." In *Minnesota Studies in the Philosophy of Science*, vol. 5, edited by Roger Stuewer. Minneapolis: University of Minnesota Press.

———. 1970d. "Problems of Empiricism, Part II." In *The Nature and Function of Scientific Theories*, edited by Robert Colodny. Pittsburgh: University of Pittsburgh Press.

———. 1978. *Science in a Free Society*. London: New Left Books.

———. 1988. *Against Method: Outline of an Anarchistic Theory of Knowledge*. 2nd ed. London: Verso. The original edition was published in 1975.

———. 1991. "Concluding Unphilosophical Conversation." 1991, In Munévar, *Beyond Reason*, 487–527.

———. 1992. *Against Method: Outline of an Anarchistic Theory of Knowledge*. 3rd ed. London: Verso.

———. 1994. "Paul K. Feyerabend: Last Interview." In *The Worst Enemy of Science? Essays in Memory of Paul Feyerabend*, edited by John Preston, Gonzalo Munévar, and David Lamb. New York: Oxford University Press.

———. 1995. *Killing Time: The Autobiography of Paul Feyerabend*. Chicago: University of Chicago Press.

Fleck, Ludwik. 1979. *The Genesis and Development of Scientific Fact*. Chicago: University of Chicago Press. The original edition was published in 1935.

Fodor, Jerry. 1975. *The Language of Thought*. Cambridge, Mass.: Harvard University Press.

———. 1983. *Modularity of the Mind*. Cambridge, Mass.: MIT Press.

———. 1985. "Précis of the Modularity of the Mind." *Behavioral and Brain Sciences* 8:1–5.

———. 1990. *A Theory Content, and Other Essays*. Cambridge, Mass.: MIT Press.

Fogelin, Robert J. 2009. *Taking Wittgenstein at His Word: A Textual Study*. Princeton: Princeton University Press.

Foster, Robert J. 1971. *Physical Geology*. New York: Charles Merrill.

Foucault, Michel. 1990. "Nietzsche, Freud, Marx." In *Transforming the Hermeneutic Context: Nietzsche to Nancy*, edited by G. L. Ormiston and A. D. Schift. Albany: SUNY Press.

Fuller, Steve. 2000. *Thomas Kuhn: A Philosophical History for Our Times*. Chicago: University of Chicago Press.

———. 2005. *Kuhn vs. Popper: The Struggle for the Soul of Science*. New York: Columbia University Press.

———. 2008. *Dissent Over Descent: Intelligent Design's Challenge to Darwinism*. London: Icon Books.

Gadamer, H.-G. 1975. *Truth and Method*. New York: Seabury Press.

———. 1976. *Philosophical Hermeneutics*. Berkeley: University of California Press.

Gallie, W. B. 1955–56. "Essentially Contested Concepts." *Proceedings of the Aristotelian Society* 56:167–98.

Gellner, Ernest. 1984. *Relativism and the Social Sciences*. Cambridge: Cambridge University Press.

Greenleaf, W. H. 1964. *Order, Empiricism, and Politics*. Oxford: Oxford University Press.

Grice, H. P. 1957. "Meaning." *Philosophical Review* 66:377–88.

———. 1968. "Utterer's Meaning, Sentence Meaning and Word Meaning." *Foundations of Language* 4:225–42.

———. 1969. "Utterer's Meaning and Intention." *Philosophical Review* 78:147–77.

———. 1975. "Logic and Convention." In *Syntax and Semantics*, edited by P. Cole and J. Morgan. New York: Academic Press.

———. 1981. "Presumption and Conversational Implicature." In *Radical Pragmatics*, edited by P. Cole. New York: Academic Press.

———. 1982. "Meaning Revisited." In *Mutual Knowledge*, edited by V. Smith. New York: Academic Press.

Gunnell, John G. 1968. "Social Science and Political Reality: The Problem of Explanation." *Social Research* 34:159–201.

———. 1975. *Philosophy, Science, and Political Inquiry*. Morristown, N.J.: General Learning Press.

———. 1986. *Between Philosophy and Politics: The Alienation of Political Theory*. Amherst: University of Massachusetts Press.

———. 1993a. *Political Theory: The Genealogy of an American Vocation*. Chicago: University of Chicago Press.

———.1993b. "Relativism and the Return of the Repressed." *Political Theory* 21:563–84.

———. 1998. *The Orders of Discourse: Philosophy, Social Science, and Politics*. Lanham, Md.: Rowman and Littlefield.

———. 2004a. *Imagining the American Polity: Political Science and the Discourse of Democracy*. University Park: Pennsylvania State University Press.

———. 2004b. "Desperately Seeking Wittgenstein." *European Journal of Political Theory* 21:563–84.

———. 2004c. "The Real Revolution in Political Science." *PS: Political Science* 37, no. 1.

———. 2007a. "The Paradoxes of Social Science: Weber, Winch, and

Wittgenstein." In *Max Weber's "Objectivity" Revisited*, edited by Laurence McFalls. Toronto: University of Toronto Press.

———. 2007b. "Are We Losing Our Minds? Cognitive Science and the Study of Politics." *Political Theory* 35:704–31.

———. 2009. "Ideology and the Philosophy of Science: An American Misunderstanding." *Journal of Political Ideologies* 14:317–37.

———. 2011. *Political Theory and Social Science: Cutting Against the Grain*. New York: Palgrave Macmillan.

———. 2012. "Unpacking Emotional Baggage in Political Theory." In *Essays on Political Theory and Neuroscience*, edited by Frank Vander Valk. New York: Routledge.

Hanson, Norwood Russell. 1958. *Patterns of Discovery*. Cambridge: Cambridge University Press.

Harré, Rom, and G. Gillett. 1994. *The Discursive Mind*. Thousand Oaks, Calif.: Sage.

Heilbron, J. L. 1998. "Thomas Samuel Kuhn." *Isis* 89:505–15.

Hempel, Carl G. 1965. *Aspects of Scientific Explanation*. Glencoe: Free Press.

Hiley, D., and J. Bohman, eds. 1991. *The Interpretive Turn: Philosophy, Science, Culture*. Ithaca: Cornell University Press.

Hirsch, E. D., Jr. 1976. *The Aims of Interpretation*. Chicago: University of Chicago Press.

Hollis, Martin, and Steven Lukes, eds. 1982. *Rationality and Relativism*. Cambridge, Mass.: MIT Press.

Holmes, Chauncey, D. 1949. *Introduction to College Geology*. New York: Macmillan.

Hoyhingen-Huene, Paul. 1993. *Reconstructing Scientific Revolutions: Thomas Kuhn's Philosophy of Science*. Chicago: University of Chicago Press.

Jarvie, Ian. 2008. "Boudon's European Diagnosis of and Prophylactic Against Relativism." *Philosophy of the Social Sciences* 38:279–92.

Kripke, Saul A. 1982. *Wittgenstein on Rules and Private Language*. Cambridge, Mass.: Harvard University Press.

Kuhn, Thomas. 1970a. "Logic of Discovery or Psychology of Research?" In Lakatos and Musgrave, *Criticism and the Growth of Knowledge*.

———. 1970b. "Reply to My Critics." In Lakatos and Musgrave, *Criticism and the Growth of Knowledge*.

———. 1970c. *The Structure of Scientific Revolutions*. 2nd ed. Chicago:

University of Chicago Press. The first edition was published in 1962.

———. 1977. *The Essential Tension.* Chicago: University of Chicago Press.

———. 1980. "The Halt and the Blind: Philosophy and History of Science." Review of *Method and Approach in the Physical Sciences, 1800–1905. British Journal of the Philosophy of Science* 31:181–92. The book under review was edited by C. Howson and published by Cambridge University Press in 1976.

———. 1984. "Revisiting Planck." *Historical Studies of the Physical Sciences* 14:231–52.

———. 1992. *The Trouble with the Historical Philosophy of Science.* Cambridge, Mass.: Department of the History of Science, Harvard University.

———. 1993. "Afterwords." In *World-Changes: Thomas Kuhn and the Nature of Science,* edited by Paul Horwich. Cambridge, Mass.: MIT Press.

———. 1997. "A Physicist Who Became a Historian for Philosophic Purposes: A Discussion Between Thomas S. Kuhn and Aristides Baltas, Kostas Gavroglu, and Vasso Kindi." *Neusis* 6:143–98.

———. 2000. *The Road Since Structure.* Edited by James Conant and John Haugeland. Chicago: University of Chicago Press.

Lakatos, Imre. 1970. "Falsification and the Methodology of Scientific Research Programmes." In Lakatos and Musgrave, *Criticism and the Growth of Knowledge.*

Lakatos, Imre, and Alan Musgrave, eds. 1970. *Criticism and the Growth of Knowledge.* Cambridge: Cambridge University Press.

Longwell, Chester R., Adolf Knopf, Richard F. Flint, Charles Schuchert, and Carl O. Dunbar. 1941. *Outlines of Geology.* New York: Wiley.

Markum, James A. 2005. *Thomas Kuhn's Revolution: An Historical Philosophy of Science.* London: Continuum.

Masterson, Margaret. 1970. "The Nature of a Paradigm." In Lakatos and Musgrave, *Criticism and the Growth of Knowledge.*

Monk, Ray. 1990. *Wittgenstein: The Duty of Genius.* New York: Free Press.

Morris, Errol. 2011. "The Ashtray." Opinionator, *New York Times,* March 6–10.

————. 2012. *A Wilderness of Error: The Trials of Jeffrey MacDonald*. New York: Penguin.

Munévar, Gonzalo. 1991. *Beyond Reason: Essays on the Philosophy of Paul Feyerabend*. Boston: Kluwer.

Nickles, Thomas, ed. 2003. *Thomas Kuhn*. New York: Cambridge University Press.

Oberheim, Eric. 2006. *Feyerabend's Philosophy*. New York: Walter de Gruyter.

Parfit, Derek. 2011. *On What Matters*. Oxford: Oxford University Press.

Pinker, Steven. 1994. *The Language Instinct*. New York: William Morrow.

————. 1997. *How the Mind Works*. New York: Norton.

————. 2002. *The Blank Slate: The Modern Denial of Human Nature*. New York: Penguin.

————. 2007. *The Stuff of Thought: Language as a Window Into Human Nature*. New York: Penguin.

Pitkin, Hanna. 1993. *Wittgenstein and Justice: On the Significance of Ludwig Wittgenstein for Social and Political Thought*. Berkeley: University of California Press. The first edition was published in 1972.

Preston, John. 1997. *Feyerabend: Philosophy, Science and Society*. Cambridge: Polity.

Putnam, Hilary. 1999. *The Three-Fold Cord: Mind, Body, and World*. New York: Columbia University Press.

Rawls, John. 1971. *A Theory of Justice*. Cambridge, Mass.: Harvard University Press.

————. 1993. *Political Liberalism: The John Dewey Essays in Philosophy*. New York: Columbia University Press.

————. 1999. *The Law of Peoples, with "The Idea of Public Reason Revisited."* Cambridge, Mass.: Harvard University Press.

Read, Rupert. 2012. *Wittgenstein Among the Sciences: Wittgensteinian Investigations Into the Scientific Method*. Edited by Simon Summers. Burlington, Vt.: Ashgate.

Reisch, George A. 2005. *How the Cold War Transformed the Philosophy of Science: To the Icy Slopes of Logic*. Chicago: University of Chicago Press.

Rhees, Rush. 1965. "Some Developments in Wittgenstein's View of Ethics." *Philosophical Review* 74:17–26.

Richardson, Alan. 2007. "That Sort of Everyday Image of Logical Positivism: Thomas Kuhn and the Decline of Logical Empiricist

Philosophy of Science." in *The Cambridge Companion to Logical Empiricism*, edited by Alan Richardson and Thomas Uebel. Cambridge: Cambridge University Press.

Rorty, Richard. 1979. *Philosophy and the Mirror of Nature*. Princeton: Princeton University Press.

Schaller, Susan. 1991. *Man Without Words*. Berkeley: University of California Press.

Scheman, Naomi. 1996. "Forms of Life: Mapping the Rough Ground." In *The Cambridge Companion to Wittgenstein*, edited by Hans Sluga and David G. Stern. Cambridge: Cambridge University Press.

Searle, John. 1992. *The Rediscovery of the Mind*. Cambridge, Mass.: MIT Press.

———. 1995. *The Construction of Social Reality*. New York: Free Press.

Sellars, Wilfrid. 1963. *Science, Perception, and Reality*. New York: Humanities Press.

Senghas, A., and M. Coppola. 2001. "Children Creating Language: How Nicaraguan Sign Language Acquired a Spatial Grammar." *Psychological Science* 12:323–28.

Sharrock, Wes, and Rupert Read. 2002. *Kuhn: Philosopher of Scientific Revolutions*. Oxford: Blackwell.

Sokal, Alan, and Jean Bricmont. 1998. *Fashionable Nonsense: Postmodern Intellectual Abuse of Science*. New York: Picador.

Taylor, Charles. 1971. "Interpretation and the Sciences of Man." *Review of Metaphysics* 25:3–51.

Toulmin, Stephen. 1958. *The Uses of Argument*. Cambridge: Cambridge University Press.

Uebel, Thomas E., ed. 1991. *Rediscovering the Forgotten Vienna Circle: Austrian Studies on Otto Neurath and the Vienna Circle*. Boston: Kluwer.

Waismann, Friedrich. 1979. *Wittgenstein and the Vienna Circle*. Edited by Brian McGuinness. New York: Barnes and Noble.

Winch, Peter. 1958. *The Idea of a Social Science and its Relation to Philosophy*. London: Routledge and Kegan Paul.

———. 1964. "Understanding a Primitive Society." *American Philosophical Quarterly* 1:307–24.

———. 1996. "Doing Justice or Giving the Devil His Due." In *Can Religion Be Explained Away?*, edited by D. Z. Phillips. Basingstoke: Macmillan.

Wittgenstein, Ludwig. 1958. *The Blue and Brown Books*. New York: Harper.

———. 1961. *Notebooks, 1914–1916*. Edited by G. H. von Wright and G. E. M. Anscombe. Translated by E. D. Klemke. Oxford: Basil Blackwell.

———. 1966. *Lectures and Conversations on Aesthetics, Psychology and Religious Belief*. Edited by Cyril Barrett. Berkeley: University of California Press.

———. 1969. *On Certainty*. Edited by G. E. M. Anscombe and G. H. von Wright. Translated by Denis Paul and G. E. M. Anscombe. New York: Harper and Row.

———. 1974. *Philosophical Grammar*. Edited by Rush Rhees. Translated by Anthony Kenny. Oxford: Basil Blackwell.

———. 1976. *Wittgenstein's Lectures on the Foundations of Mathematics, Cambridge, 1939*. Ithaca: Cornell University Press.

———. 1977. *Remarks on Colour*. Edited by G. E. M. Anscombe. Translated by Linda L. McAlister and Margarete Schättle. Berkeley: University of California Press.

———. 1978. *Remarks on the Foundations of Mathematics*. Edited by G. H von Wright, R. Rhees, and G. E. M. Anscombe. Translated by G. E. M. Anscombe. Oxford: Basil Blackwell.

———. 1980a. *Remarks on the Philosophy of Psychology*. Vol. 1. Edited by G. E. M. Anscombe and G. H. von Wright. Translated by G. E. M. Anscombe. Oxford: Blackwell.

———. 1980b. *Remarks on the Philosophy of Psychology*. Vol. 2. Edited by G. H. von Wright and Heikki Nyman. Translated by C. G. Luckhardt and Maximilian A. E Aue. Oxford: Basil Blackwell.

———. 1981. *Zettel*. Edited by G. E. M Anscombe and G. H. von Wright. Translated by G. E. M. Anscombe. Oxford: Blackwell.

———. 1992. *Last Writings on the Philosophy of Psychology*. Vols. 1 and 2. Edited by G. H. von Wright and Heikki Nyman. Translated by C. G. Luckhardt and Maximillian A. E. Aue. Oxford: Blackwell.

———. 1993. *Philosophical Occasions, 1912–1951*. Edited by James C. Klagge and Alfred Nordman. Indianapolis: Hackett.

———. 1997. *Cambridge Letters*. Edited by B. McGuinness and G. H. von Wright. Oxford: Blackwell.

———. 1998. *Culture and Value*. Edited by Georg Henrik von Wright, with Heikke Nyman. Translated by Peter Winch. Oxford: Blackwell.

————. 2003. *Public and Private Occasions*. Edited by James C. Klagge and Alfred Nordmann. Lanham, Md.: Rowman and Littlefield.

————. 2005. *The Big Typescript*. Edited and translated by C. G. Luckhardt and Maximilian A. E. Aue. Oxford: Blackwell.

————. 2009. *Philosophical Investigations*. 4th ed. Translated by G. E. M. Anscombe, P. M. S. Hacker, and J. Schulte. Oxford: Blackwell. In this edition, material formerly presented as part 2 is designated as *Philosophy of Psychology—A Fragment*, which is cited as *PPF*.

————. 2012. *Tractatus Logico-Philosophicus*. Side-by-side-by-side edition. Prepared by Kevin C. Klement. Translated by F. P. Ogden/ C. K. Ramsey and D. F. Pears/B. F. McGuinness. http://people. umass.edu/klement/tlp/. The original edition was published in 1922.

Index